An unusual and original book which will become a classic point of reference; Jo Fawkes brings a new dimension to public relations literature. Not only does she present a critical and comprehensive overview of key issues and debates, but also a reflexive piece of writing that draws in compelling autobiographical insights. This highly readable book explores public relations through a rich combination of philosophical, sociological, and psychological and psychoanalytical literature to provide a multi-level layered analysis.

Jacquie L'Etang, Professor, Queen Margaret University, Scotland

This volume is required reading, explicating ethics and performativity. Johanna Fawkes situates responsibility within a being that is embodied, thoughtful and informed by a textured Jungian perspective.

*Ronald C. Arnett, Chair and Professor, Department of Communication &
Rhetorical Studies, Duquesne University, USA*

Dr Fawkes will have none of the ethical prancing of public relations and delivers a powerful and personal narrative that takes us to the wild side of Jungian psychology and shadowy public relations. It fruitfully helps us deal with duality, complexity and contradiction.

Øyvind Ihlen, Professor, University of Oslo, Norway

You learn most about ethics not through smooth presentations that try to package the latest theory, but through the juxtaposition of perspectives that make you stop and think. This book makes you stop and think. Johanna Fawkes does that by bringing together a profession often characterised by surface image with the writings of Jung, who invites us to go deep, to look behind the image, at narratives most often not examined. It is a book both intellectually stimulating and practically honest and clear, and should be on the book shelves of all researchers, teachers, consultants and practitioners in this area.

Simon Robinson, Professor, Leeds Metropolitan University, UK

Johanna Fawkes's application of Jungian ideas relating to the 'fragmented self', the 'contradictory messiness of being' and the 'shadow' to an exploration of profes-sionalism – and public relations ethics in particular – is dazzlingly original. Moreover, her presence throughout as the overtly subjective, deeply questioning, fallible, researcher makes this text both intellectually enriching – and profoundly moving.

Richard Lance Keeble, Professor, University of Lincoln, UK

Public Relations Ethics and Professionalism

Do professions really place duty to society above clients' or their own interests? If not, how can they be trusted? While some public relations (PR) scholars claim that PR serves society and enhances the democratic process, others suggest that it is little more than propaganda, serving the interests of global corporations. This is not an argument about definitions, but about ethics – yet this topic is barely explored in texts and theories that seek to explain PR and its function in society.

This book places PR ethics in the wider context of professional ethics and the sociology of professions. By bringing together literature from fields beyond public relations – sociology, professional and philosophical ethics, and Jungian psychology – it integrates a new body of ideas into the debate. The unprecedented introduction of Jungian psychology to public relations scholarship shifts the debate beyond a traditional Western 'Good/Bad' ethical dichotomy towards a new holistic approach, with dynamic implications for theory and practice.

This thought-provoking book will be essential reading for students, academics and professionals with an interest in public relations, ethics and professionalism.

Johanna Fawkes is Senior Lecturer in Public Relations at Charles Sturt University, NSW Australia and Course Director for the Doctor of Communication. She has led PR degrees in the UK since 1990, advised the CIPR, and published in international journals and leading text books.

Routledge New Directions in Public Relations and Communication Research
Edited by Kevin Moloney

Routledge New Directions in Public Relations and Communication Research is a new forum for the publication of books of original research in PR and related types of communication. Its remit is to publish critical and challenging responses to continuities and fractures in contemporary PR thinking and practice, and its essential yet contested role in market-orientated, capitalist, liberal democracies around the world. The series reflects the multiple and inter-disciplinary forms PR takes in a post-Grunigian world; the expanding roles which it performs, and the increasing number of countries in which it is practised.

The series will examine current and explore new thinking on the key questions which impact upon PR and communications including:

- Is the evolution of persuasive communications in Central and Eastern Europe, China, Latin America, Japan, the Middle East and South East Asia developing new forms or following Western models?
- What has been the impact of postmodern sociologies, cultural studies and methodologies which are often critical of the traditional, conservative role of PR in capitalist political economies, and in patriarchy, gender and ethnic roles?
- What is the impact of digital social media on politics, individual privacy and PR practice? Is new technology changing the nature of content communicated, or simply reaching bigger audiences faster? Is digital PR a cause or a consequence of political and cultural change?

Books in this series will be of interest to academics and researchers involved in these expanding fields of study, as well as students undertaking advanced studies in this area.

Public Relations and Nation Building
Influencing Israel
Margalit Toledano and David McKie

Gender and Public Relations
Critical perspectives on voice, image and identity
Edited by Christine Daymon and Kristin Demetrious

Public Relations Ethics and Professionalism

The shadow of excellence

Johanna Fawkes

Routledge
Taylor & Francis Group

LONDON AND NEW YORK

First published 2015
by Routledge
2 Park Square, Milton Park, Abingdon, Oxon OX14 4RN

and by Routledge
711 Third Avenue, New York, NY 10017

Routledge is an imprint of the Taylor & Francis Group, an informa business

British Library Cataloguing in Publication Data
A catalogue record for this book is available from the British Library

Library of Congress Cataloging in Publication Data
Fawkes, Johanna.
Public relations ethics and professionalism: the shadow of excellence /
Johanna Fawkes.
Includes bibliographical references and index.
1. Public relations–Moral and ethical aspects. 2. Professional ethics.
3. Business ethics. I. Title.
HM1221.F39 2014
659.2–dc23
2014001737

ISBN: 978-0-415-63038-2 (hbk)
ISBN: 978-0-203-09767-0 (ebk)

Typeset in Times New Roman
by FiSH Books Ltd, Enfield

Printed and bound in the United States of America by
Edwards Brothers Malloy on sustainably sourced paper

For my parents, the late Sandy Fawkes
and, still thriving, Wally Fawkes,
from whom I learned to balance
chaos and creativity.

Contents

Foreword

It is a pleasure to write a foreword for a significantly different kind of book on PR in general and on PR ethics and professionalism in particular. As its opening sentence signals, this is an enthusiastic and committed journey to places where few PR books are bold enough to go. It is not just different in its original content – even in such a psychology-deprived field, it is, astonishingly, the first substantial contribution connecting the work of Carl Jung to PR. That alone makes it worthwhile. However, Dr Fawkes does more than just draw relevant insight from the body of work, she makes vital links to PR's ongoing struggle with ethics as a real practice in the contemporary world. Our associations from the Public Relations Society of America through to the Global Alliance present us as inherently ethical and constantly misunderstood. Dr Fawkes will have none of it. Following her Swiss master, she shows how everyone has a shadow side that has to be acknowledged before it can be understood and integrated into greater individual self-knowledge and increased group wisdom.

Inevitably, such a book is, to use its own words 'messy', and its author has the courage to tackle what are commonly called 'wicked problems' (i.e. the kind that resist solutions and persist over time). From corporate PR's origins, problems in PR ethics have consistently been met in similar fashion (e.g. by the never-ending construction and re-construction of codes of ethics). These found frequent echoes as espoused policy in corporate media releases and framed statements on board-room walls (e.g. at Enron) that continue to be contradicted by discoveries of immoral, if not illegal, business actions. To address the mess, Dr Fawkes goes back to basics and ask the question of whether PR does 'have professional ethics' and responds to it with inquiries that rightly treat the question as worthy of serious attention. Elsewhere, she explores what it really means to serve society.

Although it is genuinely exploratory, the book also offers practical and thoughtful pathways to finding sustaining and sustainable answers. Its provisional answers tend to be hard won and emerge from delving 'into the psyche', exploring 'depth ethics', and, as with all good moral responses, using human creativity. Dr Fawkes' 're-imagining' of professional ethics does not lay claim to any unattainable objectivity but goes for personal, socially transparent advances that are designed to bring about real-life change. Rejecting the dulling shadow of the Excellence Project, she drills down in a profound search for what might create PR practices that are simultaneously good in efficacy and ethics. Dr Fawkes offers a truly different voice in her honest and, sometimes, raw reflections. Her willingness to share herself in an engaging and self-critical way often takes PR academic writing to another level. But let me end with a caution to some and an endorsement to others: don't read this book unless you are prepared to radically challenge, and radically change, your perceptions of PR theory and practice in the areas of ethics and professionalism.

David McKie, Professor of Management Communication
Waikato Management School
The University of Waikato
Hamilton, New Zealand

Acknowledgements

This book was made possible by the award of a Research Fellowship from Charles Sturt University Faculty of Arts in 2013 and a Centenary Bursary from Leeds Metropolitan University (2007–10), which supported the thesis on which this book is loosely based. I'd also like to thank my supervisors, Professors Anne Gregory and Simon Robinson and Dr Steve Sayer for their contribution to the earlier work. The Jungian analyst Hester Solomon kindly read the Jungian chapters of the original thesis and this series' editor Dr Kevin Moloney provided encouraging feedback to draft chapters of this book. Everyone at Routledge was unfailingly helpful – the errors are my own.

Thanks are also due to the reviewers and editors who accepted early versions of the ideas in this book for publication, as follows:

Fawkes, J. (2006) Can ethics save public relations from the charge of propaganda? *Ethical Space, Journal of the Institute of Communication Ethics, 3*(1): 32–42.

Fawkes, J. (2007) Public relations models and persuasion ethics: a new approach. *Journal of Communication Management, 11*(4): 313–31.

Fawkes, J. and Moloney, K. (2008). Does Europe need an Institute of Propaganda Analysis? *Public Relations Review, 34*(3): 204–17.

Fawkes, J. (2009) Integrating the shadow: a Jungian approach to professional ethics in public relations. *Ethical Space, 6*(2): 30–9.

Fawkes, J. (2010a) The shadow of excellence: a Jungian approach to public relations ethics. *Review of Communication, 10*(3): 211–27.

Fawkes, J. (2010b) Cultural complexes in professional ethics. *Journal of Jungian Scholarly Studies, 6*(8). Online. Available at http://jungiansociety.org/images/e-journal/Volume-6/Fawkes-2010.pdf

Fawkes, J. (2012a) Interpreting ethics: public relations and strong hermeneutics. *Public Relations Inquiry, 1*(2): 1–24.

Fawkes, J. (2012b) Saints *and* sinners: competing identities in public relations ethics. *Public Relations Review, 38*(5): 865–72. doi: DOI 10.1016/j.pubrev.2012.07.004

Fawkes, J. (2013) Public relations' professionalism and ethics (Ch. 13) in Tench, R. and Yeomans, L., *Exploring Public Relations* (3rd edn) Harlow, Essex: Pearson Education.

Fawkes, J. and Moloney, K. (2012) Power – it's personal and public, Introduction to special edition on Public Relations and Power, *PRISM* online journal, *9*(2). Online. Available at www.prismjournal.org/powerintro.html

1 Messy ethics

An introduction

A different voice

This book builds on a lifetime of reading, writing, thinking, dreaming, failing, starting again, denying, confronting, shifting and teaching. This is an adventure in thinking – and feeling – about ethics generally and in the field of public relations (PR) particularly. It does not end in a model that will remove or resolve all ethical dilemmas henceforth. On the contrary, it aims to induce greater confusion and uncertainty at least at the beginning, before concluding that uncertainty is a healthy state to be in when reflecting on ethical situations (and, the book argues, there can be no artificial distinction between ethical and non-ethical situations). This is a book about being as much as doing.

I will do proper academic things, like provide sources and references for arguments and literature. I will also 'map' territories for which we only have partial, fragmented or contradictory information, such as the field of PR ethics. Not only that, but the book offers deeper readings and academic underpinnings for many of the ideas that are current but underexplored in the subject area.

I will also do non-academic things, like link ideas about ethics to life experiences, primarily my own. The purpose is not narcissistic self-display but to use the raw material of one PR practitioner and academic, one human life, to illustrate more general theories from philosophy and psychology. A central theme of this book is the relevance of inner experience to ethical actions and the importance of developing reflexivity to build stronger bridges between the inner and outer. Jung is the great advocate of the subjective. So it would be hypocritical not to apply such tenets in my own writing. This also means I have to own up to actions that still disturb me decades later – what was I *thinking?* Exploring these 'critical incidents' illuminates mechanisms of denial, self-righteousness and often conflicted loyalties that seem characteristic of ethical confusion. This approach aims for a more conversational than didactic tone, but risks sacrificing authority for engagement.

Given that I am drawing on my own experience as well as literature, I should briefly introduce myself: I first started work in PR in 1975 but really learned the job at the National Gas Consumer Council a year later, where my brilliant boss, Kel Hunter, and I spent most of our time in the pub, but managed to come up with headline-grabbing ideas just when our positions were looking precarious. Then a stint in publishing, some freelance journalism and, from 1983–8, campaign worker for the London Borough of Camden, including a long stint as trade union leader; the years that gave me many of the key experiences which inform this book. My last full time PR job was at the Trade Union Congress and in 1990 I joined the London College of Printing as a senior lecturer to transform a course from 'publicity and packaging' to PR. Since then I have devised, developed and delivered PR courses to undergraduates, postgraduates and professionals at universities in the UK and, since 2011, Australia. I have also advised the peak professional body, the UK's Chartered Institute of Public Relations on educational policy, and from 2005–7 was Chief Examiner for the CIPR Diploma. According to Macnamara (2012), with a similar range of experience, this allows observations to be grounded auto-ethnographically.

So many texts on ethics imply that they embody some kind of procedure for making reliable ethical decisions, whether that is the utilitarian cost/benefit analysis, a Kantian set of duties or a matrix of values and choices such as the Potter Box. Every code is normative, prescriptive: follow these precepts and you can't go wrong. The human being processing these edicts always looks, to me anyway, like a rational, educated man (probably white) who can weigh the consequences of all his actions, make lists of values and priorities, calibrate the balance between competing duties, systematically form a hierarchy of 'principal stakeholders' and so on. My experience is just so much messier.

One of the qualities that most attracted me to the work of Carl Jung was his engagement with that mess, his own and his patients'. He worked out that these experiences were not only meaningful in themselves but also had something to say to others about being human, an observation made by artists throughout time, of course. While I didn't read any of his writings until a few years ago, so claim limited expertise, I was aware from my mid-twenties that he saw growing up as a struggle between powerful inner forces. I was recovering from early addiction then, so my psyche looked like something by Hieronymus Bosch – his validation was helpful. Nevertheless, without really asking any questions, a few years later I entered into long-term psychotherapy with a neo-Freudian. This is where I finally began a relationship with the unconscious, moving from denial of the existence of some parallel personality (scary) to an acknowledgment that it sometimes had something to offer my waking self. I learned, very, very slowly, to first ask, then answer the question – how did I feel? Like many other bright young people, then and now, and of course, like many students and academics – I always knew what I *thought*, held powerful opinions on everything, particularly politics, but could barely string an emotional sentence together. My throat closed around the words I didn't know. This experience of emotional inarticulacy and the long decades of acquiring that vocabulary convince me that while the separation may have been extreme in my case, it is not uncommon. Which is why that rational ethicist described above doesn't convince. I *know* it is possible to coolly calculate why a certain course of action would be best for all concerned, while utterly denying the degree of self-interest at the heart of the decision.

So this book argues that self-awareness is a precondition for ethical action. It moves away from ethics as 'being good' or even good enough. Using Jung's ideas about the unconscious, about duality and about integrating disparate elements within the psyche, it suggests that ethics flows from self-awareness, not as a separate activity but as a way of being in the world. The central argument is that ethics stems from wholeness not goodness, and that wholeness requires the ability to recognize, acknowledge and build relationships with rejected aspects of individuals and groups. Engaging with what Jung calls the shadow is an essential stage in psychological, spiritual and ethical maturity. It is as relevant to groups as individuals and offers a new way forward for professional ethics generally, and PR in particular. As the book demonstrates, Jung's ideas are drawn from a wide range of both European and Asian literature and philosophy, and have much to contribute to current debates in ethics, though the linkage is rarely explored. They have not been discussed in the context of PR before, but a new space is opening in thinking about the field which makes such a conversation timely.

The expanding PR multi-verse

In bringing reflections from ethical philosophy and Jungian psychology to the field of PR, I hope to contribute to the sudden expansion in PR theory, which is currently becoming fluid, multi-perspectival – and hence very interesting. The creation of this Routledge series, and the 2012 launch of the SAGE journal *Public Relations Inquiry* are evidence of the wider debate available to PR scholars than was the case for most of my early teaching years (from 1990), when the only UK texts were triumphalist and simplistic how-to books. In that context the arrival of quantitative, longitudinal research into PR best practice, the beginning of the excellence project (Grunig and Hunt, 1984; Grunig *et al.*, 1992) was both a welcome aid to teaching and illustrative of the complex inter-disciplinarity of the field, drawing on management and social sciences. The four models of communication (Grunig and Hunt, 1984) provided a useful teaching tool and helped introduce concepts of history and changing roles to the classroom. In time, however, these tools seemed tired and limited, the historical assumptions increasingly implausible. It was good to have the subject taken seriously but it was essential to have it treated critically, so the publication of L'Etang and Pieczka's (1996) *Critical Perspectives in Public Relations* was pivotal in reframing the subject, allowing the articulation of power imbalances and societal perspectives that were invisible in the functionalist canon. This was followed by Moloney's two editions of *Rethinking Public Relations* (2000, 2006) and in recent years by a cascade of new ideas (Bardhan and Weaver, 2011; Curtin and Gaither, 2007; Edwards and Hodges, 2011; Holtzhausen, 2012) as well as the updated L'Etang and Pieczka (2006). Metaphorically we have stepped out of the PR office or boardroom and re-located the subject in its wider context: there are now multiple paradigms available to PR scholars with interesting points of convergence and divergence; some of these are explored later in the book when I consider how a Jungian approach 'fits' into current thinking. Much of the new writing locates public relations ethics, as I do, not in specific situations but as an expression of cultural, social and economic power. Power has raced up the agenda in the past few years of PR scholarship and I seek to enter this discussion – to a certain extent – but with a focus on ethics. While there has been some excellent critical writing on PR ethics – fully discussed in later chapters – it is still underdeveloped in many ways, dismissed by the managerialist school as something to be achieved only in symmetrical communication, and seen by others as a somewhat embarrassing, awkward subject, synonymous with being Good. (One of the joyous aspects of a Jungian approach is that it is absolutely *not* about being good.)

As I suggest later, there are voids between the ethical aspirations of codes, which are often based in idealised self-images promoted by the excellent model and happily embraced by professional associations around the world (who wouldn't want to be seen as 'serving humanity'?), and the grubbier realities of practitioners. Faced with an impossible ideal, they have largely turned away. In their stead is a vocal body of critics, often from outside the field, which remorselessly exposes the routine abuses of power that constitute 'normal' PR practice. Discussion about ethics is reduced to a slanging match, with the defenders claiming to contribute to society and the critics accusing PR of distorting the entire democratic process. While the mud-slingers often have a limited idea of how PR works, much of the mud has rightfully stuck, leading to widespread distrust of the field, its operatives and its employers. These issues are discussed fully in the opening chapters, but to summarize: in my opinion the current state of ethical thinking in the field is fragmented, contradictory – which is fine – but also philosophically thin, based on unchallenged assumptions and ultimately divorced from practice, which is not fine.

As well as engagement with multiple paradigms and a rising interest in power, there has been a recent turn away from the organizational focus of PR thinking, whether from managerial or critical perspectives (the old 'corporations are Good/Bad' dyad). Like other writers (considered in more depth in Chapter 5), I want to broaden the scope of the debate to embrace at one end of the spectrum, the PR practitioner and his/her individual experience (micro-level), and at the other, the social fabric in which we all swim (macro-level). However, for fear of losing all coherence, the focus for this book is the profession, which operates at the meso-level, the level of organization. This does not mean I consider PR from an organizational perspective, either supportively or critically. Many of the arguments and ideas here are not directly related to corporate or even organizational communications, though I do borrow from organizational psychology at various points. The unit of study is PR as a 'profession', which is of course an organization, albeit a peculiar one. Professions have 'representative' bodies that offer some organizational entity but which are neither trade unions working for members' interests nor, in the main, regulators working for society's benefit. In this sense, looking at the field as a profession or occupation (the distinction is investigated in Chapter 3) offers a lateral, cross-sectional view. The location of practitioners in agencies, corporations, voluntary bodies and so on is outside the scope of this study. It may be that there will be different applications of the central ideas in different types of workplace – and it is certainly the case that individuals in different workplaces will experience different ethical pressures and may subscribe to multiple, even conflicting codes or values systems – but the main arguments are intended to be germane across the board.

And while the scope of investigation is PR as a profession, the topic under scrutiny is not its status or value for money or relationship with the CEO or with marketing for that matter, but how it collectively considers and, to a lesser extent, practices ethics.

Research approach

Perhaps this is the place to stress that this book is based on conceptual research, not empirical study. The final chapter raises research possibilities and I certainly hope to develop some deeper understanding of how these ideas operate at local levels, but this book aims to introduce the ideas generally, to start a debate. If it lights a spark, research will follow.

Overall the book takes a hermeneutic approach, meaning that this work is one of interpretation. Briefly, hermeneutics is sometimes called the philosophy of interpretation and has been developed in the past few decades primarily by Riceour (e.g. 1981) and Gadamer (e.g. 1989) building on earlier works by Heidegger and others. Bleicher (1980) summarizes the development of traditional hermeneutic theory as a) technological understanding of language, vocabulary, grammar, etc; b) exegesis of sacred texts, such as biblical study; and c) to guide jurisdiction. These approaches focus on methodological aspects of interpretation, but hermeneutic *philosophy*, as proposed by Heidegger, questions deeper aspects of understanding, such as the impossibility of objectivity when subject and object are bound together in Being, or *Dasein*. The goal of hermeneutic investigation is *understanding through interpretation*, in which the subjective limitations and frameworks – historical and linguistic – are part of the process. It does not aim for scientific replication of interpretation; Heidegger (1926/1962) considered it *extrascientific* knowledge. It brings the subjective centrally into the discussion and thus requires reflexivity in the researcher and practitioner, because one is not only interpreting the external texts but also one's response to them. The goal of this kind of inquiry is not proof but insight; it presumes that if we acknowledge difference but engage at depth we might find what Gadamer (1989) calls a 'fusion of horizons'. This convergence is fleeting and fluid, not fixed – a moment of recognition, not a treaty, for horizons move as we change position. Different hermeneutic approaches to ethics are explored in Chapter 4, but here I'd like to stress hermeneutics as a reflexive tool, allowing the researcher to place him or herself in relation to research in developing theory and the practitioner in relation to practice in deepening understanding of those domains. In presenting my research, I am offering an interpretation of PR texts in the context of professionalism studies and schools of ethics, reframing it in the light of that work before radically framing it again from a Jungian perspective. This is particularly rich as many consider Jung himself to have taken a hermeneutic approach (e.g. Brooke, 1991), seeking points of understanding with patients rather than the rigid classification he found in contemporary practice and resisted in Freud. Again and again he envisages himself as an archaeologist, uncovering layers of meaning in the human psyche, an apt image for hermeneutics. I have also found resonance between this hermeneutic approach and the emerging socio-cultural school in PR, as will be seen later in the book. One of my central concerns is the re-engagement with the subjective, experiential aspects of ethics, in contrast to the quantified and codified approaches found in much discourse on these themes. Socio-cultural scholarship embraces the inner, the unconscious aspects of being in the world, as well as the outer aspects more traditionally covered by sociology. Throughout this text I recognize myself as the interpreter, with all the strengths and weaknesses that implies, and have tried to be explicit, citing experience and observation, so that the process is as transparent and conscious as possible.

Scope of the book

In these opening pages, I've already introduced several rather large questions:

- Can ethics be purely rational and, if not, how can we know our own motives in seeking to act ethically when self-delusion is endemic?
- Can Jung's welcoming of psychological complexity and contradiction help in this dilemma; does the move away from Good/Bad ease or complicate ethical understanding? Is a non-normative ethics possible?
- How does hermeneutic philosophy enrich or challenge our understanding of ethics and ourselves?
- To what degree do approaches to PR ethics confine themselves to 'rational' choice making, avoiding philosophical engagement?
- Is this true of other professions? What are professions, is PR one, how do they fit into society? What are their claims to ethical standards based on? What makes them tick?
- What would professional ethics in general and PR ethics in particular look like if a non-rational approach were taken? What next?

This book draws on several large, established, even ancient, bodies of thought: philosophical approaches to ethics; sociological approaches to professions; Jung's psychology and theories of the 'Self'; as well as the multiple paradigms explored in the field of PR. It is ambitious, perhaps overly ambitious, given my limited experience in these wider fields. Scholars in these disciplines may be irritated by my paraphrasing of their complex bodies of knowledge; there is a real danger of losing vital meaning in easy summary. On balance, though, this seems a risk worth taking: PR scholarship has tended towards the measurable, repeatable and safe. This book introduces some wild ideas; some may be discarded as poorly argued; others may trigger something new and unpredictable. One of the wild ideas is the introduction of the personal voice into an academic text, an approach I tested in my doctoral thesis by offering an autobiographical appendix. That was encouraged and here I am bolder, interlacing reflections throughout the book, seeking to integrate the outer and inner in form as well as content.

As part of a research series, this book is primarily aimed at students and scholars in the fields of professions, professional ethics, Jungian psychology and, above all, PR. However, the implications of much of this discussion are also relevant to thoughtful practitioners in these and other fields who may be thinking about new ways to live their own and their profession's ethics.

I have structured the book as an old-fashioned narrative, starting with an overview of PR ethics, exploring the wider context of professionalism and professional ethics, then returning to reconsider problems identified earlier more deeply. The second half of the book presents the work of Carl Jung, constructing a Jungian ethic, which is then synthesised with earlier discussions in the final chapters of the book, in the hope of generating new solutions or at least discussions.

You are of course free to consume this book in any order, skipping the Jung, or reading only the autobiographical material. You may be interested in professions or professional ethics not PR at all. Or focused on how Jung's ideas of cultural complexes can be translated into wider social debates, an important and emerging area of scholarship. You will construct your own meaning. The following summarizes my narrative so you can decide for yourself how to read this book.

Overview

The book is informally divided into three distinct parts, each forming an element in the conversation:

- *Part One* (Chapters 2–5) critically examines the assumptions and particularly power dimensions embedded in current approaches to PR ethics. To understand why so many of these approaches lack depth, we take a step back to look at the role of professions in society and how professional codes of ethics are used to bolster claims for social status and autonomy. Having established the parameters of professional ethics, we then look more deeply into the underlying philosophies, noting that much of this discussion is absent from PR literature. The section concludes by repositioning PR ethics in its sociological and philosophical context and identifying a range of questions requiring attention.
- *Part Two* (Chapters 6–7) introduces the psychology and philosophy of Carl Jung and the post-Jungian scholars, in particular the key components of the psyche, together with the multiple interpretations of these key concepts. In engaging with the work of Carl Jung, I suggest means for raising self-awareness in groups such as professions, as well as justifications for such effort, creating a 'space' where conflicting or parallel ideas might meet and the ethical implications of such a conversation. It is tricky terrain but certain common ground emerges from the discussion, which is fashioned into a foundational ethic. These ideas are also located in their historical and philosophical context, drawing on themes and literature established in Part One.
- *Part Three* (Chapters 8–10) finally brings the elements together, demonstrating the impact of Jungian ideas on concepts of professions, professional ethics and in particular the field of PR and its idea of ethics. It re-examines the issues problematized in its first third to discover what emerges from such a fusion of horizons, producing a depth approach to PR ethics located in Jungian

psychology and hermeneutic philosophy. As stated earlier, the goal is not a solution or a new set of rules, far from it – the idea is re-locate the centre of ethical debates from the code to the profession, individually and collectively.

Chapter outlines

2 What's wrong with PR ethics?

Public relations' ethics and its relationship to society are examined, and the main schools of thought in the field are introduced, together with their approaches to ethics. The chapter highlights the schisms between these schools and also those between academics and practitioners. It concludes that PR ethics is often incoherent and aspirational rather than grounded either in practice or ethical theory.

3 Trust me, I'm a professional

Placing PR in the context of the sociology of professions helps illuminate arguments between its defenders and critics, and explains the insistence on social good, as this is one hallmark of a profession. Professions are suffering a real crisis as the combination of scandals and managerialism erode public trust, their traditional base for authority; hence the turn to ethics.

4 To serve society

The wider discussion of professional ethics and contemporary debates in ethical philosophy demonstrates the range of ideas that might be of value in developing a more grounded and coherent approach to PR ethics. This discussion emphasizes shifts from reliance on external codes and rules to inner guidance and explores the tensions between these frameworks.

5 Does public relations have professional ethics?

Having set the background, the book returns to PR and delves deeper into the nature of the arguments within the field. This remarks on the lack of engagement with either professional or modern ethical literature in much PR writing. Growing resistance to the dominance of the excellence model and the arrival of non-US voices in recent years suggest a new dynamic within the field. A range of questions is raised as worthy of attention.

6 Into the psyche

This chapter introduces key Jungian concepts, such as ego, animus/anima, collective consciousness, and archetypes of shadow and persona. The process of individuation – the coming to terms with one's own shadow – is shown to be applicable to organizations, groups and, here, professions.

7 Depth ethics

A Jungian approach to ethics is grounded in individuation, starting with acceptance of internal dualities – in individuals and in groups. By withdrawing projections and accepting the shadow material, a more developed, ethical ego function can offer a deeper understanding of the 'other' and alter the ethical relationship with society. This is about process not outcomes.

8 Re-imagining professional ethics

Professions and professional ethics are here re-viewed through a Jungian lens, suggesting a reconceptualization of the profession as a psychic entity, with methods for self-enquiry to identify and re-own the shadow aspects of the field. The impact for theory and practice is explored, providing an opportunity for ethical leadership if so desired, and at least a more honest appraisal of its role in society if ethical leadership is eschewed.

9 The shadow of excellence

The status of PR as a profession and its professional ethics are re-evaluated and some preliminary suggestions are made concerning the likely shadow aspects of the field and how a new ethics might integrate, or at least address, the question of persuasion. Points of conflict or tension are explored between disciplines and between academics and practitioners, with a view to suggesting a Jungian approach to some of the problems identified at the outset.

10 What next? Reflections and directions

The final chapter summarizes the main findings of the book, discusses implications for practice and theory, and identifies a range of research possibilities for PR and professions generally.

References

Bardhan, N. and Weaver, C. K. (2011) *Public Relations in Global Cultural Contexts: multi-paradigmatic perspectives*. New York, NY and London: Routledge.

Bleicher, J. (1980) *Contemporary Hermeneutics*. London and Boston: Routledge & Kegan Paul.

Brooke, R. (1991) *Jung and Phenomonology*. London: Routledge.

Curtin, P. A. and Gaither, T. K. (2007) *International Public Relations: negotiating culture, identity and power*. Thousand Oaks, CA: Sage.

Edwards, L. and Hodges, C. E. M. (eds) (2011) *Public Relations, Society & Culture: theoretical and empirical explorations* (1st edn) London: Routledge.

Gadamer, H. -G. (1989) *Truth and Method* (2nd rev. edn) New York, NY: Crossroad.

Grunig, J. E. and Hunt, T. (1984) *Managing Public Relations*. New York, NY and London: Holt, Rinehart and Winston.

Grunig, J. E., Dozier, D. M., Ehling, W. P., Grunig, L. A., Repper, F. C. and White, J. (1992) *Excellence in Public Relations and Communication Management*. Hillsdale, NJ: Lawrence Erlbaum Associates.

Heidegger, M. (1926/1962) *Being and Time*. J. McQuarrie and E. Robinson (trans.) San Fransisco, CA: HarperSanFrancisco.

Holtzhausen, D. (2012) *Public Relations as Activism: postmodern approaches to theory and practice*. New York, NY: Routledge.

L'Etang, J. and Pieczka, M. (1996) *Critical Perspectives in Public Relations*. London: International Thomson Business Press.

L'Etang, J. and Pieczka, M. (2006) *Public Relations: critical debates and contemporary practice*. Mahwah, NJ and London: Lawrence Erlbaum Associates.

Macnamara, J. (2012) The global shadow of functionalism and Excellence Theory: an analysis of Australasian PR. *Public Relations Inquiry,* 1(3): 367–402.

Moloney, K. (2000) *Rethinking Public Relations: the spin and the substance*. London: Routledge.

Moloney, K. (2006) *Rethinking Public Relations: PR propaganda and democracy* (2nd edn) London: Routledge.

Riceour, P. (1981) *Hermeneutics and the Human Sciences: essays on language, action and interpretation*. Cambridge: Cambridge University Press.

2   What's wrong with public relations ethics?

Introduction

Any student, practitioner or researcher professing an interest in public relations (PR) ethics will have encountered the scathing remarks and dismissive smirks of colleagues from other disciplines. 'Ethics? What ethics?' is the usual response. Others will refer to spin, seeing the field as synonymous with media relations or perhaps political huckstering. Others will cite information scandals emanating from global corporations, or – and this is a favourite at PR conferences – reduce the entire discussion to whether they would work for tobacco/arms/oil industries. These reductionist reactions fuel the problem by underestimating the scope and range of PR activities, worldwide. As Dean Kruckeberg said (about US practice) nearly twenty years ago, given the scope for global PR, now become reality,

> public relations practitioners must first acknowledge and articulate their own values and belief systems and ideologies … at a level far beyond any broad-based acceptance and defense of Judeo-Christian values and traditional Western concepts about freedom and flow of information.
>
> (1995: 38)

So this chapter offers a very brief summary of the field in the second decade of the twenty-first century, including estimates of numbers and professional bodies to illustrate the scale of its global operation. It then presents a typology of PR schools of thought, including their approaches to ethics. Tensions between these groups are highlighted, as are divisions between self-images held and promoted by some academics and those offered by some practitioners. So this chapter is a kind of 'map' of the field. Without such a map, it will be impossible to navigate a path through the ideas that follow. I want to highlight areas of PR where assumptions or habits remain unchallenged and identify emerging themes in PR scholarship. These will then be revisited in Chapter 5, following an excursion into professionalism studies and approaches to professional ethics.

Public relations as a social and economic force

The following section offers an overview of global public relations, for readers new to the field. The sources are limited and reflect resources available to Anglo-American professional bodies. I am not going to explore definitions and other introductory tropes (see Fawkes, 2011 or the very useful www.cipr.co.uk/content/about-us/about-pr, for that), just to indicate the spread and range of PR activities in order to highlight its significance as a social force. For example, the largest umbrella body, the Global Alliance for Public Relations and Communication Management, claims to represent 160,000 practitioners through its network of national professional bodies. It offers a useful country-by-country breakdown which may be of interest to those seeking to understand better the distribution of PR practitioners in their own nation (see www.globalalliancepr.org/website/page/country-landscapes). For more detailed investigation of PR around the world see van Ruler and Vercic (2004), Zerfass *et al.* (2013) and Sriramesh and Vercic (2009). Insights into PR in the UK are offered by Gregory (2011) and the Annual Benchmarking Survey run by the UK professional body for individual practitioners (as opposed to agencies), the Chartered Institute of Public Relations (www.cipr.co.uk/content/state-of-the-pr-profession-2013). There is also data on the percentage of graduate practitioners in various countries (Macnamara, 2012; Sriramesh and Verçic, 2009) but while education is a central element of the professional scaffolding, and deserves greater attention, I am not considering the role of education in the profession here. The Global Alliance for Public Relations and Communications Management estimates that there are over three million practitioners worldwide, though issues of title and domain vary enormously globally (Macnamara, 2012). Australian figures suggest a sector of over 21,000 in 2009, of whom about 3000 individual members belonged to the Public Relations Institute of Australia (Macnamara, 2012); 2011 figures for the UK suggest a total number of over 60,000 practitioners (Bussey, 2011), of whom about 10,000 are members of the Chartered Institute of Public Relations (CIPR). The UK professional body has had Chartered status since 2005, which increases its own status and that of members but does not confer the power to control practice or license practitioners, only to recommend its members over non-members. The CIPR summarizes approaches to the field:

> Public relations is conceived of in a number of ways:
>
> - As a marketing discipline (part of the marketing mix) – a view often expressed in *PR Week* in the UK.
> - As the management of communication between an organization and its publics (a view attributed in the past to US academics such as James Grunig).
> - As the management of reputation (a view developed in the mid-1990s as the then Institute of Public Relations in the UK tried to redefine public relations).
> - As the management of relationships between an organization and its publics (a view arrived at by academics and practitioners associated with the US Institute for Public Relations).

- As a practice with a significant contribution to make to the performance and success of organizations.

(www.cipr.co.uk/content/about-us/about-pr)

This is helpful in highlighting the multiple perspectives on PR but it is the second, Grunigian, definition that dominates discussion in both professional and academic contexts, as will be explored in this chapter and indeed book. For example, at the 2012 World Public Relations Forum in Melbourne, Australia, the following mandate was adopted setting out the social obligations of practitioners:

Public relations and communication professionals have a mandate to:

- define and maintain an organization's character and values;
- build a culture of listening and engagement; and
- instill responsible behaviours by individuals and organizations.

These roles are essential and interconnected: an organization must understand its character and responsibility to have meaningful engagement with its stakeholders. Taken together, these roles form an essential contribution to organisational strategy, and to society.

(Global Alliance, 2012)

This is a fascinating document, worth reading closely, but here I just point out that global definitions of PR and its societal role are remarkably close to those proposed by the excellence project (see below).

Again, my intention is not to offer definitions or enter the discussion on whether the practice should be called PR, organizational communication or some other variant; I am considering the totality of practitioners, in and outside professional bodies, in agencies, in government and organizational departments, working for multinational corporations or local grass-roots campaigns. Even more broadly, I am including PR academics and their students, all of whom have an interest in the direction of the field as a whole. In Chapter 3 I look at the literature on professions, from which I borrow the term 'community of practice' (Brown and Duguid, 2001) to describe this coalition of related groups. This enables a wider discussion of the role of PR in society than would be possible if I concentrated on the specific actions of specific sections. It also reflects new narratives of the development of PR as a profession that are currently emerging; for example, Jacquie L'Etang's historical research (2004) into the development of the field in Britain found closer entanglement with journalism, due to the prevalence of local government communication in the early and mid-twentieth century, than in the US model, which was more closely connected to the growth of capitalism and the promotional or marketing aspects of PR.

Recent writing, as the overview below outlines, has expanded the field of study to consider PR in its wider social role and I follow that trend. Second, the ubiquity of PR practitioners in every aspect of contemporary life, from global corporations to local activists, illustrates the significance of PR ethics to wider society. Given the centrality of communication to modern economic and social life, the ethics of those who craft that communication warrants closer scrutiny than it currently receives.

Competing schools of public relations scholarship

When I started developing and delivering PR courses at the London College of Printing (now University of Arts) in 1990, there were very few texts available other than 'how-to' books by Frank Jefkin or Sam Black, which saw the practice of PR as wholly unproblematic and amounted to tips on being a good 'PR man'. They bore no relation to the complexities and demands of my own recent experience. Then key US texts (Cutlip *et al.*, 1985; Grunig and Hunt, 1984; Wilcox *et al.*, 1986) filtered into specialist bookshops and hence into my curriculum, as they were well-written, clearly laid out and contained some resemblance to the world I had previously worked in. I was grateful for the lists of qualities, tasks, functions and relationships that could easily be converted to hand-outs and slides, and which positioned PR education as part of a wider discourse than the anecdotal material previously at my disposal. However, it took a long time to understand that these and other texts issued from particular worldviews; like many other practitioner-turned academics, I had a humanities background and paradigms were creatures of the social sciences. Until Pieczka's (1996) key chapter 'Paradigms, system theory and public relations', I was merely irritated by the assumptions and Panglossian reassurance; afterwards I was a critical scholar. As Weaver (2011: 257) notes, 'It is vital that we also understand the cultural worldviews that public relations theorists promote through their methodologies and research agendas. Too infrequently do theorists articulate these agendas in their research projects and resulting publications'. She's right; only recently have scholars clearly identified their allegiances to particular paradigms. Encouraged and enlightened, I started sketching a taxonomy of PR thinking in regard to persuasion and hence ethics in conference papers and an article published in the *Journal of Communication Management* (*JCM*) (Fawkes, 2007). Reviewing this matrix of schools illuminated tensions and polarities that have underpinned all my subsequent writing, allowing me to view a variety of issues through those different lenses. It made visible the hidden structures of PR scholarship, and enabled me to challenge the authority of some of the 'definitive' texts (though I faltered in delivering the conference paper to the authors of those texts: it was like presenting to my bookshelf). It was my second sole-authored paper and part of my personal exploration of the field, but has now been one of the *JCM*'s top downloaded papers every year since publication (personal communication), suggesting its value to others. The popularity of this paper, often used as a teaching aid, also persuaded me of the value of asking obvious questions – clearly, many fellow academics were as confused as I was.

So this chapter proceeds from the same motive – a desire to understand the layout of the field before entering into a detailed critique. Building on that earlier writing, it presents the field of PR as comprising a set of schools: excellence, advocacy (rhetorical and marketplace), relationship management and critical/ cultural. Each of these has a different stance on the idea of PR, the role of the practitioner and, in particular, on PR ethics, ranging from the idealized image of the ethical guardian found in the excellence school to the demonic propagandist described by the most vehement critics. Other writers (e.g. Edwards, 2011) simplify the division into normative and cultural, which has attractions, and there has recently been an extraordinary expansion of the field as issues of globalization, identity, power and culture have entered the debate (Bardhan and Weaver, 2011; Curtin and Gaither, 2007; Edwards and Hodges, 2011). These contributions are briefly considered under the critical umbrella, but suggest the need for an extension to this grouping. Indeed, recent writings (Curtin, 2012; Edwards, 2012) review the core paradigms for PR, contributing to a deeper philosophical examination of competing world views. But as this grouping has proved useful to me and others, I'll use it as a starting point for considering the theoretical foundations and directions of current PR thinking.

The excellence project

The Symmetrical/Excellence theory of PR emerged from a USD 400,000 International Association of Business Communicators-sponsored research project in the 1980s and 1990s, designed to make the value of PR work explicit (Mackey, 2009: 52). This generated a set of dimensions of 'best practice' that were then offered as a universal framework for 'excellent' PR (see Weaver, 2011: 252ff). It built on the work of Grunig and Hunt (1984), who wrote the first serious book about the theoretical and strategic principles of PR and formulated the famous 'four models of public relations communication' (1984: 22). They characterized PR as falling into four categories: publicity, information (both one-way communication) and asymmetrical and symmetrical communication (both two-way but with only the latter representing equality). These were originally presented as a historical progress from unethical hucksterism to ethical symmetry, though this has been modified by Grunig (2001). The excellent communicator serves a management function and has access to key internal stakeholders via the dominant coalition (such as the boardroom) and salient external stakeholders, making the core role that of 'boundary spanner'. Public relations practitioners interact with an organization's environment to 'gather, select, and relay information from the environment to decision makers in the dominant coalition' (White and Dozier, 1992: 93). This role achieves its highest level in symmetric communication when the full range of negotiating and diplomatic skills is deployed to secure positive outcomes for all parties: 'In the two-way symmetric model ... practitioners serve as mediators between organisations and their publics. Their goal is mutual understanding between practitioners and their publics' (Grunig and Hunt, 1984: 22), where each party is willing to alter their behaviour to accommodate the needs of the other. While the other models are characterized by monologue-type communication, communication in this model is fully reciprocal and power relationships are balanced. Critics (Pieczka 1996; Moloney 2000, 2006, for example) argue that it is so rarely practised as to be unhelpful. Weaver (2011: 254) points out that the excellence approach is 'both managerialist (in that it emphasises the causal value of efficient management to organisational success) and "scientific" (in presenting a universal law of causality between how public relations is practiced and organisational effectiveness)'. In many ways the focus on organizations' desires, goals and strategies is only just being challenged by new approaches (see critical section below). The emphasis on scientific method – the theories are grounded in large-scale, longitudinal, international interviews with practitioners – has also had a major impact on the field. Indeed, Grunig and White (1992: 31) extol the virtues of scientific method as forcing people to 'think logically and systematically' and 'ground' the profession, reflecting a transatlantic divide between the post-war US preference for quantitative methods in all their academic subjects and long European traditions of reflection, interpretation and qualitative forms of research. As Weaver (2011: 253) points out, systems theory – the foundation of the excellence project – was developed in the biological sciences and exported to PR, where it 'represents the organisation as a complex social system made up of interdependent parts, and as linked to and dependent on the environment in which it operates'.

In summary, excellence theory emerged from management theories in the mid-twentieth century, with very low critical awareness of its own ideological bias and an insistence on PR's social value, an assumption that is foundational in its ethics (see below). Yet despite these inadequacies the excellent approach has been the dominant paradigm for several decades, so it should not be dismissed without an examination of its attractions to academics and practitioners. First, the attractions of the scientific method are considerable when teaching a subject as hybrid and ill-defined as PR; the longitudinal, international nature of the data collected gave a powerful boost to the hitherto anecdotal and disorganized writing on PR. It also positioned the field as a significant one, albeit with organizations rather than society at its heart (the dominant coalition is clearly seated in the boardroom, not in any elected chamber or voluntary organization). As Moloney (2006: 3) says, 'James Grunig … drew an intellectual route map that in its stages distanced PR from propaganda and made public relations intellectually respectable, decently practicable, and legitimately teachable'. Like others, I leapt upon the lovely diagram, the historical examples, the simplicity it offered to students perplexed by PR's lack of definition, especially if they were simultaneously being told by marketing lecturers that PR equals publicity and is a subset of marketing. Here was an idea that put PR up with the bosses and moreover asserted that in so doing it was playing a crucial role in the very fabric of society. What's not to like?

The puzzle for me, and for many others (L'Etang and Pieczka, 1996; Moloney, 2006; Pfau and Wan, 2006; Porter, 2010; Weaver *et al.*, 2006) was that it refused to acknowledge PR's role in propaganda, its dubious record on many issues and, crucially, its central task of persuasion (which is explored more fully later in the book). As a campaigner in UK local government and trade union movements during the conflict-ridden Thatcher years, I had no pretensions to 'objectivity' and understood that I used communication persuasively to win arguments and influence opinions in a democratic arena, either in person through speeches and debates or indirectly through communication channels. It was the only non-violent means available to those lacking power. In some ways, my desire to articulate an alternative view, to find ethical room for persuasion, has fuelled my academic journey to date.

The critical scholars cited above supplied the missing piece of the jigsaw: power. Omit power dynamics and not only is two-way symmetrical communication eminently achievable but persuasion must be demonized as an intruder from the murky world of politics. Over the years I have noticed that the colleagues who are most enthusiastic about the Grunigian paradigm are most resistant to any ideological analysis of society: 'I'm just not political' they'd say while explaining to students how advertising/marketing/accounting was essential for the smooth operation of free-market capitalism. The US texts, like the excellence writings, echoed this claim and the two arguments seemed connected: a) persuasion is peripheral; b) PR is apolitical. I didn't buy either position.

The popularity of Grunig's theoretical approach in classrooms and lecture halls is evident from the number of courses and texts that rely on it 'not only because it offers a clear framework for analysis but also because it has been used to underpin ideas about the role and ethics of public relations practice' (Pieczka and L'Etang, 2001: 229). Holtzhausen (2000) critiques PR academics' reliance on Grunig's management theories and excellence study, which she describes as 'a metanarrative … lack[ing] in reflexivity' (2000: 256), a view shared by others (Cheney and Christianson, 2001; McKie, 2001) who urge scholars to expand their conceptual framework. Developments in theory, particularly from critical and cultural scholars, hint that the Age of Excellence may be drawing to a close. Edwards and Hodges (2011: 12) note that through such work 'the limitations of normative scholarship are being addressed gradually, but more is required'. After all, excellence still shapes global curricula and codes of ethics, and is presented as a norm in many recent text books (Chia and Synnott, 2009; Johnston and Zawawi, 2009), meaning its influence has years if not decades to run and therefore deserves continuing scrutiny and challenge. Moreover, while critical scholars (see below) are dismantling the core claims of the excellence project, and particularly exposing the power dynamics at the heart of PR, ethics are still underexplored, an omission that this book seeks in part to correct.

Excellence and ethics

The two-way symmetric level of communication (the fourth model) is the only one which is seen as inherently ethical, meaning that the excellence approach to ethics relies on structural issues. 'It is difficult, if not impossible, to practice public relations in a way that is ethical and socially responsible using an asymmetrical model' (Grunig *et al.*, 1992: 175). As the primary asymmetrical communication is persuasion, the bulk of PR content is thus dismissed as inherently unethical. Grunig and Hunt (1984) offer nebulous advice that practitioners should have the 'will to be ethical' and should not adversely affect others, but concentrate on following Codes of Conduct. Although detailed systems theory approaches to ethics are developed by McElreath (1996) and Bowen (2007), many references to ethics are idealized, with references to 'best practice', 'excellence' and codes rather than principles. For example, Bowen (2007: 275) finds that 'ethics is a single excellent factor and the common underpinning of all factors that predict excellent public relations', concluding that 'public relations is serving a larger and more ethically responsible role by communicating for the good of society, both for the benefit of specific groups and for the maintenance of society itself' (2007: 279). The prominence given to the symmetrical models (despite its rarity in reality) has led to an elevated ideal: 'There is an implied judgement that PR has become two-way respectful dialogue with others—or that it soon will' (Moloney, 2006: 168). Yet, as Bivins (1993) argued two decades ago, this claim rests on no clear idea of what is in the 'public interest' or the means by which PR serves it. In particular he highlights the 'additional burden' (1993: 118) on the practitioner of serving both client and society as a whole. As Bivins points out, these tensions are not addressed by Grunig's two-way symmetric model or by the 'entirely insufficient' (1993: 119) Public Relations Society of America (PRSA) code of professional standards. As the latter has been constructed on the principles of the former (Parkinson, 2001), this is hardly surprising. Moreover, having established these 'truths', the model was then exported globally as the universal ideal for all PR (Parkinson, 2001).

The emphasis on two-way symmetric communication as the sole ethical position has been revised somewhat (Grunig, 2001) following extensive criticism of the idealism inherent in promoting the symmetrical model as a norm (especially by critical scholars L'Etang and Piezcka, see above), so that symmetry and asymmetry are presented as a continuum rather than as binary oppositions. In the revision, Grunig accepts that persuasion is part of current, not merely historical, practice and suggests a spectrum of communication from asymmetric to mutually beneficial, rather than discrete categories, but the central system is still that of the organization, not its societal context, as others have noted, and the distaste for persuasion persists.

However, while excellence may be the dominant paradigm (Botan and Hazleton, 2006) it is not the only game in town.

Rhetorical theory

While excellence was the first body of PR theory I was exposed to, over time it became clear that rhetorical approaches were highly influential in US academic discourse, though it is not established widely in other countries' PR curricula (Fawkes and Tench, 2004). The curricula, organization and location of US PR education is set out in two major research reports, *Port of Entry* (PRSA, 1999) and *The Professional Bond* (PRSA, 2006), and is outside the scope of this book. Contributors to the *Port of Entry* report, Miller and Kernisky (1999) stress the centrality of theory in the persuasive/rhetorical tradition, which leads to examination of audience role and motives, ethical advocacy, interactive rhetoric, intrapersonal, interpersonal, intra-organizational and mass media channels of communication. However, while some European scholars, such as Ihlen (2002, 2011) have promoted the rhetorical approach, it is still primarily a US-based school (Toth and Heath, 1992; Heath, 2001, 2010). I suspect the European equivalent is semiotic approaches to the exchange of meaning in text and symbol, another underdeveloped area of PR as communication (though see Burkart, 2007; Mickey, 2003). A key aspect of rhetorical theory (Heath, 2007; Porter, 2010; Toth and Heath, 1992) is that it does address the role of persuasion in communication, dating back to Aristotle and strongly linked to concepts of democracy. The communicator uses words and symbols to influence the perceptions of others, with varying outcomes. The roles of speaker, audience, the choice of message, and the dynamics and characteristics of each provides the focus of study, lending itself to the examination of PR as shapers of organizational rhetoric. Here, persuasion is seen as central, not peripheral, and the exchange of ideas in the public arena as an essential element in democratic discourse, so persuasion is not inherently unethical. Thus the central image for rhetorical approaches is that of the advocate, though this is not the cab-rank version promoted by marketplace theory (see below) but a more refined, educated Aristotelian (I see Gore Vidal here) using sophisticated persuasion techniques in a forum of equals who have all been educated in such tropes. Rhetoric is often located in speech or linguistic schools and may involve deconstructing and constructing language in political campaigns, for example (see Marsh, 2013).

Rhetorical ethics

Writers on PR from the rhetorical perspective, such as Baker and Martinson (2002), Edgett (2002) and Porter (2010), have deepened understanding of how persuasive communication might be ethical, generally drawing on virtue ethics, which is explored more fully in Chapter 4. The virtues and vices of PR and advertising practitioners are contrasted in Baker (2008), offering a model for good and bad practice, but recognizing that this is a continuum. Heath (2007) explores the tension between the symmetry proposed as the basis of ethics in the excellence approach and the ethical aspects of advocacy, noting Grunig's (2001) acceptance that not all ethical dialogue can be symmetrical, or there would be no room for debate. Rather, argues Heath, ethical advocacy requires equal access to the structures and platforms of debate. Porter (2010) goes further, suggesting that PR *is* rhetoric (2010: 129) and that 'rhetoric provides a framework for ethical public relations' (2010: 128), illustrating the earlier comment that ethical approaches to PR are framed by competing theoretical lenses. While rhetorical approaches do help redress the balance on persuasion and therefore have a more nuanced ethical stance, there are problems here, too. As Holtzhausen (2012: 6) points out, Heath's (2009) use of the 'wrangle in the marketplace' metaphor for developing theory treats theory building as a form of capitalism, an ideological position. Virtue ethics has its limitations too, which are considered in Chapter 4.

Marketplace theory

A second version of the PR advocate is more reliant on marketplace theory than rhetoric. Here advocacy is the act of

> publicly representing an individual, organisation or idea with the object of persuading targeted audiences to look favourably upon, or to accept the point of view of, the individual, the organisation or the idea. In this respect, public relations practitioners share the general nature of their purpose with lawyers.
>
> (Johnston and Zawawi, 2009: 119)

The attorney-advocate is a model of PR that was put forward by Barney and Black (1994) and developed by Fitzpatrick and Bronstein (2006). This model recognizes that PR often plays a more asymmetrical or persuasive role than is encompassed by the Grunigian boundary spanner. Fitzpatrick and Bronstein (2006) argue that all organizations are entitled to have a voice:

> Marketplace theory is predicated, first on the existence of an objective truth which will emerge from a cacophony of voices promoting various interests; second on a marketplace in which all citizens have the right – and perhaps the means – to be both heard and informed; and third, on the rational ability of people to discern 'truth'.
>
> (Fitzpatrick, 2006: 4)

It is strongly USA-based, citing the First Amendment as inspiration, as well as social responsibility theory. The problems with the 'objectivity' of truth (despite the inverted commas) are not explored.

Public relations practitioners' comments (see below) suggest that this is the image with most resonance for those outside academe. It may not be enshrined in core texts or have a developed theoretical base but many PR practitioners model themselves on lawyers. However, they do so on a false premise: unlike lawyers, PR people are not licensed and, while they too have to make the best case for the client, the court of public opinion, let alone behind-the-scenes influence, is very different to a court of law. Again, the presumption of equity between parties omits the power dimension and renders the theory attractive but fantastical.

Marketplace ethics

The advocacy approach presented by Fitzpatrick and Bronstein (2006), is fairly uncritical of the workings and morality of the free market, but does recognize the need for ethical constraints within the marketplace and suggests that these should involve awareness of factors such as access, process, truth and disclosure (Fitzpatrick, 2006: 3). Seib and Fitzpatrick (1995) talk about the five duties of PR professionals as being to oneself, the client, the employer, the profession and society. These are not necessarily listed in rank order, but emphasize awareness of the multiple levels of ethical consideration practitioners face. But the conundrum identified by Bivins (1993) remains: how to balance duty to client and to society?

Relationship management theory

Audiences move to centre-stage in relationship theory, which conceptualizes PR professionals as negotiating a complex set of relationships inside and outside client/employer organizations (Ledingham and Bruning, 2001). Relationship management draws on a variety of theoretical disciplines to identify the elements that make up a positive relationship, such as control mutuality, trust, satisfaction, commitment, exchange relationship and communal relationship (Hon and Grunig, 1999). Unlike the organization-centred perspective of systems theory approaches to PR, it can take the standpoint of the publics (Leitch and Nielson, 2001), though it shares similar managerialist objectives of improving business goals by harnessing relationships more effectively, making them instrumental and functionalist rather than mutually transformative. Jahansoozi (2006) suggests that the focus on publics follows cultural and technological shifts which have empowered service and media users and facilitated international dialogue and/or coalitions. It also follows the excellence approach in many respects, methodologically, as it seeks to map and measure the nature and content of relationships according to a number of variables, such as the wants and needs of parties; the degree of mutual understanding; past, existing and desired relationships, and the role of symbols and interaction in the relationship. Like excellence it focuses on best practice and the needs of organizations, lacking the critical perspective, and there is a sense of convergence between these two approaches.

Relationship management ethics

The ethics of relationship management seem underexplored, particularly in the lack of a developed theory of relationship dialogue. An emerging theme in PR ethics is ethical dialogue (Day *et al.*, 2001; Kent and Taylor, 2002), though Pieczka (2011) suggests that while many PR scholars have stressed the centrality of dialogue to the field, there has only been superficial engagement with dialogic theory, unlike related disciplines such as political science and organizational communication, which have developed a range of techniques and applications that have changed their practice. In contrast, she says, 'there is very little in public relations scholarship to help the discipline think about how dialogue can become an expert communication skill' (2011: 117). Hodges and McGrath (2011) also suggest that these recent invocations of dialogue lack scrutiny and are deployed to serve organizational ends; for example, in Kent and Taylor's (2002: 30) emphasis on dialogue as generating 'public support, enhanced image/reputation and decreased governmental interference'.

Critical/cultural perspectives

In 1995, I had been running PR courses from scratch for nearly five years (with a year out to do an MA in creative writing) and wondering how long I could go on deconstructing my own experience and improvising student campaigns and projects. I had developed teaching methods that challenged students' ingenuity, problem-solving skills and communication talents but not really found a way to raise my uncertainty about the field as a whole. Then I went to the Bled International conference in 1995, where I first met Jacquie L'Etang, Magda Pieczka and others (including James and Larissa Grunig); we were a group of about 50 PR academics, as it was still a tiny field. This is where I learned that I belonged in the critical school, as it was these writers who voiced my unease and ambivalence.

Critical approaches, including postmodernism, political economy and, at the outer reaches, propaganda studies, are sceptical of the PR role; L'Etang summarizes this grouping as 'an interdisciplinary approach which seeks to define assumptions which are taken-for-granted with a view to challenging their source and legitimacy' (2005: 521). The key differential from the previous approaches is that critical writers scrutinize the power dynamics of organizations and their publics, and often reveal the persistent involvement of PR practitioners in propaganda and deception, past and present. While the previously covered models share an optimistic view of PR's contribution to democracy and tend to minimize the role of propaganda in the formation of the field (Moloney, 2000), critical scholars are more sceptical of such claims (Fawkes and Moloney, 2008; L'Etang, 2006; Moloney, 2006; Weaver *et al.*, 2006).

Critical theory emerged from the Frankfurt school of scholars in the 1930s, with a base in Marxism and a (well-founded) fear of media manipulation; later proponents included Jurgen Habermas, who developed concepts of the public sphere and communicative action and derides the persuasive elements in PR, as he strives for a communication equality. His approach to ethics is considered in Chapter 4. The propaganda model (Chomsky, 2002; Herman and Chomsky, 1988) suggests that 'free' press can be manipulated to serve governmental and business interests, and that PR is inherently propagandist, an argument repeatedly made by PR's greatest critics, Stauber and Rampton (2004) in the USA and Miller and Dinan (2008) in the UK. They particularly highlight the distortions to the democratic process, caused by PR firms' fake grass-roots campaigns (astroturfing), or questions planted in media conferences by PR people masquerading as journalists. However, they provide little insight into what might constitute legitimate PR, and tend to conflate corporate business interests with communication, without considering the promotional activities of voluntary, charity or trade union groups, for example.

There are also PR scholars who take a critical perspective from *within* the field, such as Pieczka, L'Etang, Edwards, Moloney, Weaver, Pfau, Holtzhausen and McKie, and this is where I locate my own work. This involves the tricky stance of criticizing an occupation that you are educating others to join. My own rationale is that the field desperately needs practitioners who can think as well as act, who are prepared to challenge assumptions and are capable of seeing the bigger picture.

Some (Edwards, 2012; Weaver, 2011) note that critical scholarship can prove better at demolition than construction and I am conscious of a need to correct my own negativity towards PR when in full critical flow. Rather than dismiss PR as wholly ideological, as do some critics, I prefer to see communication as inherently neutral, capable of being deployed ideologically of course, but not essentially so. Many critics seem to conflate the organizational or sectoral interests with their communication strategy, blaming PR for inequalities in capitalism. On the other hand, many examples of gross distortion of communication, amounting to corporate propaganda, do originate in organizations with considerable economic power. These issues are explored throughout the book and go to the heart of PR ethics.

Critical scholars have many differences between them but share a rejection of the normative influence of the excellence approach, arguing for greater reflexivity, acceptance of the role of propaganda in the formation of PR, and reaching outside the field to bring aspects of postmodernism (Holtzhausen, 2012), chaos theory/complexity (McKie, 2001; McKie and Munshi, 2007; McKie and Willis, 2012) and social theory (Ihlen *et al.*, 2009) for example, into discussion of PR. There is general agreement among these scholars that PR needs to engage with a wider range of theory to develop a greater understanding of its role in society. Edwards (2011) calls this the socio-cultural turn, and it looks as if the field is heading in some interesting directions.

Critical ethics

Critical scholars have written about ethics: for example, Curtin and Boynton (2001) provide a critical overview of PR ethics; L'Etang (2003) raises serious reservations about the PR function as the 'ethical conscience' of the organization; and Weaver, Motion and Roper (2006: 21) examine the role of propaganda in shaping PR practice and theory, concluding that

> the critical theory perspective … finds no substantive difference between propaganda and public relations … this is a consequence of a rejection of the notions that propaganda necessarily operates counter to the public interest, and that public relations necessarily works for the public interest.

Others have looked at PR ethics from the perspectives of political economy (Moloney, 2006), narrative theory (Breit and Demetrious, 2010) and a Weberian approach (Waeraas, 2009). Yet overall, critical scholars tend to foreground social, political or economic theory rather than ethical issues, which may be explained by Kersten's (1994) comment that 'a critical perspective on the ethics of PR … maintains that the question of ethics cannot be examined without exploring the social context in which PR practice takes place' (cited in Bowen *et al.*, 2006: 126). It is also natural that critical scholars are primarily engaged in de-constructing and challenging normative assumptions in theory and practice, rather than constructing alternatives.

Curtin and Gaither (2005, 2007) do however move from critique to construction, with a proposal for the 'circuit of culture' as a new paradigm for PR scholarship, including ethics. This borrows concepts from cultural and sociological study (du Gay *et al.*, 1997), and shows how a circuit of 'moments' (comprising representation, identity, production, consumption and regulation) offers a powerful model of interrelated, continuing, process-based communication with strong foundations in and implications for PR. Practitioners are envisioned as 'cultural intermediaries' (Bourdieu, 1984) and key players in the 'cultural economy' (both terms are fully explored in Curtin and Gaither, 2007). Ethics comes under the regulatory heading, as it involves cultural norms, an insight that could encourage a move away from reliance on codes to examining 'what meanings codes have as cultural artefacts ... for example, ethics codes may play quite different roles in different cultures ... [and] ... in constructing the identities of public relations practitioners and the profession' (Curtin and Gaither, 2005: 104).

A postmodern approach to ethics is taken by Holtzhausen (2012), who usefully rejects 'metanarratives' such as ethical guardian or advocate, embracing instead the contradictions and complexity of contemporary practice. As she says, drawing on Bauman (1993), '[t]he postmodern rejection of universal ethics thus focuses on the moral responsibility of the individual to the *Other* without an institutionally created ethical framework' (1993: 33). I would agree that ethical debate needs to shift from reliance on external codes to an internalized, owned set of – unfixed – ethical principles, though would suggest that these can be developed collectively, in professional bodies or organizational settings. A simple increase in reflexivity – Is this OK? Why do I feel uncomfortable? – would be an advance on some of the arguments put forward by practitioners (see below). These issues are explored from the field of professional ethics in Chapter 4, then relocated in PR in Chapter 5.

Competing ethical identities in public relations

The above comparative analysis of the different approaches to PR suggests that: a) each approach contains its own ethical stance; b) approaches tend to treat their own version of PR as absolute – only the critical theorists have taken a step back to compare views; and c) there is very little engagement with other perspectives in the field of ethics or professional ethics, leading to fragmented and contradictory ethics. In particular, the idealized version of PR promoted by the Grunigian approach and supported by many key texts is incompatible with the enthusiastic embrace of the advocacy role by practitioners. The next section draws on a recent paper for the *Public Relations Review* (Fawkes, 2012) to consider not only the competing views within academic approaches to PR but to highlight the tensions between academics and practitioners.

While the 'ethical guardian' image dominates textbooks, the languages of professional bodies and codes of conduct, the 'advocate' role emerges clearly from practitioner voices. These images or representations move beyond description to constitute identity, in the fluid sense envisaged by Curtin and Gaither (2005, 2007) and described above, explicitly linking identity and ethics. The binary opposition between guardian (sometimes 'angel') and advocate is of course simplistic and reductive; Curtin and Gaither (2007) note that the focus on the 'public relations practitioner as sole ethical decision-maker in the organization ... is typical of the modernist perspective of the powerful individual who can control and direct his environment' (2007: 33). But this polarity will be helpful later in the book, where a Jungian perspective will be offered as a bridge between these extremes. It also reflects the divide between academics and practitioners in PR towards profession-alization, which van Ruler (2005) sees as a Mars/Venus schism, an idea considered in the next chapter. In contrasting approaches to ethics by academics and practi-tioners, I am illuminating the lacuna between the ideal and the lived experience of the field.

Academic views of public relations' ethical role

There is a strong claim in PR texts that the PR function should play the role of organizational ethical guardian, usually citing the excellence approach in support. For example: 'As ethics are important to organisational excellence on the one hand and to public relations on the other, practitioners should be at the forefront of the movement for ethical organisational conduct' (Johnston and Zawawi, 2009: 115). Or: 'A public relations officer who is also a corporate conscience helps mold a corporation so that its goals and actions are consisted with the public good' (Ryan and Martinson, 1983, cited in Bowen, 2008: 277). This view of PR, as a force for public good, underpins the development of excellence theory (Grunig *et al.*, 1992) and, consequentially, its ethical approach. Bowen's (2008) analysis is firmly bounded by systems theory, which, she asserts, 'provides a normative theoretical framework to explain why public relations is the best suited function to advise senior management on matters of ethics' (2008: 273). Having established the desirability of this function and the suitability of PR to execute it, she is naturally perplexed that so many practitioners reject the role (see below). The idea of PR's ethical advocacy informs documents such as the Global Alliance Melbourne Mandate (Global Alliance, 2012), mentioned above, where practitioners are given detailed guidance on conducting a workplace 'integrity index', and their respon-sibility to self, organization and profession is stressed – ideas that are explored in Chapters 4 and 5. However, L'Etang (2003) raises serious reservations about this concept, given the lack of moral philosophy in the educational or training back-grounds of most practitioners: 'An important question to ask is whether the public relations practitioner is qualified to be "an ethical guardian". This claim is questionable' (2003: 64). Interestingly, as Bowen (2008) discovered, the main opposition comes not from scholars but from the equally powerful, if less academ-ically investigated, image of the PR function as advocate, paid to promote the interests of the employer, not other publics or society as a whole. This marketplace approach (sketched above) is a view marginalized by PR academics but embraced by practitioners. A further division has been recently identified between European and North American scholars (Bowen and Erzikova, 2013), finding the former tend to stress philosophical bases for ethical reflection and decision-making, while the latter are more orientated towards industry and the application of professional ethics in practice. This research helps explain some of the tensions explored throughout this book, and while the contribution of ethical scholars from outside these two arenas has yet to be fully realized, the Asian roots of Jungian ethics provide a new perspective.

Practitioner views of public relations' ethics

The views of practitioners are taken from three main sources: media coverage of a debate about ethics hosted by the University of Westminster in the UK and reported by one of the organizers (Goldsworthy, 2007); the International Association of Business Communicators' (IABC) quantitative and qualitative research into practitioner views on ethics (Bowen, 2008; Bowen *et al.*, 2006) and an online essay by practitioner Paul Seaman (2011). Obviously directly quoted practitioner voices lack the academic credibility of peer-reviewed sources and only the Bowen works constitute empirical research, but these voices do help illustrate some themes in general discourse, so seem worth reporting, albeit with health warnings.

The Westminster debate was covered in the UK PR trade magazine, *PR Week*, the CIPR newsletter and leadership blogs and various other blogs from the UK and USA (kindly supplied by Simon Goldsworthy). The motion 'PR has a duty to tell the truth' was defeated by 138 to 124 votes, and, according to commentators, the winning arguments (put forward by Goldsworthy and leading publicist Max Clifford) were that PR professionals have a primary duty to clients not the truth and that media hostility made it impossible for clients to tell the truth. Subsequent comments illustrate the tension referred to earlier between the advocate and excellence roles:

- Are you telling the truth by creating a campaign that highlights the amazing focus of customer care and philanthropic nature of a client … and leaving out pending lawsuits by upset clients, former employees and product defects (comment on blog, Jarvis, 2007)?
- I was dismayed. Truth and integrity have to be the cornerstones of our profession if we are to have any credibility with the media and the wider world (Peter Crumpler, Director of Communication, Church of England, *PR Week*, 21 February, 2007).
- The victorious Clifford insisted that lying was sometimes necessary to achieve the greater good (*PR Week*, 21 February, 2007).
- I hope any CIPR members in the audience were aware of the requirements of the Code and that they had voted accordingly (CIPR President, Lionel Zetter, from his blog, cited in Goldsworthy, 2007: 5).
- To survive as a useful marketing tool, it is a necessity that PR should be seen as a truthful medium: if we cannot rescue our reputation for honesty, we have no commercial future (John Mounsey, director, Trail Communications, Letter, *PR Week*, 9 March, 2007).

- The fact that PR people admit they need to lie occasionally is a sign of growing honesty and confidence in what they do (Daniel Rogers, Opinion, *PR Week*, 21 February, 2007).
- Industry maxim: 'ethical PR consultancy = small PR consultancy' (Goldsworthy, 2007: 5).

The purpose of these quotes is not to raise issues of truth, lies and loyalty but to illustrate the confusion that exists in the field, much of which is tied to conceptions of role. In this cut-throat version of advocacy (as suggested, reflecting the marketplace rather than rhetorical approaches) ethics are purely reputational, a 'marketing tool' at best, a liability at worst. Those who see themselves as advocates experience their loyalty as primarily to the client, while those who write codes base their conceptualization in the idealized symmetrical communication of the excellence project, in which persuasion is inherently unethical. Codes are used as a rhetorical weapon from CIPR officers but this voice sounds desperate rather than threatening. It should also be noted that the main arguments recorded (Goldsworthy, 2007) were pragmatic: lying tends to be found out in the long term; and debates like this are damaging to the reputation of PR. Despite being framed as an ethical debate, it would seem that core concepts of ethics were almost entirely absent and that the main dialogue was a competition between self-serving arguments. It is also interesting to note here that advocacy becomes grounds for abdicating moral responsibility, which is placed with the employer/client not the practitioner. This echoes the sterile debate that erupts whenever PR ethics is raised: would you work for tobacco/arms/oil/bad people? As if ethics consists of a one-off employment choice rather than a process that affects the decisions communicators make all day every day.

Trust and corporate reputation are also drivers behind the IABC report, *The Business of Truth, a guide to ethical communication* (Bowen *et al.*, 2006), which surveyed just under 2000 senior practitioners in north America, New Zealand, Israel and Australia, as well as qualitative interviews and focus groups. Their key findings were a) that practitioners considered dealing with ethical concerns to be part of their everyday practice, though it was frequently not labeled as such and b) that practitioners distinguish between the ethical counseling role, which involves advising management on particular situations, and managing core values by embedding relevant qualities in all communications and other activities. This could be seen as differentiating between ethical acts and ethical agents. Nevertheless the research found a sizeable proportion of respondents rejected the 'ethical counselor' role, feeling that was the province of the legal department or the board itself, particularly where communications was not represented at board level. The research also found that while many wished to be considered as ethical counselors, there was very little training in ethical theory or practice. One respondent is quoted as saying: 'It's simple stuff. Fundamentally you're either a good person or you're not' (2006: 8). On the other hand, another respondent commented, 'My job is filled with ethical issues. Who we are, what we've done, what we'd like to do, and what do we want to do in the future', which is echoed by another, 'I do ethics stuff all the time – they just don't call it that' (2006: 9). The report stresses that ethics matters because of its relationship to communication credibility, organizational reputation and relationships to publics (2006: 13), but that practitioners are ill-equipped to participate fully in such roles due to inadequate training and lack of discussion on such issues by employers. Bowen's (2008) exploration of this material concludes that the strongly polarized views of respondents reflect divergent views on ethics among practitioners, between those who sought to offer counsel and those who embraced the advocacy model. She groups these respondents into 'pro-ethical' and 'anti-ethical' camps, implying that there is no alternative ethical approach to the counselor role.

Such a position is vigorously rejected by Paul Seaman (2011), an experienced practitioner who writes regular articles on issues of practice and theory; in his essay 'A new moral agenda for PR' he attacks the concept of ethical guardian, suggesting that the idea of PRs as 'moral keepers of their organization' (2011: 6) is rather grand. Indeed, he says that 'Grunig, in common with many PR thinkers, mistakenly believes that PR is about establishing mutual understanding between publics and clients. Actually, PR is about advocacy on behalf of clients' (2011: 8). He also notes the export of Grunigian views of the world (which, unusually, he treats as congruent with those of L'Etang) to the development of stakeholder doctrine, corporate social responsibility, sustainability and as embedded in the Stockholm Accords – all of which he sees as falsely claiming to serve social rather than corporate or shareholder interests. Seaman's views raise interesting questions about the role and image of the practitioner, and seem to articulate some of the voices found in the Westminster debate and IABC research. It is important to note that Seaman does not condone amoral behavior, but asks for a more robust defense of what PR advocacy contributes.

I'd also like to mention here a small study (Thurlow, 2009) which found practitioners distancing themselves from PR as an identity, described as a stigmatized or 'tainted' occupation. They expressed particular concern about the effect of the term 'spin doctor' and the unethical behaviour of a minority of practitioners on communication professionals generally. They are of course right – most practitioners make a contribution to their organizations and act responsibly – but denial is not a solution to stigma, as some defenders of PR seem to believe. One respondent illustrates the dilemma expressed by Seaman, above: '[a] code of ethics requires us to respect the confidentiality of our clients and protect their relationships. Sometimes that might preclude us from actually taking something to the media … like an issue that might hurt the client' (2009: 258).

The key problem raised in the practitioner debates is the absence of any engagement with ethical issues at all beyond the self-serving and pragmatic 'don't get caught' maxims that concern survival rather than ethics. The abdication of responsibility to legal departments or the organization/board cannot be reconciled with claims to professionalism. However, I suggest that the poverty of these arguments may be, at least partially, attributed to the insistence on ideals promoted by texts, codes and professional bodies. The emphasis on the excellent ethical guardian may have widened the gap: refusing to engage with persuasion leaves practitioners, to whom it is the daily business, with nowhere to go for guidance. They have to adopt the ethical guardian role or condemn themselves to the unethical outlands. They choose the latter.

Codes

Public relations codes of ethics are largely based on the excellence approaches to the field, explicitly or implicitly. Their content and function are explored more fully in Chapter 5, following consideration of the role of ethical codes in professions generally. Here I will merely cite Parkinson (2001), who suggests that the PRSA code of ethics is strongly influenced by the excellence model in its emphasis on symmetry and avoidance of persuasion. He argues that this in turn has influenced models exported around the world: the Global Alliance approach to ethics is broadly similar in tone and content, for example (Breit and Demetrious, 2010), as can be seen by the wording of the 2012 Melbourne Mandate mentioned earlier. This suggests that the ethical guardian ideal has been promoted as a universal norm and written into professional codes around the world. Yet the absence of detailed discussion of ethics from the core excellence texts (Grunig *et al.*, 1992; Grunig and Hunt, 1984) is striking: codes are presented as sufficient to handle the complex conflicts of duty that constitute real ethical debate. As Kruckeberg (2000: 37) says: 'Contemporary codified public relations professional ethics would seem a grossly inadequate primary referent for practitioners serving in the role of interpreter and ethicist and social policy-maker in guiding organiza- tional behavior as well as in influencing and reconciling public perceptions'. Moreover they are rarely used as a disciplinary tool, making them doubly idealistic, not to say hypothetical, both in content and application. Perhaps the primary power of professional codes lies in their embodiment of an imagined identity, both individually and collectively, as the counsel who offers wise words to the dominant coalition and refrains from doing harm.

Conclusions

This chapter has introduced, briefly, some of the themes that will be explored in more depth throughout this book, such as the effect of competing schools of PR scholarship with their separate approaches to ethics. In particular the ethical concept of guardian versus advocate was explored to illustrate the gap between dominant academic and professional body concepts of the field and those often expressed by practitioners. Further, I began to suggest that the emphasis on ideal versions of practitioners has actually hindered ethical dialogue by denying the complex reality that confronts most PR people on a daily basis.

To explore these ideas further, the next two chapters widen the context to consider the nature of professionalism and the kinds of approaches to professional ethics found across professions generally. These contextual chapters then help set the scene for a return to PR ethics in Chapter 5, in order to define more accurately the core problems with PR ethics.

References

Baker, S. (2008) The model of the principled advocate and the pathological partisan: a virtue ethics construct of opposing archetypes of public relations and advertising practitioners. *Journal of Mass Media Ethics, 23*(3): 235–53.

Baker, S. and Martinson, D. L. (2002) Out of the red-light district: five principles for ethically proactive public relations. *Public Relations Quarterly, 47*(3): 15–19.

Bardhan, N. and Weaver, C. K. (2011) *Public Relations in Global Cultural Contexts: multiparadigmatic perspectives*. New York, NY and London: Routledge.

Barney, R. and Black, J. (1994) Ethics and professional persuasive communications. *Public Relations Review, 20*: 233–48.

Bauman, Z. (1993) *Postmodern Ethics*. Oxford: Blackwell.

Bivins, T. H. (1993) Public relations, professionalism and the public interest. *Journal of Business Ethics, 12*: 117–26.

Botan, C. H. and Hazleton, V. (2006) *Public Relations Theory II*. Mahwah, NJ and London: Lawrence Erlbaum Associates.

Bourdieu, P. (1984) *Distinction: a social critique of the judgement of taste*. Cambridge, MA: Harvard University Press.

Bowen, S. A. (2007) The extent of ethics. E. L. Toth (ed.) *The Future of Excellence in Public Relations and Communication Management*. Mahweh, NJ: Lawrence Erlbaum Associates, pp. 275–97.

Bowen, S. A. (2008) A state of neglect: public relations as 'corporate conscience' or ethics counsel. *Journal of Public Relations Research, 20*(3): 271–96. doi: 10.1080/106272 60801962749

Bowen, S. A. and Erzikova, E. (2013) The international divide in public relations ethics education: advocacy versus autonomy. *Public Relations Journal, 7*(1). Online. Available at www.prsa.org/Intelligence/PRJournal/Vol7/No1/#.UyRJzvmSwbA

Bowen, S. A., Heath, R. L., Lee, J., Painter, G., Agraz, F. J., McKie, D. and Toledano, M. (2006) *The Business of Truth: a guide to ethical communication*. San Francisco: International Association of Business Communicators.

Breit, R. and Demetrious, K. (2010) Professionalisation and public relations: an ethical mismatch. *Ethical Space, 7*(4): 20–9.

Brown, J. S. and Duguid, P. (2001) Knowledge and organization: a social-practice perspective. *Organization Science, 12*(2): 198–213.

Burkart, R. (2007) On Jurgen Habermas and public relations. *Public Relations Review, 33:* 249–54.

Bussey, C. (2011) UK PR industry worth £7.5 billion data from PR Census 2011 reveals, *PR Week*.

Cheney, G. and Christianson, L. T. (2001) Public relations as contested terrain: a critical response. In R. L. Heath (ed.) *Handbook of Public Relations*. Thousand Oaks, CA: Sage, pp. 167–82.

Chia, J. and Synnott, G. (2009) *An Introduction to Public Relations*. Oxford: Oxford University Press.

Chomsky, N. (2002) *Media Control: the spectacular achievements of propaganda* (2nd edn) New York, NY: Seven Stories Press.

Curtin, P. A. (2012) Public relations and philosophy: parsing paradigms. *Public Relations Inquiry, 1*(1): 31–47.

Curtin, P. A. and Boynton, L. A. (2001) Ethics in public relations: theory and practice. In R. L. Heath (ed.) *Handbook of Public Relations*. Thousand Oaks, CA: Sage, pp. 411–22.

Curtin, P. A. and Gaither, T. K. (2005) Privileging identity, difference and power: the circuit of culture as a basis for public relations theory. *Journal of Public Relations Research,* *17*(2): 91–115.

Curtin, P. A. and Gaither, T. K. (2007) *International Public Relations: negotiating culture, identity and power.* Thousand Oaks, CA: Sage.

Cutlip, S. M., Center, A. H. and Broom, G. M. (eds) (1985) *Effective Public Relations* (6th edn) London: Prentice-Hall International.

Day, K. D., Dong, Q. and Robins, C. (2001) Public relations ethics: an overview and discussion of issues for the twenty-first century. In R. L. Heath (ed.) *Handbook of Public Relations.* Thousand Oaks, CA: Sage, pp. 403–10.

du Gay, P., Hall, S., Janes, L., Mackay, H. and Negus, K. (1997) *Doing Cultural Studies: the story of the Sony Walkman.* London: Sage.

Edgett, R. (2002) Toward an ethical framework for advocacy. *Journal of Public Relations Research, 14*(1): 1–26.

Edwards, L. (2011) Critical perspectives in global public relations, theorizing power. In N. Bardhan and C. K. Weaver (eds) *Public Relations in Global Cultural Contexts.* New York, NY: Routledge, pp. 29–49.

Edwards, L. (2012) Defining the 'object' of public relations research: a new starting point. *Public Relations Inquiry, 1*(1): 7–30.

Edwards, L. and Hodges, C. E. M. (eds) (2011) *Public Relations, Society & Culture: theoretical and empirical explorations* (1st edn) London: Routledge.

Fawkes, J. (2007) Public relations models and persuasion ethics: a new approach. *Journal of Communication Management, 11*(4): 313–31.

Fawkes, J. (2011) What is public relations? A. Theaker (ed.) *The Public Relations Handbook* (4th edn) London: Routledge, pp. 3–20.

Fawkes, J. (2012) Saints and sinners: competing identities in public relations ethics. *Public Relations Review, 38*(5): 865–72. doi: 10.1016/j.pubrev.2012.07.004

Fawkes, J. and Moloney, K. (2008) Does the European Union (EU) need a propaganda watchdog like the US Institute of Propaganda Analysis to strengthen its democratic civil society and free markets? *Public Relations Review, 34*: 207–14.

Fawkes, J. and Tench, R. (2004) Does employer resistance to theory threaten the future of public relations? A consideration of research findings, comparing UK practitioner, academic and alumni attitudes to public relations education. Paper presented at the 11th International Public Relations Research Symposium, Bled, Slovenia.

Fitzpatrick, K. (2006) Baselines for ethical advocacy in the 'marketplace of ideas'. In K. Fitzpatrick and C. Bronstein (eds) *Ethics in Public Relations: responsible advocacy.* Thousand Oaks, CA: Sage.

Fitzpatrick, K. and Bronstein, C. (2006) *Ethics in Public Relations: responsible advocacy.* Thousand Oaks, CA and London: Sage.

Global Alliance (2012) Online. Available at http://melbournemandate.globalalliancepr.org/wp-content/uploads/2012/11/Melbourne-Mandate-Text-final.pdf, retrieved 18 November, 2013.

Goldsworthy, S. (2007) I'm a liar and so are you: reflections on the aftermath of a famous victory. *Ethical Space, 4*(1/2): 5–7.

Gregory, A. (2011) The state of the public relations profession in the UK: a review of the first decade of the twenty-first century. *Corporate Communications: an international journal, 16*(2): 89–104.

Grunig, J. E. (2001) Two-way symmetrical public relations: past, present and future. In R. L. Heath (ed.) *Handbook of Public Relations.* Thousand Oaks, CA: Sage, pp. 11–30.

Grunig, J. E. and Hunt, T. (1984) *Managing Public Relations*. New York, NY and London: Holt, Rinehart and Winston.

Grunig, J. E. and White, J. (1992) The effect of worldviews on public relations theory and practice. In J. E. Grunig (ed.) *Excellence in Public Relations and Communication Management*. Hillsdale, NJ: Lawrence Erlbaum Associates, pp. 31–64.

Grunig, J. E., Dozier, D. M., Ehling, W. P., Grunig, L. A., Repper, F. C. and White, J. (1992) *Excellence in Public Relations and Communication Management*. Hillsdale, NJ: Lawrence Erlbaum Associates.

Heath, R. L. (2001) A rhetorical enactment rationale for public relations: the good organisation communicating well. In R. L. Heath (ed.) *Handbook of Public Relations*. Thousand Oaks, CA: Sage, pp. 31–50.

Heath, R. L. (2007) Management through advocacy: reflection rather than domination. In J. E. Grunig, E. L. Toth and L. A. Grunig (eds) *The Future of Excellence in Public Relations and Communications Management*. Mahwah, NJ: Lawrence Erlbaum Associates.

Heath, R. L. (2009) The rhetorical tradition: wrangle in the marketplace. In R. L. Heath, E. L. Toth and D. Waymer (eds) *Rhetorical and Critical Approaches to Public Relations II*. New York, NY: Routledge, pp. 17–47.

Heath, R. L. (2010) Mind, self and society. In R. L. Heath (ed.) *The SAGE Handbook of Public Relations*. Thousand Oaks, CA: Sage, pp. 1–4.

Herman, E. S. and Chomsky, N. (1988) *Manufacturing Consent: the political economy of the mass media*. New York, NY: Pantheon Books.

Hodges, C. E. M. and McGrath, N. (2011) Communication for social transformation. In L. Edwards and C. E. M. Hodges (eds) *Public Relations, Society and Culture: theoretical and empirical explorations*. Abingdon: Routledge, pp. 90–104.

Holtzhausen, D. (2000) Postmodern values in public relations. *Journal of Public Relations Research, 12*(1): 251–64.

Holtzhausen, D. R. (2012) *Public Relations as Activism: postmodern approaches to theory & practice*. New York, NY: Routledge.

Hon, L. C. and Grunig, J. E. (1999) Guidelines for measuring relationships in public relations. Online. Available at www.instituteforpr.com.

Ihlen, Ø. (2002) Rhetoric and resources: notes for a new approach to public relations and issues management. *Journal of Public Affairs, 2*(4): 259–69.

Ihlen, Ø. (2011) On barnyard scrambles: toward a rhetoric of public relations. *Management Communication Quarterly, 25*(3): 455–73.

Ihlen, Ø., Fredriksson, M. and Ruler, B. v. (2009) *Public Relations and Social Theory: key figures and concepts*. New York, NY and London: Routledge.

Jahansoozi, J. (2006) Relationships, transparency and evaluation: the implications for public relations. In J. L'Etang and M. Pieczka (eds) *Public Relations, Critical Debates and Contemporary Practice*. Mahweh, NJ: Lawrence Erlbaum Associates, pp. 61–91.

Johnston, J. and Zawawi, C. (2009) *Public Relations: theory and practice*. Crows Nest, NSW, Australia: Allen & Unwin.

Kent, M. L. and Taylor, M. (2002) Toward a dialogic theory of public relations. *Public Relations Review, 14*(28): 21–37.

Kruckeberg, D. (1995) The challenge for public relations in the era of globalization. *Public Relations Quarterly, 40*(4): 36–40.

Kruckeberg, D. (Fall 2000) The public relations practitioner's role in practicing strategic ethics. *Public Relations Quarterly, 45*: 35–9.

L'Etang, J. (2003) The myth of the 'ethical guardian': an examination of its origins, potency and illusions. *Journal of Communication Management, 8*(1): 53–67.

L'Etang, J. (2004) *Public Relations in Britain: a history of professional practice in the twentieth century.* Mahwah, NJ and London: Lawrence Erlbaum Associates.

L'Etang, J. (2005) Critical public relations: some reflections. *Public Relations Review, 31*(4): 521–6.

L'Etang, J. (2006) Public relations and propaganda: conceptual issues, methodological problems and public relations discourse. In J. L'Etang and M. Pieczka (eds) *Public Relations, Critical Debates and Contemporary Practice.* Mahweh, NJ: Lawrence Erlbaum Associates, pp. 23–40.

L'Etang, J. and Pieczka, M. (1996) *Critical Perspectives in Public Relations.* London: International Thomson Business Press.

Ledingham, J. A. and Bruning, S. D. (2001) *Public Relations as Relationship Management: a relational approach to the study and practice of public relations* (2nd edn) Mahwah, NJ and London: Lawrence Erlbaum Associates.

Leitch, S. and Nielson, D. (2001) Bringing publics into public relations: new theoretical frameworks for practice. In R. L. Heath (ed.) *Handbook of Public Relations.* Thousand Oaks, CA: Sage, pp. 127–38.

McElreath, M. P. (1996) *Managing Systematic and Ethical Public Relations* (2nd edn) Madison, WI: Brown and Benchmark.

Mackey, S. (2009) Public relations theory. In J. Johnston and C. Zawawi (eds) *Public Relations: theory and practice.* Crows Nest, NSW, Australia: Allen & Unwin, pp. 47–7.

McKie, D. (2001) Updating public relations: 'new science' research paradigms and uneven developments. In R. L. Heath (ed.) *Handbook of Public Relations.* Thousand Oaks, CA: Sage, pp. 75–91.

McKie, D. and Munshi, D. (2007) *Reconfiguring Public Relations: ecology, equity and enterprise.* London: Routledge.

McKie, D. and Willis, P. (2012) Renegotiating the terms of engagement: public relations, marketing and contemporary challenges. *Public Relations Review, 38*(5): 846–52. doi: http://dx.doi.org/10.1016/j.pubrev.2012.03.008

Macnamara, J. R. (2012) *Public Relations: theories, practices, critiques.* Frenchs Forest, NSW: Pearson Australia.

Marsh, C. (2013) *Classical Rhetoric and Modern Public Relations: an Isocratean model.* Hoboken, NJ: Taylor & Francis.

Mickey, T. J. (2003) *Deconstructing Public Relations: public relations criticism.* Mahwah, NJ and London: Lawrence Erlbaum Associates.

Miller, D. and Dinan, W. (2008) *A Century of Spin: how public relations became the cutting edge of corporate power.* London: Pluto.

Miller, D. P. and Kernisky, D. A. (1999) Opportunity realized: undergraduate education within Departments of Communication. *Public Relations Review, 25*(1): 87–100.

Moloney, K. (2000) *Rethinking Public Relations: the spin and the substance.* London: Routledge.

Moloney, K. (2006) *Rethinking Public Relations: PR propaganda and democracy* (2nd edn) London: Routledge.

Parkinson, M. (2001) The PRSA Code of Professional Standards and Member Code of Ethics: why they are neither professional nor ethical. *Public Relations Quarterly, 46*(3): 27–31.

Pfau, M. and Wan, H. (2006) Persuasion: an intrinsic function in public relations. In C. H. Botan and V. Hazleton (eds) *Public Relations Theory II*. Mahweh NJ: Lawrence Erlbaum Associates, pp. 101–36.

Pieczka, M. (1996) Paradigms, systems theory and public relations. In J. L'Etang and M. Pieczka (eds) *Critical Perspectives in Public Relations*. London: International Thomson Business Press, pp. 124–56.

Pieczka, M. (2011) Public relations as dialogic expertise? *Journal of Communication Management, 15*(2): 108–24.

Pieczka, M. and L'Etang, J. (2001) Public relations and the question of professionalism. In R. L. Heath (ed.) *Handbook of Public Relations*. Thousand Oaks, CA: Sage, pp. 223–35.

Porter, L. (2010) Communicating for the good of the state: a post-symmetrical polemic on persuasion in ethical public relations. *Public Relations Review, 36:* 127–33.

PRSA (1999) *A Port of Entry: public relations education in the 21st century*. New York, NY: Public Relations Society of America.

PRSA (2006) *The Professional Bond: public relations education in the 21st century*. New York, NY: Public Relations Society of America.

Seaman, P. (2011) A new moral agenda for PR. *21st Century PR Issues*. Online. Available at http://paulseaman.eu/wp-content/uploads/2011/04/a-new-moral-agenda-for-PR1.pdf, retrieved 20 June, 2011.

Seib, P. M. and Fitzpatrick, K. (1995) *Public Relations Ethics*. Fort Worth, TX and London: Harcourt Brace College Publishers.

Sriramesh, K. and Verçic, D. (ed.) (2009) *The Global Public Relations Handbook: theory, research, and practice* (expanded and rev. edn) London: Routledge.

Stauber, J. C. and Rampton, S. (2004) *Toxic Sludge is Good for You: lies, damn lies and the public relations industry*. London: Robinson.

Thurlow, A. B. (2009) 'I Just Say I'm in Advertising': a public relations identity crisis? *Canadian Journal of Communication, 34*(2): 245–64.

Toth, E. L. and Heath, R. L. (1992) *Rhetorical and Critical Approaches to Public Relations*. Hillsdale, NJ: Lawrence Erlbaum Associates.

van Ruler, B. (2005) Professionals are from Venus, scholars are from Mars. *Public Relations Review, 31:* 159–73.

van Ruler, B. and Vercic, D. (2004) *Public Relations and Communication Management in Europe: a nation-by-nation introduction to public relations theory and practice*. Berlin: Walter Guyter.

Waeraas, A. (2009) On Weber: legitimacy and legitimation in public relations. In Ø. Ihlen, B. van Ruler and M. Fredriksson (eds) *Public Relations and Social Theory*. New York, NY, NY and Abingdon: Routledge, pp. 301–22.

Weaver, C. K. (2011) Public relations, globalisation and culture: framing methodological debates and future directions. In N. Bardhan and C. K. Weaver (eds) *Public Relations in Global Cultural Contexts: multi-paradigmatic perspectives*. New York, NY and London: Routledge, pp. 250–74.

Weaver, C. K., Motion, J. and Roper, J. (2006) From propaganda to discourse (and back again): truth, power the public interest and public relations. In J. L'Etang and M. Pieczka (eds) *Public Relations, Critical Debates and Contemporary Practice*. Mahwah, NJ: Lawrence Erlbaum Associates, pp. 7–21.

White, J. and Dozier, D. M. (1992) Public relations and management decision making. In J. E. Grunig (ed.) *Excellence in Public Relations and Communication Management*. Hillsdale, NJ: Lawrence Erlbaum Associates, pp. 91–108.

Wilcox, D. L., Cameron, G. T., Ault, P. H. and Agee, W. K. (2003) *Public Relations, Strategies and Tactics* (7th edn) Boston, MA: Allyn and Bacon.

Zerfass, A., Vercic, D., Tench, R., Verhoeven, P. and Moreno, A. (2013) European communication monitor: annual survey on future trends in communication management and public relations. Online. Available at www.communicationmonitor.eu/

3 Trust me, I'm a professional

Introduction

One of the leading sociologists of the professions, Andrew Abbott (2010), says that those writing about professions fall into one of several 'varieties of ignorance' – amateur, professional and expert ignorance – of which the first is excusable and is marked by enthusiastic disregard for all preceding literature on the subject and an inability to think clearly about social life; the second, less forgivably, is practised by scholars, often from adjacent fields, who over-cite but under-engage with research in the field (especially Abbott's) or, worse, misrepresent central arguments; finally, expert ignorance is often found in authors who have synthesized and reinforced key theories over time but selectively forgotten the materials in which those ideas were grounded. I suspect I belong in the second circle of ignorance, that of the inter-disciplinary academic who reaches into a nearby library to acquaint herself with the fundamentals of a body of literature but fails to appreciate the schools and sub-strata in the field. However, given that most discussion in public relations (PR) literature regarding professions (notable exceptions will be honoured in Chapter 5) more closely resembles the ragbag of amateur, anecdotal and self-serving ramblings Abbott finds in the Wikipedia entry on the professions, I will proceed on the basis that I have brought back something of value from my library outing.

The term professional is used very loosely in PR literature, yet is the foundation of many claims to reputation, autonomy and social value. It is used as if its meaning is self-evident, though associations may vary from 'doing a decent job' or 'getting paid' through 'objectivity' to aspects of appearance, such as suits and briefcases or even masculinity and whiteness. Of course, PR is not alone in finding the concept elusive and this book does not aim to replace the existing definitions. Indeed, having suggested that 'profession' is used loosely in PR texts, I will continue the offence, with two justifications. As Cheney (2010: 7) points out, 'occupation … is not as suggestive of lifestyle, social pressures and one's place in society'. The second defence is that I am working towards the idea of a profession as a cultural construct, a nebulous entity but one capable of generating identity and containing conflict. I particularly like Brown and Duguid's (1991; 2001) development of the concept of communities of practice, because it includes academics and other commentators, not just practitioners. Moreover, this chapter's exploration of the complexities of usage illustrates the various usages underpinning 'professional', meaning the term is not used carelessly.

This chapter unpacks the construction of professional, taking first a sociological overview of what a profession is and how it is perceived as functioning in society, then a deeper investigation of how the very notion of 'professional' is constructed and finally an exploration of professions' inner, cultural and psychological aspects. It is interesting that many early sociologists considered psychological dimensions of professionalism, and in some ways socio-cultural approaches suggest a return to this synthesis, as well as linking to socio-cultural developments in PR theory. The interrogation of professionalism is an important prerequisite for rebuilding professional ethics in the field – if we under-examine the role of professions in society, how can we make the exalted claims of service outlined in the last chapter? Likewise, if we assume that a professional identity is uncontested, we fail to realize either the particular ethical approaches or conflicts it embodies. This exploration of professionalism sets the scene for examining professional ethics in the next chapter, as the latter is firmly founded in competing views of the former, as we shall see. One of my key propositions is that professions have to choose between maintaining societal status on false grounds or dropping their claims to serve society and concentrating on the core business of serving members. I am also interested in the argument that old notions of professions have been rendered obsolete by current social and market forces, reducing the badge to a promotional tool or logo, and raising the question of their social status and contribution. In stripping away the artifice, I hope to reveal what may still be of value.

There is urgency to this discussion as the loss of trust in professions has accelerated in recent years. A survey of leading Chief Executive Officers (Arthur W. Page Society, 2009) found that their most pressing issue was public lack of trust; the 2013 Edelman Trust Barometer (an annual international survey of trust and credibility based on a sample of 26,000 'informed' people across 26 countries) found a massive drop in trust in governments, with fewer than one in five respondents claiming to believe that business leaders and government officials can be relied upon to tell the truth in difficult circumstances (Edelman, 2012). The 2009 Mori/Ipsos survey exploring trust in professions found that '[c]ynicism also surrounds business leaders. They registered their worst net trust score – the percentage of people who trust them minus those who do not – since the yearly veracity index began in 1983' (Campbell, 2009). It is worth noting that most of these business-led reports problematize the public rather than the organizations or professions under scrutiny. It is about our lack of trust not their lack of trustworthiness. This framing has ethical implications: if the public is the 'problem', better communication might be the solution; but if the professions and/or organizations were to reflect more deeply on what changes *they* need to make, then ethics not communication is the key. This leads to the kind of apology offered 'to those who have taken offence', evidenced in the sense of grievance found in many of the cited reports, that we, the taxpayers, have failed to understand their situation, together with the hope that PR can bridge this failure of communication. It seems that the traditional claim to work for the benefit of society, by which professionals secure social status, no longer has credibility. What Larson (1977) calls the 'professional project' is under threat, and professional identity is in crisis (Broadbent *et al.*, 1997; Dent and Whitehead, 2002; Watson, 2002). It should not therefore be surprising that many professional bodies are looking to ethics for validation. As Sama and Shoaf (2008: 39) put it:

> As scandal continues to rock the professional business sector, questions abound as to cause and effect, while clients' trust and business legitimacy wear down. Understanding the fundamental drivers of ethical lapses in the professions is a critical pursuit of academics and practitioners alike.

As a crisis is a good time to take stock, this chapter looks at a range of traditional and more recent approaches to professions, from the trait approach to socio-cultural frameworks.

What is a profession?

It may be comforting to PR scholars to discover that the field of professional studies is wracked by conflict over approaches, definitions and validity, though our frequent discussion of 'profession' as unproblematic should give pause. Sciulli (2005) says that one problem is that 'most contributors to the sociology of professions have either proposed ideal types or taxonomies based on empirical generalisations' (2005: 3), which tend to describe existing phenomena but offer limited conceptual foundations for analysis. Further, most theories derive from the four exemplars of professionalism – law, medicine, science and engineering – and, even more restrictively, Anglo-American histories of these fields. Thus, professions are traditionally described as emerging from medieval guilds, through the establishment of educational courses and standards, and the creation of professional bodies to oversee or uphold those claims (Larson, 1977). The simplest definitions set out core tasks, called the *trait approach*, a means of differentiating one group from another as specialisms emerged, such as the difference between a pharmacist and a general practitioner under the general heading of medicine (Freidson, 1970). Although more sophisticated sociological approaches to professions emerged in the twentieth century (see below), descriptive approaches still abound, coupled with attempts to 'fit' every emerging occupational group into the revered professional template (Sciulli, 2005). For example, such analysis often produces taxonomies like Greenwood's (1957) ranking of:

a) Well-recognised and undisputed professions, such as medicine, the law, college teaching, and science, which are bunched at the top of the continuum and possess the attributes to a maximum;
b) Less developed professions, including social work, which possess them to a lesser degree;
c) The mid-region, with the less skilled and less prestigeful clerical, sales, and craft occupations; and

d) The least skilled and least attractive occupations, bunched at the lower end, such as those of the watchman, truckloader, farm labourer, scrub woman, and busboy.

(cited in Kultgen, 1988: 61–2)

This is in many ways a class-based, as well as gender-specific, hierarchy of occupations rather than a forensic tool and despite being written half a century ago, the sentiment persists in much writing in the field. As the chapter explores later, such a rigid set of definitions is increasingly unworkable in any event, as professionals become subject to new management systems and managers gain something close to professional status, echoing Sciulli's (2005) point about the limitations of empirical generalizations as poorly adaptable to changes in the field of study.

Accepting these theoretical limitations, it is still worth exploring how professions have traditionally been described, not least because, as suggested above, such approaches are still influential. Cooper (2004: 61–3) summarizes key texts (Johnson, 1972; Greenwood, 1957) as suggesting that professions must comprise the following elements to qualify for the term:

- esoteric knowledge – theoretical or technical – not available to the general population;
- commitment to social values, such as health or justice;
- national organization to set standards, control membership, liaise with wider society;
- extra-strong moral commitment to support professional values.

This echoes Freidson's (1970) clarification of the privileges enjoyed by professions, particularly regarding self-government, in exchange for their perceived social value. Another version suggests professions possess:

- a claim to represent, to have a level of mastery over, and to practise a particular discipline, skill, vocation or 'calling';
- advanced learning, usually represented by higher education qualifications (showing an ability to learn and amass knowledge);
- high-level intellectual skills (showing an ability to grasp new events quickly and to respond effectively);
- independence and discretion within the working context (showing allegiance to an ethical framework and often to specific codes of practice that govern relationships between the profession, the professional, his/her clients and the wider society.

(Broadbent *et al.*, 1997: 51)

Here the claim to autonomy is explicitly linked to the claim to observe ethical standards, reflecting, in turn, the centrality of the relationship between the profession and wider society. While these definitions emphasize a 'body of knowledge' and commitment to society, and while the most hallowed forms are those like medicine, the law and clergy (Freidson, 1994) which licence practitioners in their fields, they are clearly not restricted to licensed occupational groups. Freidson (2001: 127) describes the ideal typical profession as consisting of a range of inter-dependent elements, namely:

1   specialized work in the officially recognized economy that is believed to be grounded in a body of theoretically based, discretionary knowledge and skills, and which is accordingly given special status in the labour force;
2   exclusive jurisdiction in a particular division of labour created and controlled by occupational negotiation;
3   a sheltered position in both external and internal labour markets that is based on qualifying credentials, which is controlled by the occupation and associated with higher education; and
4   an ideology that asserts greater commitment to doing good work than to economic gain and to the quality rather than the economic efficiency of work.

Some of these ideas will be revisited in Chapter 5 when considering whether PR meets these criteria for a profession, but rather than attempt to create and/or impose a definition of profession on PR or any other field, I am, as noted earlier, using the concept loosely in line with 'community of practice' (Brown and Duguid, 2001), which itself reflects Larson's (1977: x) comment that professionals are perceived as 'possessing some of the characteristics of community'. A related concept is Bourdieu's 'field' (see below), the informal gathering of practitioners and aca-demics, within and without professional bodies, who have a shared interest (supportive and critical) in the values and practices of an occupational group. This is also what Kemmis (2009) considers a discursive approach, making a distinction between objective examination of discourses and language from the outside and the 'subjective perspective of a particular participant in a community of practitioners who attaches particular meaning, significance, values and intentions to their ideas or utterances' (2009: 29). I value this subjective perspective – a theme that runs through this book – and am interested in professions as entities in society, as locations both of power struggles between groups and as sources of identity. This allows a distance from the traditional examination of professions as upholders of social value – given that the more one looks, the flimsier such claims appear – but retains the focus on professions as groupings of practitioners, academics and others with either shared or conflicting aspirations and identity issues. The next section looks more closely at the profession-in-society, taking a meta-perspective, rather than a comparative analysis of different professions.

Sociological approaches to professionalism

Concepts of professions can be very broadly divided into those scholars who argue that professions play a supportive role in maintaining social order, such as Durkheim and Parsons, and those who see professions as lacking intrinsic worth but emerging as the result of power struggles, like Weber, Abbott and Larson. Sciulli (2005) terms these groups functionalists and revisionists in his overview of professionalism studies. In one corner is Emile Durkheim (1858–1917), considered one of the founding fathers of the sociology of the professions (and sociology in general); Giddens (1978) describes his approach as moving between philosophy and sociology in its engagement with issues of morality in society, some aspects of which Durkheim believed to be applicable across varying cultures. While Kant emphasized the negative sanctions of duty, Durkheim stresses the positive rewards of social duty, including the creation of 'solidariness' within groups and societies. He theorizes the role of groups and institutions as buffers between excessive state domination and individual alienation (which he termed 'anomie'), including the family, religious institutions and 'occupational groups' or professions.

> Here again Durkheim looked towards professional and occupational associations to form this necessary intermediate stratum of institutions between the individual and the state. Indeed, these professional associations would become, according to Durkheim, the very foundation of political life. These institutions were necessary to avoid what we might usefully call 'political anomie'.
>
> (B. S. Turner, 1992: xxxxiv)

Durkheim sees professions as linking individuals, through their professional groups, to the larger goals of society and thus possessing moral agency, according to Watts-Miller (1996: 5) in his book, *Durkheim, Morals and Modernity*:

> occupational groups of the socio-economic division of labour, reconstituted as self-governing corporations … are definite but interlinking groups, in a central sphere of life, that offer the cohesion we need in the arguments in which we work out and work for the aspirations to freedom and justice of the modern human ideal. They can take on a whole range of functions. But they are above all a moral force and the road, not least, to the active, meaningful and informed involvement of democratic citizenship.

This benign moral agency is seen by Durkheim's critics as offering a rather idealized view of the modern state in which religion, family and occupational groups are offered as the primary means for securing social stability, without considering the competing or conflicting demands they may make on the state (Giddens, 1978). However, B.S. Turner (1992) highlights Durkheim's critiques of class injustice and believes Durkheim has been misrepresented as a conservative because he emphasizes the desirability of social stability and the role of professions in maintaining social order. Durkheim was not, then, merely supporting existing elites but considering which structures might enhance the experience of everyday life, given the marginalization of religious institutions in the west and the related disappearance of the sacred from contemporary life. Similar concerns are found in Weber and Jung, among others, suggesting that European scholars in the early twentieth century took a broad and humane overview of their topics, linking sociology with psychology (as will be explored shortly), philosophy and a range of what would now be seen as cross-disciplinary issues – how compartmentalized academic life has since become. It is hard to imagine a contemporary writer on professions and society invoking the sacred – though it does glimmer through discussion on ethics, as the next chapter illustrates.

While Durkheim offers a philosophical basis for examining the role of professions in society, his idealistic approach was adopted – and adapted – as part of the wider, functionalist approach spearheaded by US scholar Talcott Parsons (1951). This endowed professions with moral purpose that was not always evident empirically (Sciulli, 2005), while the detailed discussion focused on definitions and descriptions of professional work, rather than scrutiny of moral claims. This view dominates the field, and underpins the role of professional bodies and codes of ethics in most western professional or occupational groups. From the mid-1960s, this concept of professionalism was critiqued and challenged by the power approach (or revisionists, to use Sciulli's term), drawing on the seminal work of Max Weber (1864–1920) following the English translation of his *Theory of Social and Economic Organisation* in 1964. While both are concerned with the division of labour in society, Weber is more critical than Durkheim about the role of professions and their acquisition and maintenance of power over others. As Sciulli (2005: 917) puts it,

> revisionists also consider the rise of expert occupations with monopolies in the services market to be, if anything, a malevolent force in civil society, not a salutary addition. They reject outright as apologetic and ideological Parsons' conjecture that professions contribute in any way, let alone intrinsically, to social integration as opposed to social control.

One of the leading scholars of professionalism, Magali Larson (1977) draws on Weberian analysis to critique what she terms the 'professional project', the means whereby a group of workers evolve from a collection of workers through occupational status to form a profession, a movement that involves creating professional monopolies, guarding them in jurisdictional contests and mythologizing their achievements. She argues that 'a successful project of professionalization, one that comes close to attaining the goals of market monopoly, social status and work autonomy, must be able to combine certain structural elements' (1977: 49). These elements include the body of knowledge – identified in the trait definitions too – and the market for services, which is determined by a range of social and economic and cultural factors. Larson deploys Weber's model of the ideal-typical profession, by which desired characteristics and domains are outlined, not as a descriptor of reality but as a benchmark or reference point, suggesting professions have proceeded as if the idealized version was descriptive rather than prescriptive. This is the conceptualization that is revisited in chapters on professional ethics, especially from a Jungian perspective; the emphasis on the ideal aspects of a profession – the angelic nurse, the devoted nun, the impartial judge – may blind us to the nurse who rewards and punishes patients at will, the nun who despises those less devout than her, the judge who indignantly denies bias.

Larson emphasizes professionalism as a dynamic process of securing and maintaining social status, 'the process by which producers of special services sought to constitute *and control* a market for their expertise ... Professionalization appears also as a collective assertion of special social status and as a collective process of upward social mobility' (1977: xvi, emphasis in original). Leicht and Fennell (2001) argue that there is an overemphasis on the actions of the elite and under-examination of the demands of consumers in conferring that social status, but they agree that the 'decoupling of knowledge from the specific organisational forms seeking to use it' (2001: 94) has opened up the arena for considering professions in society, rather than individually. This is also the interstitial space in which Bourdieu and others explore the construction of professionalism not as deriving from knowledge but from practice, as is explored more fully below.

Professions can also be seen as sites for control, as Freidson (1994; 2001) points out, a negotiation between members of an occupation, the users of that service and the state that chooses whether or not to regulate the provision of the service. Freidson calls professionalism 'the third logic', an intermediary between the polarities of a centrally planned service delivery and a wholly free-market-driven activity, echoing Durkheim's buffer, but to different intent. This emphasizes the degree of autonomy professions have about the nature, timing and direction of their work, being in thrall neither to employing nor state organizations on the one hand or to consumers on the other. Of course this autonomy is not absolute but it does help distinguish professional work from everyday labour (see Freidson 2001 for more about the economic and institutional aspects of professions). It is this autonomy that is threatened by managerialism and regulatory threats (see below). The relationship between occupational groups is explored further by sociologist Andrew Abbott, whose *The System of Professions* (1988) analysed the social dynamics of professions, and who also developed theories of legitimacy and jurisdictional struggle (Abbott, 1995).

> A jurisdictional claim made before the public is generally a claim for the legitimate control of a particular kind of work. This control means first and foremost a right to perform the work as professionals see fit. Along with the right to perform the work as it wishes, a profession normally also claims rights to exclude other workers as deemed necessary, to dominate public definitions of the tasks concerned, and indeed to impose professional definitions of the tasks on competing professions. Public jurisdiction, in short, is a claim of both social and cultural authority.
>
> (Abbott, 1988: 60)

Abbott makes three observations that are particularly relevant for this book: one concerns the use of 'entities' as a metaphor for professions; the next looks at 'difference'; and the third asks why professional ethics are primarily considered as pertaining to individuals rather than the collective, and is considered in the next chapter. The discussion of entities arises in Abbott (1995), where professional groups are described as evolving from undifferentiated to distinct bodies, formed in and against other societal pressures, helping set the scene for conceptualizing professions as psychological entities later in the book and is in contrast to the individualized approach to describing the professional found elsewhere in the literature (Cheney, 2010):

> I am here suggesting that we reverse the whole flow of metaphor. Rather than taking the individual human being as metaphor for the social actor, let us take the social actor as metaphor for the individual human being. Not only is there much biological evidence for this – the world is full of organisms like slime molds and jellyfish that appear to be individuals but are actually societies – but also, under such an assumption, the fruitful belief that there might be social boundaries without social entities becomes possible.
>
> (Abbott, 1995: 861)

Professions are then defined as emerging entities in which 'dimensions of difference' (1995: 870) – such as the introduction of examinations for apothecaries – form a boundary between surgeons and apothecaries, but within the larger entity of physicians. Abbott shows how social work emerged and defined itself against other occupational groups from the 1920s onwards. This view sees professional fields as engaged in a constant struggle for control of segments of the market, where definitions are crucial to the task of accruing professional status and distancing the group from other, competing sectors. However, such claims are now subject to even greater pressures from economic, social, technological and other global factors, contributing to what many scholars see as the end of professions (Adams, 2010; Broadbent *et al.*, 1997; Leicht and Fennell, 2001). In particular, easy access to the traditional 'body of knowledge', widespread vocational training and the proliferation of professional bodies (see below) mean the claim to elite status is no longer sustainable. Undaunted, Dingwall (2008) points out that just as professions were transformed from their mediaeval versions by the industrialization of western societies in the eighteenth and nineteenth centuries, their role needs to be re-appraised in the light of contemporary global shifts in state, individual and corporate power. However, instead of suggesting that professions have outlived their social relevance (as do other writers, cited above), Dingwall calls for global professional networks, because 'the global order may find that it needs trust-promoting groups much as nation-states did' (2008: 110). This sentiment illustrates Abbott's (2010) observation that many writers about professions are over-attached to a Whiggish idea of social cohesion, the neo-liberal fantasy of bourgeois professional stability, ideas rooted in the century before last. As will be suggested in Chapter 5, PR has voted for the globalization of professionalism rather than reconsider its viability.

Recently, a new approach to studying professions as institutions has emerged (Bartlett, 2007; Leicht and Fennell, 2001), drawing on new social institutional theory (DiMaggio and Powell, 1991) which is primarily a means of understanding the development of organizations and their tendency to resemble each other more closely over time, a process termed *isomorphism*. Institutions are seen as having organic properties, allowing them to be' influenced by each other in a meaningful way' (Greenwood *et al.*, 2002: 59) and raising issues of boundaries and jurisdiction, similar to those addressed by Abbott (see above).

> Organizations, initially at least, behave in accordance with this socially constructed reality because to do so reduces ambiguity and uncertainty ... Over time, these shared understandings, or collective beliefs, become reinforced by regulatory processes involving state agencies and professional bodies.
>
> (Greenwood, Suddaby and Hinings, 2002: 59)

As well as generating organizational legitimacy, institutional theory, applied globally, explains the struggle for local, national and transnational legitimacy among professions (Covaleski *et al.*, 2003: 328), stressing the agency of professions in this contest, as well as the effect of outsourcing on the development of global professional services.

In summary, the alternative ways of seeing professions sketched above shed some light on the societal and organizational dynamics of professional status, jurisdiction and norms. The primary schism lies between the idealistic functionalists and the sceptical revisionists, underpinning nearly all the writing on professions, including concepts of professional ethics, which the former group find unproblematic and the latter oxymoronic.

This book does not aim to resolve this dispute, though my inclination is towards those who claim professionalism is an increasingly empty concept, sociologically. Regardless of the continuing validity of the profession as a social entity, it is clearly part of social discourse (as will be seen from the field of PR) and can be seen as a cultural element in society, a source of meaning, identity and kinship for some. Professional practice is summarized by Kemmis (2009: 25) as consisting of practices as materially and economically formed; practices as discursively formed and practices as socially formed. The above section has looked at the sociological aspects of professions; the lens now shifts to a more socio-cultural perspective.

Socio-cultural and psychological approaches to professionalism

Edwards and Hodges (2011: 3) draw on Geertz (1973) to define culture as the 'historically transmitted pattern of meanings (symbolic and linguistic) by which we (as human beings) communicate, develop and transform our knowledge about and attitudes towards'. They suggest that a socio-cultural approach to a field (PR) raises issues of discourse, context and 'must interrogate the profession itself as a social group, a social function and a status project that itself emerges from and sustains a particular set of social and cultural norms and structures' (2011: 7). This section attempts to see professions as cultural constructs and also to consider the collective aspects of professional meaning-making, invoking a range of cultural and psychological approaches that interrogate the inner life of organizations and which are here applied to professions. There is a continuity between the sociological approaches outlined above, of course; for example, Abbott's (1995) idea of difference as an engine of change echoes the socio-cultural writer Pierre Bourdieu's use of *différence* in the more nebulous French meaning and both authors demonstrate how the Other (to use a Jungian term) plays a crucial part in the evolution of professional groups. Bourdieu's sociology (Bourdieu, 1984, 1977; Bourdieu and Wacquant, 1992) includes analysis of the social function of professions, and is more subtle and nuanced than most of the approaches already considered. Green (2009a: 44) considers him to offer 'a sustained and particularly creative engagement with the problematics and aporias that are involved in trying to understand practice'. Bourdieu sees practice as a combination of several dynamics, each of which is multilayered, much of which is rooted in unconscious, reflexive behaviours, some acquired from past experience (family, school, church, for example); others from present experience (the way things are done in this workplace, for example):

> For Bourdieu practice is habitual, primarily non-discursive and un-reflexive, routinised behaviours, scripts not scripted, regular but not rule-bound. Bourdieu's is not a sociology of action, centred on rational or meaningful behaviour of a knowing subject, nor a behavioural sociology centred on determined repertoires that can be described independently of their meaning for those who act them out. It is in between, objectively meaningful without intention, patterned without rules, logics of action not governed by logic.
>
> (Friedland, 2009: 889)

Practice encompasses several variables: a) *habitus,* b) capital and c) field. *Habitus* is seen as the means by which society reproduces itself, by generating in the individual and collective a set of behaviours, expectations and relations that are not absolutely fixed but which tend to repetition unless consciously examined (Ihlen, 2007). Gray (2008) states that Bourdieu's concept of *habitus* requires that its structures and demands are not conscious, and Fries (2009) describes it as consisting of deeply set patterns of belief, value, attitude and attribute that help structure understanding of self and society. Bourdieu's concept of 'capital' is seen as comprising knowledge capital, social capital and cultural capital, which may consist of material goods, such as paintings and books, credentials, like academic degrees, and/or social skills (Adkins and Corus, 2009). Others (such as Fries, 2009) also identify symbolic capital, which can emerge when any object or attribution acquires inherent value, and physical capital, the role of the body in securing social value. Field denotes the 'social space or network of relationships between the positions occupied by actors' (Ihlen, 2009: 65), positions that are partially distributed on the grounds of power or capital. Actors are seen to compete for positions of power within a field. Bourdieu's concept of 'fields' is organized around behaviour and identity:

> identity and professional development entail habituation to a discursive and symbolic field, the production of disciplined bodies, within which must be

objectified those 'durable dispositions that recognise and comply with the specific demands of a given institutional area of activity' ... A Bourdieusian perspective is also supported by empirical studies which reveal workplace organizations as systems of power relations imbued with race, class, gender, and other social categories, producing cultures that, even whilst they change, remain largely unwelcoming to outsiders, inducing assimilation or exit.

(Sommerlad, 2007: 194)

These concepts are well suited to explain and describe the acquisition of power by professional groups and the creation of norms in, for example, law (Sommerlad, 2007), health education (Adkins and Corus, 2009), professional practice (Green 2009) and PR (Edwards, 2006; Ihlen, 2009).

Bourdieu advocates a relational mode of thinking, where the meaning of social attributes (such as professions, gender, educational qualifications, appearance) can only be understood within the context of the relationships in which they are relevant (Bourdieu, 1992). These relationships exist within fields, where members of a particular group practice according to unconscious rules and norms informed by habitus ... The structures of these fields are homologous with the systems of domination and symbolic power that define relations in wider society—for example, economic and political relations of domination.

(Edwards, 2006: 229)

Professions can now be seen as fields, governed by social relations between members with varying capital who come together to acquire capital or status in wider society, creating cultural and psychological depth to the power struggles observed by Larson, Abbott and others. Interestingly, according to Edwards (2006: 230),

Bourdieu (1998) characterises certain professionals – journalists, politicians, public relations practitioners – for whom language is at the heart of their work, as symbolic producers, transforming or disguising interests into disinterested meanings and legitimizing arbitrary power relations.

Importantly for this book, the landscape is expanded by Bourdieu to encompass the unconscious in conceptualizing professional practice and here I dig a little deeper. In the early twentieth century the divisions between fields of psychology and sociology were not as pronounced as they are now and both fields drew from the other. For example, one of the founding fathers of sociology, Durkheim, demonstrates interest and engagement with psychological theory and non-material topics such as the role of the sacred in society. In his introduction to the first edition of Durkheim's *Professional Ethics and Civic Morals* (1957), Davy comments on the nature of collective consciousness in society:

> There is no doubt that the sub-stratum does not consist of one sole organ. It is diffused, by definition, through the whole range of society. But none the less, it possesses specific features which make a separate reality of it. It is indeed independent of the particular conditions in which individuals are placed: they pass on and it remains … It is therefore something quite different from the individual consciousnesses, although it only becomes reality through the individuals. It is the psychological type of society, the type which has its own properties, its conditions of existence, its own way of development, exactly as the individual types have, but in a different way.
>
> (Davy, 1957: xlvi–xlvii)

As will be seen later, there is resonance between Durkheim's and Jung's world views and it is clear that early sociologists were interested in the psychological or inner, as well as outer circumstances. Indeed, although they offered different insights, Durkheim and Weber both theorized on the role of religion in society, a linkage pursued by Parsons (1951), as Chriss (1995: 545) points out:

> Parsons argued that the process of allocating roles in society was analogous to the internalization, through socialization, of cultural norms and values in the individual. As Parsons (1951) states, 'The allocation of personnel between roles in the social system and the socialization processes of the individual are clearly the same processes viewed in different perspectives (207). Both processes, then, have similar functional significances at their respective levels of generality or specificity, namely that of integration.'

Other examples of cross-disciplinary enquiry include Habermas's (1972) chapter on psychoanalysis and social theory, which draws on Freud's conception of sociology as applied psychology and compares his work with that of Marx. As Freud is seen as taking a normative position, his position is rejected, but interesting points are made about the links between the two fields. There is also wide literature on the psychology of organizations, which looks at both the psychology of the individual and groups in workplaces and at organizational characteristics or personality as a whole (Haslam, 2004; Kets de Vries, 1991; Lefkowitz, 2003). The following synthesis of definitions illustrates the relationship between psychology and sociology:

> An organisation is: a) a group with a social identity so that it has psychological meaning for all the individuals who belong to it … b) characterised by coordination so that the behaviour of individuals is arranged and structured rather than idiosyncratic; and c) goal directed so that this structure is oriented towards a particular outcome.
>
> (Statt, 1994, cited in Haslam, 2004: 2)

While these approaches focus on the psychology of and within organizations, some ideas can be easily transferred to the study of professions. For example, J. C. Turner

(2004: xix) talks about social identity theory as a theory of intergroup relations 'where people make social comparisons between groups, they seek positive distinctiveness for their ingroups compared to outgroups in order to achieve a positive social identity'. This echoes previous discussion about professions defining themselves against other professions in jurisdictional disputes and resonates with neo-institutional theory. It is important, however, to remember that social identity theory places the group firmly in its social context, and that there are significant differences between professions and organizations, not least because the former are trans-organizational. There appears to be a lacuna in the study of organizational psychology in that the cited authors do not consider the role of professional bodies as a particular manifestation of organizational dynamics (there is no index reference for professions in Haslam, 2004, for example). This does not seem to be attributable to any category problem, although of course professional bodies have a different relationship to their members than organizations do to employees. Bucher and Stelling (1969) bemoan this lack of communication between fields of scholarship, especially as they found most professionals in their studies worked in organizations so that characteristics of professionals may also be characteristics of organizations, and vice versa. Moreover, leading professional theorist Freidson (1970), argues that 'First, one must understand how the profession's self-direction or autonomy is developed, organised and maintained. Second, one must understand the relations of the profession's knowledge and procedures to professional organisation as such and the lay world' (cited in Pieczka and L'Etang, 2001: 227). Although this exhortation seems to invoke psychological approaches, such as social identity theory, it has led primarily to sociological analysis.

However, the absence of a thriving literature does not mean that psychological concepts and insights should not be applied to professions as groups, just as they are to organizations, nations and other groupings. Indeed, Goodpaster (2007: 19) is clear that that 'organisations are in many ways macro-versions (projections) of ourselves as individuals – human beings writ large. Because of this, we can sometimes see more clearly in organisations certain features we want to understand better in ourselves'. And, as noted earlier, Abbott (1995) reflects on the meta-phorical mirroring of individuals and organizations, so this linkage is not unique, though it does not appear to have been applied to professions before. In earlier versions of writing on this topic I have argued for a new psychological approach to professions, but in writing this book I realize that the umbrella of socio-cultural thinking actually embraces both elements and is centrally involved with the negotiation between the inner and the outer worlds, the individual and the collective, the creation of norms and compliance or resistance (or both) to those norms. Writers such as Bourdieu, Goffman and du Gay create frameworks like the concepts of habitus, performativity or the circuit of culture (see below) that are both sociological in their portrayal of how social institutions and norms are reproduced but also engage with the lived experience of integrating or rejecting such norms.

A socio-cultural approach thus connects the role of a profession in relation to society and to the individual with new directions in PR research (indicated in

Chapter 2, and which are revisited in Chapter 5) and also to cultural approaches to ethics and to Jung, as will be seen elsewhere. Moving from generalized discussion of the inner life of professions, we now turn to the more specific question of professional identity – what is it? How is it structured and maintained? How empty is it?

Professional identity

Green (2009b: 6–7) suggests four concepts of 'professional practice': the notion of practising a profession, as in medicine or law; the idea of practising professionalism, that is enacting aspects of identity associated with being or been seen as a professional; the moral-ethical quality, the sense of ethical responsibility in one's practice; and finally, in opposition to 'amateur', implying some reward for services. This section is most engaged with the second, performative aspect of identity, though the moral-ethical aspects will be explored more deeply in the next chapter. After all, the question 'what does it mean to be a professional?' has a real impact on how we act out our ideas about ethics. It also raises some of the issues that will come up again in thinking about Jung's concepts of the Self. For example, for many years I was surprised to be treated as a professional on the basis of experience and expertise when I felt so unsure of my position in the workplace, sector or conference platform; I reached for accessories – heels, jacket, manicure – to do the job, relying on external props to construct a performance of professional, like an actor. Perhaps for this reason I am drawn to Goffman's (1959) dramaturgical approach to professional identity, which I read long after these experiences but which shed light on both my individual and the collective approach to constructing professional identity. Goffman explores how individual and team performances are constructed, maintained – and disrupted; he talks about impression management in professions as a 'rhetoric of training' (1959: 46) for example. This is not to suggest a manipulative intent, more the mechanisms by which cultural norms are observed and reproduced in professional (*inter alia*) settings. Some of these themes will be revisited in later chapters on the construction of the self, where connections with Jung will be explored; they are introduced here to suggest the richness and depth available to students of professionalism but rarely reflected in discussions of PR professionalism.

> When an individual appears before others, he knowingly and unwittingly projects a definition of the situation, of which a conception of himself is an important part. When an event occurs which is expressively incompatible with this fostered impression, significant consequences are simultaneously felt in three levels of social reality.
>
> (Goffman, 1959: 242)

These levels are social structure, interaction and personality (ibid: 243). The first affects teams which may become confused by the disruption; then, audiences may question the individual's projected performance and indeed legitimacy; finally, the person may find his ego identified with this aspect and the consequences affect 'his' sense of self – all aspects that will be revisited in the chapters on Jungian ideas. Here, performance also resonates with Bourdieu's concept of *habitus*, the unconscious ways of doing things which only become visible when disrupted. As Edwards (2010: 206) puts it:

> The professional habitus plays a significant role in defining what it is to be 'a professional' and, like the other processes that define professional jurisdiction, its character is linked to the political, social and economic circumstances from which the profession has emerged.

Bourdieu observes that new entrants to a profession 'fall into line with the role … try to put the group on one's side by declaring one's recognition of the rule of the group and therefore of the group itself' (2000, cited in Edwards, 2010: 206) and goes on to explore how whiteness is established in one profession, PR, as a norm, requiring black and minority ethnic practitioners to marginalize their racial identities. Bourdieu's exploration of difference focuses on the variations between members of the dominant class, where relative status acquires greater significance, rather than the gross inequalities between differences of class, race and gender: 'Social identity lies in difference, and difference is asserted against what is closest, which represents the greatest threat' (1984, cited in Friedland, 2009: 892).

So professional identity includes learning how to 'perform' the role, as established by that group's history and cultural norms. Moreover, the professional role is only one of the identities that a 'professional' worker may need to negotiate: as an employee, parent, partner, child, a member of a union, a member of voluntary organizations, faith groups, political parties and so on. A review of literature on teachers' professional identity explores these issues and concludes:

> What these various meanings have in common is the idea that identity is not a fixed attribute of a person, but a relational phenomenon. Identity development occurs in an intersubjective field and can be best characterised as an ongoing process, a process of interpreting oneself as a certain kind of person and being recognised as such in a given context.
>
> (Beijaard *et al.*, 2004: 108)

Their review found divergent interpretations of identity, examining self-image, professional roles in the workplace and images of teachers held by society, and suggests similar variations could be found in other professions' discussions of identity,

> with different voices of discourse: the personal, professional, and institutional. Roberts argued that the notion of multiple selves and different ways of talking connect with current research on teacher socialization and professional identity, where induction into teaching is seen as similar to the process of learning to talk.
>
> (Roberts, 2000, cited in Beijaard *et al.*, 2004: 114)

These approaches emphasize that being professional involves acting the role of the professional as much as, possibly more than, the traditional acquisition of knowledge or expertise. However, this acculturation may minimize, even prevent, reflection on the desired outcome:

> Thus, what comes to be considered 'true' and of 'value' will be that which is considered to 'work' in the so-called 'real world'. However, as countless organizational actors are only too well aware, the ubiquitous 'real world' against which they and others are appraised often turns out to be at best elusive, and at worst a fiction sustained in part by their own silence and complicity.
>
> (Dent and Whitehead, 2002: 4)

Other writers on professional identity explore the social construction of identity; for example, Broadbent *et al.,* (1997) claim that the professional has to 'navigate the increasingly choppy waters of organisational life' (1997: 4) and that narratives of self are shaped by professional identity, which extends far beyond remuneration: 'The "I" cannot talk with the authority of a professional, cannot give an account of itself as a professional, unless the discursive association is prior held and legitimised in the eyes of others' (1997: 4). This echoes Kemmis's (2009) concept of the profession as a discursive field, and reinforces the socio-cultural sense of profession as a fluid, dynamic and elusive construction, generating both outer sociological observations but also inner experiences of personal identity and meaning. This constructed meaning is further disrupted by the emergence in recent decades of managerialism throughout the Anglo-American bureaucracies, which threatens professionalism in a number of ways.

Half a century ago, 'the professionalization of everyone' (Wilensky, 1964) was predicted, but in recent decades this could be recast as the 'managerialization' of everyone, following the introduction of targets and performance indicators particularly in the public sector for all sectors regardless of their professional status. This is largely an Anglo-American phenomenon but the impact of what is termed New Public Management (NPM) on Australian social welfare is described as undermining professional identity (Healy, 2009). NPM is seen as a response to changing structures in public service since the 1990s in many countries, and Healy argues that the increased demands for accountability and transparency coupled with traditional gender bias in areas such as social work amount to a 'de-professionalization agenda' (2009: 402). Dent and Whitehead (2002) find that professionalism has become fatally managerialized, embedded in the employing organization, just as management has become professionalized, so that the boundaries of what constitutes a profession referred to earlier are now blurred beyond recognition:

> As the notion of professionalism has become reconfigured, emerging as a ubiquitous, compelling icon for all organizational players, so has the ideology/ discourse of managerialism risen to ascendancy. The subsequent blurring of the boundaries between professionalism and managerialism has been profound

across both the public and private sectors, leading to a significant slippage of identity for those professionals who previously saw themselves as exclusive and privileged and, thus, somewhat removed from the messy business of managing resources ... Whether in the public or private sector, the professional has no escape from being managed nor, indeed, from managing others.

(Dent and Whitehead, 2002: 1)

Bradley (2009: 65) echoes this, suggesting that managerialism constitutes a new model of professional practice, where 'professionalism consists less in expert practical judgment than in meeting general standards for effective practice ... They bring an alien type of authority into the professional arena'. This alien authority shifts the professional identity, then, creating pressure for evidence-based quantifiable practice. I suspect this has profound implications for professional ethics, as it reinforces the supremacy of the outwards, objective realm of things and numbers, diminishing the role of experience, value and inner direction. This suspicion is reinforced by the approach to identity proposed by the 'circuit of culture' (Curtin and Gaither, 2005, 2007), which borrows concepts from cultural and sociological study (du Gay *et al.*, 1997) to reconceptualize PR. Curtin and Gaither (2005: 101) describe identity as 'meanings given to a particular object or group through the process of production and consumption'. Identity is imagined at the individual, organizational and national levels, and comprises one in a circuit of 'moments' (made up of representation, identity, production, consumption and regulation), offering a powerful model of interrelated, continuing, process-based communication with strong foundations in, and with implications for, PR. This interrelated, experiential and fluid approach is closer to that found in identity debates in other professions, and supports my suggestion that professional identity is deeply challenged by managerialism. It also reflects the erosion of borders and status that professions used to enjoy, leading to confusion at all stages of the circuit of culture: images of professions become emptier as identity is eroded, production and consumption of professionalism is located on the external context of management, and regulation becomes notional, almost empty in the process, as the next chapter reveals. This blurring is explored by Bauman and Vecchi (2004), who also note the loss of meaningful identity through class solidarity and its replacement by emphasis on individual attributes such as gender and race. While Bauman does not address the role of professions in the following, his approach is applicable to the discussion of the question of professional identity in a fast changing or 'liquid' world:

Locations where the feeling of belonging was traditionally invested (job, family, neighbourhood) are either not available, or untrustworthy ... Hence the growing demand for what may be called 'cloakroom communities' – conjured into being ... by hanging up individual troubles, as theatregoers do with their coats, in one room.

(Bauman, 2004: 30–1)

As the individual professional's identity dissolves, the role of professional bodies – the key repository and promoter of professional self-images, comes into view.

Professional bodies

According to the Professional Associations Research Network (PARN), there are over 450 professional associations in the United Kingdom, representing 6.5 million professionals –some 23 per cent of the workforce (Friedman and Phillips, 2004). PARN also estimates there are between 6,000 and 7,000 such bodies in the USA and that most professional bodies are traditionally run by volunteers from the profession, with a small number of serving officers or paid employees and large, cumbersome ruling bodies. They face conflicting duties, as between those to society and those to members; there may be conflicts of interest between sub-groups of members; and between the short-term demands of members and the long-term requirements of the profession. Moreover, the external environment has become more hostile in recent years: the loss of trust outlined elsewhere in this chapter has led to demands for greater government regulation of professions. Evetts (2002: 343), for example, comments on the self-regulation of professions as a strategy 'to prevent intervention by state governments', as the attempts of the British media to maintain autonomy in the wake of the 2012 Leveson Report illustrate. Professional bodies are often cited as an indicator of an occupational group aspiring to or acquiring professional status:

> Professional associations have long been seen as a marker of professional-ization. The establishment of a professional association does not necessarily precede or cause the achievement of professional goals. But an organizational representative, in particular the existence of a single, identifiable national association is clearly a prerequisite of public or legal claims on the part of a would-be profession ... organizational representatives play an indispensable role in making professionalization possible.
>
> (Berman, 2006: 159)

Larson (1977) sees professional bodies as an aspect of the internal hierarchy of professions, with the body as the ruling elite that speaks for but does not always represent its members. Given that most work is undertaken by volunteers, it would be interesting to explore their psychological make-up (desire to enact change or acquire extra status?) as compared with the non-active membership. The role of the professional association as the main control mechanism for the field, through admission and expulsion of members, is explored by Freidson (1988). He cites a range of literature which suggests that professional bodies have exercised diminishing controls over members, at least formally, with rare examples of disciplinary measures and reliance on the creation of professional 'norms' to encourage standards of behaviour. Evetts (2002) notes, however, that in the UK, professional bodies are increasing their scrutiny of member behaviour and standards, largely through professional training. It is not clear whether such scrutiny reflects increased control over membership or is intended to justify continued self-regulation. The primary control mechanism is through disciplinary procedures enforcing codes of conduct, which are rarely invoked, as will be seen in the next chapter. The discussion of managerialism, above, illustrates what Friedman (2006) calls the *marketisation* of professions following the dismantling of professional jurisdictions by government directives, as in the removal of advertising restrictions for legal services. Professionals are now called on to market themselves more efficiently to regain their 'market share' by competition. Managerialism also contributes to pressures on the professional body's ability to control membership and standards through accreditation, licensing (in some cases) and disciplinary procedures. However, most critics of managerialism do not address the reasons why authorities have sought to impose external controls on professions, which Kaye (2006) argues are designed, but may fail, to mitigate the loss of trust in professions' ability to control themselves. He suggests that the pattern of accountability has shifted from that of the professional body, representing the practice community, to that of the professional as an individual, accountable through the representative body, to various regulating authorities, a new system which he terms 'regulated (self) regulation'. This is particularly evident in the new systems of revalidation required for medical staff, but in more general application indicates the desire for new control mechanisms as a corollary to the loss of trust in professions. This shift in gravity also reflects a shift in responsibility for professional ethics (see next chapter). While professional bodies may not use sanctions to control member behaviour, they can influence it through the production and maintenance of norms. One of the ways in which a professional body can generate norms, according to Galaskiewicz (1985) is through the creation of 'mindsets', a concept he examines through social network theory. This suggests that actors with similar interests and backgrounds will form loose networks through which to transmit information, particularly well-suited to professional structures:

> One of the latent functions of professional associations is to put people together in committees, panels, task forces, and study groups who might not otherwise be attracted to one another based on their background characteristics alone. Recruitment to these associations is not based on ascribed criteria (e.g., race, sex, etc.) but on interest, achievement, and talent. The association filters out the 'untrustworthy' and presents a slate of 'safe' candidates to whom its membership can relate.
>
> (Galaskiewicz, 1985: 640)

Galaskiewicz notes challenges to the notion of free shared access to these networks, but the potential for screening on race, gender and class is rather blithely dismissed, an assumption that would be challenged by Sommerlad (2007) and Edwards (2006), for example. While Galaskiewicz sees this 'isomorphism' as largely benign, Goodpaster's (2007) analysis finds that mindsets tend to become myopic and over-idealistic. Despite this idealism, Galaskiewicz's suggestion that professional associations 'contribute to value consensus and shared norms; that is, they can help create a professional subculture' (1985: 641) resonates with Bourdieu's concept of *habitus*, discussed earlier. Oliver and Montgomery (2005) also deploy social network theory to understand the development of professional bodies, examining the precise transition from disorganized groups of individuals with shared interests to formal professional organizations. Their four stages of development of a professional body are worth repeating:

> Stage one represents the nascent moments of boundary construction, when an informal group of like-minded individuals becomes aware that they share interests and wish to mobilise those interests in some fashion. At this stage, the networking activities are undifferentiated, rather than specifically aimed either inward toward the nascent group or outward toward actors in the environment.
>
> Stage two is marked by the beginning of coordinated efforts to communicate the core group's initial interests to a wider group of potential members and to a group of key actors who can be energised to aid in construction of both membership and domain boundaries. During this stage, outward-directed networking forces predominate.
>
> Stage three is marked by the point at which membership and domain boundaries begin to solidify. A critical mass of members has been established, enabling the group to shift from an open membership, outward-directed model, to a more restricted one. At this point, inward-directed networking activities take over to establish more exclusive membership boundaries, raising commitment to the emerging entity and reducing exit interests. Simultaneously, outward-directed networking activities continue toward more sophisticated efforts to formalise and institutionalise the legitimacy of domain claims within the relevant professional or organisational field.
>
> Stage four represents a point when the group is recognised by influential external bodies as a distinct social entity, often signalled by the acceptance of credentials and licenses. This stage requires efforts to maintain a dynamic equilibrium through ongoing dual-directed networking activities to avoid risks and challenges to both membership and domain boundaries, such as membership complacency or obsolescence and domain intrusion or diffusion.
>
> (2005: 1170)

This description of a professional body taking shape and its inwards and outwards orientation will be helpful in later chapters as it demonstrates the methods by which collective attitudes may be formed and maintained, and has parallels with individual developmental theories, though Sciulli's (2010) dismissal of this process approach as over-reliant on data from a handful of Anglo-American professions should also be remembered. Similar themes emerge from framing professional bodies within institutional theory (see above), as a mechanism for generating isomorphism:

We suggest that at those moments, associations can legitimate change by hosting a process of discourse through which change is debated and endorsed: first by negotiating and managing debate within the profession; and, second, by reframing professional identities as they are presented to others outside the profession. This discourse enables professional identities to be reconstituted.

(Greenwood *et al.*, 2002: 59)

Here it is argued that, while professional associations are generally characterized as conservative and risk-averse, because of their regulatory functions, their discursive roles may contribute to change both within a profession and in its wider context. This social constructivist view sees meaning as generated through social structures and locates the professional body as one such site for sharing and negotiating the meaning of the profession, a useful insight for later discussion, one that leads neatly into the next chapter on the role of ethics in professions.

Conclusions

This chapter has explored some of the key concepts around the notion of professionalism, noting the range of approaches and tending to favour those with a socio-cultural perspective as offering a synthesis of sociological observations of the behaviour of professions in society with deeper, unconscious motivations of individual professionals in constructing and conforming to their collective identities. Ideas from Goffman and Bourdieu open a space in the discourse of professionalism that encourages the Jungian insights explored later in the book. The shift from fixed social roles to shifting constructions of meaning reflects wider debates in various academic disciplines and is consistent with the hermeneutic approach outlined in the introduction. Technological, political and governance-related engines of change, such as managerialism, were explored to demonstrate this fluidity of professionalism in the twenty-first century, and issues of lost status and confused identity highlighted uncertainty in professional standing. The ideological divide between those who see professions as agents in social cohesion and those who see them as the successful outcome of occupational struggles, with promotional rather than substantial contributions to society, was explored and will be revisited in the next chapter, which considers how images of professions have shaped approaches to professional ethics. While sharing the critical perspective, I do not want altogether to lose the potential that professions have for moral agency in social discourse. They are sites of social significance to practitioners in that field, whether affiliated to professional bodies or not, and to wider society. The part that professional bodies play in generating or maintaining professional status was also discussed and will be the focus of later speculation regarding their potential for developing a more challenging and collective approach to professional ethics.

At the beginning of the chapter, I reported some of the concerns expressed by organizations, businesses and professions about the public loss of trust. This chapter has shown how flimsy the grounds for professions are; the next shows that while many are turning to ethics as the salvation of reputation, the foundations on which they do so are even shakier.

References

Abbott, A. (1995) Things of boundaries. *Social Research, 62*(4): 857–82.

Abbott, A. (2010) Varieties of ignorance. *American Sociologist, 41:* 174–89.

Abbott, A. D. (1988) *The System of Professions: an essay on the division of expert labor.* Chicago, IL: University of Chicago Press.

Adams, T. L. (2010) Profession: a useful concept for sociological analysis? *Canadian Review of Sociology/Revue canadienne de sociologie, 47*(1): 49–70.

Adkins, N. and Corus, C. (2009) Health literacy for improved health outcomes: effective capital in the marketplace. *Journal of Consumer Affairs, 43*(2): 199–222.

Arthur W. Page Society (2009) The dynamics of public trust in business – emerging opportunities for leaders.

Bartlett, J. (2007) Creating legitimacy as a central rationale for public relations. Paper presented at the International Communications Association, San Francisco, CA.

Bartlett, J., Tywoniak, S. and Hatcher, C. (2007) Public relations professional practice and the insitutionalisation of CSR. *Journal of Communication Management, 11*(4): 281–99.

Bauman, Z. and Vecchi, B. (2004) *Identity: conversations with Benedetto Vecchi.* Cambridge: Polity.

Beijaard, D., Meijer, P. and Verloop, P. (2004) Reconsidering research on teachers' professional identity. *Teaching and Teacher Education, 20*(2): 107–28.

Berman, E. P. (2006) Before the professional project: success and failure at creating an organizational representative for English doctors. *Theory and Society, 35*(2): 157–91.

Bourdieu, P. (1984) *Distinction: a social critique of the judgement of taste.* Cambridge, MA: Harvard University Press.

Bourdieu, P. and Nice, R. (1977) *Outline of a Theory of Practice.* Cambridge: Cambridge University Press.

Bourdieu, P. and Wacquant, L. J. D. (1992) *An Invitation to Reflexive Sociology.* Chicago, IL: University of Chicago Press.

Bradley, B. (2009) Rethinking 'experience' in professional practice: lessons from clinical psychology. *Understanding and Researching Professional Practice.* Rotterdam, Netherlands: Sense Publishers, pp. 65–82.

Broadbent, J., Dietrich, M. and Roberts, J. (1997) *The End of the Professions?: the restructuring of professional work.* London: Routledge.

Brown, J. S. and Duguid, P. (2001) Knowledge and organization: a social-practice perspective. *Organization Science, 12*(2): 198–213.

Brown, T. S. and Duguid, P. (1991) Organizational learning and communities of practice: towards a unified view of working, learning and innovation. *Organizational Science, 2*(1): 40–57.

Bucher, R. and Stelling, J. (1969) Characteristics of professional organizations. *Journal of Health and Social Behavior, 10*(1): 3–15. Online. Available at www.jstor.org/stable/2948501

Campbell, D. (27 September, 2009) Trust in politicians hits an all-time low, *The Observer.* Online. Available at www.guardian.co.uk/politics/2009/sep/27/trust-politicians-all-time-low

Cheney, G. (2010) *Just a Job? Communication, ethics, and professional life.* Oxford and New York, NY: Oxford University Press.

Chriss, J. J. (1995) Habermas, Goffman and communicative action: implications for professional practice. *American Sociological Review, 60*(4): 545–65.

Cooper, D. E. (2004) *Ethics for Professionals in a Multicultural World*. Upper Saddle River, NJ: Prentice Hall.

Covaleski, M. A., Dirsmith, M. W. and Rittenberg, L. (2003) Jurisdictional disputes over professional work: the institutionalization of the global knowledge expert. *Accounting, Organizations and Society, 28*(4): 323–55.

Curtin, P. A. and Gaither, T. K. (2005) Privileging identity, difference and power: the circuit of culture as a basis for public relations theory. *Journal of Public Relations Research, 17*(2): 91–115.

Curtin, P. A. and Gaither, T. K. (2007) *International Public Relations: negotiating culture, identity and power*. Thousand Oaks, CA: Sage.

Davy, G. (1957) Introduction. In C. Brookfield, (trans.) E. Durkheim. *Professional Ethics and Civic Morals*. London: Routledge & Kegan Paul, pp. xliii–lxxiv.

Dent, M. and Whitehead, S. (2002) *Managing Professional Identities: knowledge, performativity and the "new" professional*. London: Routledge.

DiMaggio, P. J. and Powell, W. W. (1991) *The New Institutionalism in Organizational Analysis*. Chicago, IL: University of Chicago Press.

Dingwall, R. (2008) *Essays on Professions*. Farnham: Ashgate Publishing.

du Gay, P., Hall, S., Janes, L., Mackay, H. and Negus, K. (1997) *Doing Cultural Studies: the story of the Sony Walkman*. London: Sage.

Durkheim, E. (1957/1992) In C. Brookfield, (trans.) E. Durkheim. *Professional Ethics and Civic Morals*. London: Routledge & Kegan Paul.

Edelman. (2012) Trust Barometer: Edelman Public Relations.

Edwards, L. (2006) Rethinking power in public relations. *Public Relations Review, 32*(3): 229–31.

Edwards, L. (2010) 'Race' in public relations. In R. L. Heath (ed.) *The SAGE Handbook of Public Relations*. Thousand Oaks, CA: Sage, pp. 205–22.

Edwards, L. and Hodges, C. E. M. (eds) (2011) *Public Relations, Society & Culture: theoretical and empirical explorations* (1st edn) London: Routledge.

Evetts, J. (2002) New directions in state and international professional occupations: discretionary decision-making and acquired regulation. *Work, Employment and Society, 16*(2): 341–53.

Freidson, E. (1970) *Profession of Medicine: a study of the sociology of applied knowledge*. New York, NY: Dodd.

Freidson, E. (1988) *Professional Powers: a study of the institutionalization of formal knowledge*. Chicago, IL: University of Chicago Press.

Freidson, E. (1994) *Professionalism Reborn: theory, prophecy, and policy*. Cambridge: Polity.

Freidson, E. (2001) *Professionalism: the third logic*. Cambridge: Polity.

Friedland, R. (2009) The endless fields of Pierre Bourdieu. *Organization, 16*(6): 887–917.

Friedman, A. (2006) Strengthening professionalism: ethical competence as an alternative to the market path towards the public good. In J. Craig (ed.) *Production Values: futures for professionalism*. London: Demos.

Friedman, A. and Phillips, M. (2004) Balancing strategy and accountability: a model for the governance of professional associations. *Nonprofit Management and Leadership, 15*(2): 187–204.

Fries, C. (2009) Bourdieu's reflexive sociology as a theoretical basis for mixed methods research. *Journal of Mixed Methods Research, 3*(4): 326–48.

Galaskiewicz, J. (1985) Professional networks and the institutionalization of a single mind set. *American Sociological Review, 50*(5): 639–58.

Geertz, C. (1973) *The Interpretation of Cultures: selected essays*. New York, NY: Basic Books.

Giddens, A. (1978) *Durkheim*. Hassocks: Harvester Press.

Goffman, E. (1959) *The Presentation of Self in Everyday Life*. New York, NY: Doubleday Anchor.

Goodpaster, K. E. (2007) *Conscience and Corporate Culture*. Malden, MA and Oxford: Blackwell.

Gray, F. (2008) *Jung, Irigaray, Individuation: philosophy, analytical psychology, and the question of the feminine*. London: Routledge.

Green, B. (2009a) The primacy of practice and the problem of representation. In B. Green (ed.) *Understanding and Researching Professional Practice*. Rotterdam, Netherlands: Sense.

Green, B. (2009b) Introduction. In B. Green (ed.) *Understanding and Researching Professional Practice*. Rotterdam, Netherlands: Sense, pp. 1–18.

Greenwood, R., Suddaby, R. and Hinings, C. R. (2002) Theorizing change: the role of professional associations in the transformation of institutionalized fields. *Academy of Management Journal, 45*(1): 58–80. doi:10.2307/3069285

Habermas, J. R. (1972) *Knowledge and Human Interests*. J. J. Shapiro (trans.). London: Heinemann.

Haslam, S. A. (ed.) (2004) *Psychology in Organizations: the social identity approach* (2nd edn) London: SAGE.

Healy, K. (2009) A case of mistaken identity: the social welfare professions and New Public Management. *Journal of Sociology, 45*(4): 401–18.

Ihlen, Ø. (2007) Building on Bourdieu: a sociological grasp of public relations. *Public Relations Review, 33*(3): 269–74.

Ihlen, Ø. (2009) On Bourdieu: public relations in field struggles. In Ø. Ihlen, M. Fredriksson and B. v. Ruler (eds) *Public Relations and Social Theory: key figures and concepts*. New York, NY and London: Routledge, pp. 62–82.

Kaye, R. P. (2006) Regulated (self-)regulation: a new paradigm for controlling the professions. *Public Policy and Administration, 21*(3): 105–19.

Kemmis, S. (2009) Understanding professional practice: a synoptic framework. In B. Green (ed.) *Understanding and Researching Professional Practice*. Rotterdam, Netherlands: Sense, pp. 19–38.

Kets de Vries, M. F. R. (ed.) (1991) *Organizations on the Couch: clinical perspectives on organizational behavior and change* (1st edn) San Francisco: Jossey-Bass.

Kultgen, J. (1988) *Ethics and Professionalism*. Philadeplhia: University of Philadelphia Press.

Larson, M. S. (1977) *The Rise of Professionalism: a sociological analysis*. Berkeley and London: University of California Press.

Lefkowitz. (2003) *Ethics and Values in Industrial-Organisational Psychology*. Mahwah, NJ: Lawrence Erlbaum Associates.

Leicht, K. T. and Fennell, M. L. (2001) *Professional Work: a sociological approach*. Malden, MA: Blackwell.

Oliver, A. L. and Montgomery, K. (2005) Toward the construction of a profession's boundaries: creating a networking agenda. *Human Relations, 58*(9): 1167–84.

Parsons, T. (1951) *The Social System*. London: Routledge & Kegan Paul.

Pieczka, M. and L'Etang, J. (2001) Public relations and the question of professionalism. In

R. L. Heath (ed.) *Handbook of Public Relations*. Thousand Oaks, CA: Sage, pp. 223–35.

Sama, L. M. and Shoaf, V. (2008) Ethical leadership for the professions: fostering a moral community. *Journal of Business Ethics, 78:* 39–46.

Sciulli, D. (2005) Continental sociology of professions today: conceptual contributions. *Current Sociology, 53*(6): 915–42.

Sciulli, D. (2010) Why professions matter: structural invariance, institutional consequences, bias. *Comparative Sociology, 9*(6): 744–803.

Sommerlad, H. (2007) Researching and theorizing the processes of professional identity formation. *Journal of Law and Society, 3*(2): 190–217.

Turner, B. S. (1992) Preface to the second edition. In B. S. Turner and C. Brookfield (eds) *Professional Ethics and Civic Morals*. London: Routledge, pp. xiii–xlii.

Turner, J. C. (2004) (Foreword) What the social identity approach is and why it matters. In S. A. Haslam (ed.) *Psychology in Organizations: the social identity approach*. London: Sage, pp. xvii–xx.

Watson, T. (2002) Speaking professionally: occupational anxiety and discursive ingenuity in human resourcing specialists. In M. Dent and S. Whitehead (eds) *Managing Professional Identities, Knowledge, Performativity and the 'New' Professional*. London: Routledge, pp. 99–115.

Watts-Miller, W. (1996) *Durkheim, Morals and Modernity*. London: UCL Press.

Wilensky, H. L. (1964) The professionalization of everyone? *American Journal of Sociology, 70:* 137–58.

4   To serve society

Introduction

Scandals of abuse, negligence and corruption have hit journalism, banking, clergy, sports, accounting and other groups around the world in recent years: all these sectors are covered by professional or legal codes; all showed that such frameworks were comprehensively disregarded where the cultural norms of the newsroom, trading floor or seminary set other standards. So one question for this chapter is: what is the point of professional ethics if the members they aim to influence hold them in such low esteem? Scrabbling to restore ruined reputations, professional bodies and committees, such as the UK's Press Complaints Commission, desperately seek to bolster their ethical codes and procedures in the hope of staving off state intervention. Another question, then, is: are professional ethics a key instrument in enacting or *avoiding* responsibility to society?

This chapter looks at the role of ethics in establishing and maintaining professional status, and then digs deeper into the range of ethical approaches that inform professional ethics as a whole – again, the level here is a meta-narrative, so the literature that explores the ethics of nursing, law, social work and so on is not covered, though examples are occasionally taken from such fields to illustrate more general points. The gap between philosophical approaches to ethics and the ethical foundations of most professional codes is investigated, and the two questions above inform much of the discussion. General trends, such as the move to incorporate non-rational approaches are welcomed, as they open up room for discussion of a deeper, interior consideration of ethics, such as that offered by hermeneutic approaches in general and, as will be seen in later chapters, Jungian ethics in particular. The over-reliance on and disregard for codes of conduct are also important in this chapter, as they encapsulate the contradictions at the heart of professional ethics.

My personal starting point was the inadequacy of codes for resolving the kinds of ethical dilemmas I experienced at work, both as a public relations (PR) practitioner and later as an academic. One particular example springs to mind: students returning from their first internships at various local PR agencies routinely reported doing really interesting work calling media outlets and competitors, announcing that they were undertaking research for the university and requesting commercially sensitive information. This was clearly obtaining information under false pretences, which compromised the university, the student and the agency. But the norm was so widespread and so entrenched that a conscientious student would have looked absurd objecting to the task, and for me – with all my extra power – to have made a fuss would have jeopardized future internships, as colleagues made clear. I did nothing.

This scepticism about professional ethics was reinforced by the ease with which core texts and professional codes presumed ethical conflict could be addressed and resolved; the language implied clear choices between wrong and right in which the Good practitioner would do the Right thing. Yet, as I had discovered in building an ethical framework on the moral wasteland of my early addiction and early recovery, not all compasses are set to North. Grappling with my own behaviour meant slowly, messily and painfully re-interpreting my actions against my motives, understanding that self-serving actions often wore altruistic guises. At the heart of addiction is self-delusion, and in the decades since, I have learned to be watchful for it in myself and others – and most professional ethics reeks of the stuff. I discovered I needed operating principles rather than situation-specific guidance, sets of questions to ask myself when in a quandary, the main one being not 'what is the right action?' because it begged the question, but 'what (hidden) gains might be influencing my choices?'. Because I have experience of this inner construction of ethical navigation tools, I am attracted to depth approaches to ethics, as I'll set out later, and wary of those schools of ethics that locate wisdom and judgement in the mind alone; I know how profoundly unreliable that organ can be.

A brief consideration of terms: most of the literature cited here uses the terms 'ethics' and 'morality' interchangeably, though some distinguish between individual and social duties. Appiah (2008) draws on Aristotle's idea of *eudemonia*, or what it means to live well, as the basis for ethics, reserving the term morality for normative ideas about 'how we should and should not treat other people' (2008: 37). Proulx (1994) notes that the words originally meant the same thing in Latin and Greek, and this book argues that the two aspects are profoundly interrelated, and follows the bulk of literature in using the terms interchangeably, except when discussing Jung's approach as he seeks to differentiate personal ethics from social *mores*. In the introduction, the distinction between different levels of ethical discussion was made, making it clear that this book is primarily concerned with the meso level, between the society-wide macro level and that of individual (micro) ethics. Considering professional ethics at this level is desirable, as Mount (1990: 27) points out:

> Many treatments of professional ethics today focus on the standards of behavior expected of people with particular professional roles and responsibilities or on specific ethical quandaries they face as individuals … Enlarging the scope of professional ethics moves us beyond the ethics of individuals in institutions and professions to the ethics of institutions and professions and to the images and myths they embody and transmit.

The role of ethics in professions

Ethics have long been seen as a central plank in establishing – or re-establishing – professional legitimacy, as a defining element is the responsibility of the professional to society at large, as well as to the particular client or patient. In order to justify their social credit, they appeal to general ideological rationales, according to Larson (1977), as promoters of social values, rather than mere monetary reward. But Cooper (2004) argues that professional ethics are failing to respond adequately to societal changes, and that professions tend to claim either that there are no moral frameworks anymore or create situation-specific codes lacking an underlying philosophy, leading to 'moral drift and banal choices' (2004: viii). A key quote for this chapter – and book – comes from Kultgen (1988: 120), who sees professional ethics as part of the professional mythology:

> The *Urmythos* from which all of the myths in the professional mythology spring is that professions are oriented to the service of humanity. Professions avow in their official pronouncements and the functionalist typification endorses the view that professions are oriented to service rather than to profit or the interest of any patron group. Handsome rewards are required to entice recruits, compensate for the cost of education, and provide equipment and trappings for effective practice. It is simple justice that those who serve well should be paid well. But they serve to serve, not to be paid.

Exploration of the content of codes later in the chapter provides ample support for this view; they are littered with claims to serve humankind, placing duty to others always above self-interest, eschewing monetary reward for respect. There may indeed be noble exemplars of all professions amongst their members; but this chapter suggests that it is unlikely to be a result of their profession's ethics. The term 'professional ethics' contains three interpretations, according to Kultgen (1988: 209):

> first, to the norms required by the moral point of view for the kind of work that professionals do, that is, an ideal rational ethic. This is what moral theorists try to formulate. It does not yet exist in perfected form acceptable to everyone. 'Professional ethics' means, second, common norms actually followed by most professionals. Sociologists describe widespread practices; an ethic exists to the extent that professions regard such practices as morally obligatory. Since the norms for these practices are not necessarily acceptable from the moral point of view, this sense of 'professional ethics' differs from the first. The term means, third, common elements of codes of professional associations.

I am interested in the gap between the first and second definitions, as well as the promotional aspect of the third; it seems to me that there is a gulf between the ideal rational ethic promoted and the common norms actually practised. This contrast between academic views of ethics and practitioner voices in PR was explored in

Chapter 2, and will be revisited in the next chapter. It is this interstitial territory that intrigues me, where grand claims are made but not enacted, where dubious decisions are rationalized away, leading to an increasingly empty *performance* of professional ethics. The literature on professional ethics as a whole reflects the divide outlined in the last chapter between the functionalists and what Sciulli (2005) calls revisionists and others call the power approach. The former tend to look for improvements in codes and analyse or compare ethics in particular professional groups, using historical or case study methods. The latter often dismiss the whole enterprise as oxymoronic at best, pernicious at worst. There are dangers in both positions, as Abbott (1983) points out. He suggests that the shortcomings in the former approach, which he describes as evolving ethics as a mechanism to protect ignorant clients from unethical experts, have led the latter, intent on exposing the self-aggrandisement of professions, to ignore its virtues.

Before exploring those avenues, it is worth considering the fundamental question raised by some Western critics and scholars of Asian ethics: why do professionals require 'extra' moral duties at all? This debate was played out in the academic dialogue between Freedman (1978) and Gewirth (1986) in which Freedman argued that there were circumstances – he cited instances of medical confidentiality – where professionals carried an 'extraprofessional' responsibility that licensed them to deviate from 'normal' ethical standards. Gewirth rejected this, arguing for 'ordinary' ethics in which professional status does not offer exemption from generalized ethics. This is closer to some approaches in Asian ethics (Koehn, 2001) in which the duty of care is universal and not segregated into particular professional groups; in China, for example, 'medicine was never the exclusive province of a trained class of doctors' because healing is a 'kind gesture performed by an exemplary child who understands what is owed to a parent' (2001: 145). Brecher (2010: 354) also raises the question of whether there is a need for professional ethics, asking to what extent a nurse, mechanic or engineer requires ethics beyond those required between all humans:

> The very notion of professional ethics makes a false distinction, namely one between people's moral responsibilities qua person and their putative ethical responsibilities qua professional: the incongruity of 'professional morals' or 'professional morality' – in contrast to 'professional ethics' – already hints at this.

The counterargument is offered by Kultgen (1988: 259), who, despite demolishing many claims to professional ethics (see below), nevertheless concludes that

> professions should foster higher aspirations in their members than they can or should enforce. In particular they should inculcate ideals that impose open obligations. Such obligations include those unenforceable by nature, supererogatory, more likely to be observed if left to personal conscience, requiring individual initiative and insight, or simply providing opportunities for the individual to acquire moral dignity by going beyond what is required by law.

I am both a critic and an optimist, and therefore hope that in exposing the pretensions behind most approaches to professional ethics, we can start a debate about what a reflexive ethical approach might really resemble and how practitioners and professional bodies might participate in such a debate. The dispute between Freedman and Gewirth could be bridged by an approach that recognizes particular professional responsibilities but locates its ethics in everyday experience. It is re-phrased by Green (2009: 5) as a debate between neo-Aristoleanism and post-Cartesian thinking; that is, there are those who see the 'internal goods' of professions, their commitment to health, justice and education, for example, and those who challenge the assumptions of modernity and seek to re-connect with the subjective world. I feel myself straddling this divide, willing to see collective goods but more likely to jump into the sceptics' camp if a choice must be made. Eventually, over the course of the book, I hope to show how professions could enact their discursive claims and prove the critics wrong.

For now, it seems that professional ethics have become an aspect of marketplace economics, embraced where they offer some competitive advantage, dropped where they do not, as embodied in Bauman's (2008) plaintive book title: *Does Ethics have a Chance in a World of Consumers?* My optimism is grounded in the current crisis in trust in professional groups (as suggested in this chapter's introduction); the failure of current approaches creates space for a new one. As Sama and Shoaf (2008: 39) put it:

> As scandal continues to rock the professional business sector, questions abound as to cause and effect, while clients' trust and business legitimacy wear down. Understanding the fundamental drivers of ethical lapses in the professions is a critical pursuit of academics and practitioners alike.

It is also notable that most professional ethics pays scant regard to current developments or arguments in the world of moral philosophy, despite drawing its principles from these fields. Instead, there is a pre-occupation with solving problems, ethics as *doing* rather than *being*, a question of act not agent.

> Currently it is popular to treat ethical and moral issues as problems to be solved ... Quandary ethics concern tangible and concrete moral dilemmas, case studies, engaging in role playing, or solving critical incidents ... The step beyond quandary ethics in schools of business curricula is moral discourse.
> (Mitchell and Scott, 1990, cited in Lefkowitz, 2003: 4)

A survey of the literature on professional ethics does reveal a fascination for case studies and practical examples, with little analysis of underlying philosophical reasoning. Goodpaster (2007) describes his move from a philosophy department to a business school as the transition from abstract reflection to an engagement with outcomes and measurement of results. Eventually, he found the strengths in both approaches and argues strongly for greater engagement across this divide; this book tries to reverse his journey by introducing more philosophy than is common in discussion of PR's professional ethics. Koehn (1994) is also concerned with issues lying beneath definitions to explore the *ground* of professional ethics, by which she means both well-spring and legitimacy: 'Grounding professional authority entails specifying the source of the standards governing professional actions undertaken or authored on behalf of the client' (1994: 8). In order to discover the ground of professional ethics, it is necessary to chart its theoretical underpinnings. The next section explores a range of fundamental ethical concepts, some of which are reflected in professional ethics texts and codes, some of which are ignored. This will help in identifying the philosophical strengths and weaknesses of the codes so central to professional ethics in general and PR in particular.

Philosophical debates in professional ethics

For the first half of the twentieth century, professional ethics focused on the specific conflicts facing particular professions, such as patient confidentiality or accounting procedures, following the trait approach described earlier (Cooper, 2004). Then, wider reading of philosophy introduced the established schools of consequentialism and deontology, as developed by Bentham and Kant, respectively, which have since dominated the development of professional ethics (Lefkowitz, 2003). These approaches focus on either the consequences of actions as the ground for ethics or the duty of professionals to groups such as clients, patients or society generally, or even more often, an ad-hoc combination of both. Lucas (2005: 41) suggests that 'utilitarian thinking has infiltrated all levels of public decision making, through the widespread use of economic methods such as cost-benefit analysis', and examples of this thinking can be found in health policy and in weighing civil liberties against perceived terrorist threats. There are, however, philosophical and practical problems in basing professional ethics on either of these approaches: Lucas points out the dehumanizing and de-professionalizing aspects of consequentialism in that it takes a mechanical approach to calculating relative harms and goods issuing from actions (at least in its most reductionist form, as is sometimes found in codes). The problem with Kantian ethics on the other hand (again, as often summarized and applied to professional ethics) is the lack of flexibility in managing conflicts of ethical duty, where two choices are both morally justified but opposing. Lucas (2005) finds that the emphasis on reason and universalism can tend to dehumanize ethical decision-making, and concludes that Aristotle's virtue ethics offers a more human foundation for professional ethics (see below). Utilitarianism is particularly popular because it lends itself to calculations, cost-benefit analysis, as Lucas (2005) suggests. But this increases the sense that rules can be objective and impartial, compounding the moral drift referred to above by Cooper (2004). For example, Rowson (2006: 52) comments:

> Portraying ethics in the professions as obedience to rules can have undesirable effects … As regulatory codes have proliferated in recent years, and as examples of unethical behaviour in professions have increasingly made the

headlines, the cry has gone up that what is needed is fewer rules and a greater sense of individual moral responsibility among professionals.

The response to this rule-based ethics is to adopt a deontological or duty-based approach, based on Kant, by which ethical decisions are evaluated by consideration of whether one would wish such actions to be taken by all others in similar circumstances. This approach also emphasizes the importance of treating others as ends in themselves, not means to achieve particular goals. This is valuable in imagining a society where ethical rules are universalized and resembles the precepts invoked across any number of faiths, including the Golden Rule to Do Unto Others as You would be Done By (Cooper, 2004: 221). Looking back, I now see that my activist years were predicated in a Kantian perspective, drawn to absolutes and imperatives, and always seeking the principle underlying decisions we made. I was fierce about ensuring that decisions had universal validity and did not depend on particular variables; for example, I insisted on actively representing union members whose views I found noxious because they were entitled to such services and it was not my place to veto access. (Of course, this is Voltaire as much as Kant.) In recent years, my conviction regarding right and wrong has blurred as I've embraced my own and others' ambiguity, but I am still influenced by the need for universal laws, even if I now think the main one is that there are no universal laws. As a result, I find myself uneasy about situationist ethics. Situationist ethics modifies both consequentialist and deontological approaches by starting not from abstract principles, but from the specifics of the ethical dilemma, before reaching back into underlying principles, combining both theories in a complex evaluation of principle and likely outcomes. It emphasizes pragmatic decision-making and underpins quandary ethics, as suggested above. Rather than operating from generalizable principles, it deploys procedures such as the moral reasoning model set out by Cooper (2004) or the Potter Box (as described by McElreath, 1996), which provide a matrix for evaluating the relative salience of values/stakeholders and other claims for ethical attention. This is sometimes called contingency ethics (Curtin and Boynton, 2001), but suggests that the situation is subject to rational analysis, when social psychological experiments have demonstrated the degree to which individual ethical behaviour is influenced by such variables as a pleasant aroma (Appiah, 2008). Moreover, as Day *et al.* (2001) point out, it is often confused with situational ethics, loosely translated as 'it depends', a term embraced by many students (and teachers) of ethics, but which is often evidence of a reluctance to engage with underlying ethical principles. Philosophically, all these approaches are predicated on justifying ethical choices, either through fear of consequences or sense of duty, though as Bauman (2008: 62) states, 'the question why should I be moral is the end, not the beginning, of ethical dialogue'. If a person needs a motivation or reward, their act is inherently de-ethicized, he says, adding that 'morality is nothing but an innately prompted manifestation of humanity' (2008: 62). This illustrates the tension between theoretical ethicists seeking to construct philosophically sound overarching frameworks (what Cooper, 2004, calls 'justification discourse') and professional bodies that primarily require everyday tools for decision-making (Cooper, 2004, terms this 'application discourse'). The ability to bridge abstract and concrete approaches to ethics is one of the reasons why virtue ethics has been embraced by so many professional ethicists in recent decades.

The virtue approach (MacIntyre, 1984), which derives from Aristotle's writing on ethics, is particularly useful in its lack of reliance on external rules to prescribe acceptable ethical behaviour, focusing instead on character and reflection, and has had a considerable impact on the field of professional ethics in recent decades. The main ideas are summarized as:

> (a) An action is right if and only if it is what an agent with a virtuous character would do in the circumstances; (b) Goodness is prior to rightness; (c) The virtues are irreducibly plural intrinsic goods; (d) The virtues are objectively good; (e) Some intrinsic goods are agent-relative; (f) Acting rightly does not require that we maximise the good.
>
> (Adapted from Oakley and Cocking, 2001: 9ff.)

Aristotle uses the term *phronesis* to describe practical wisdom, which results not from being right, but from finding a midpoint between extremes, so that courage lies somewhere between cowardice and recklessness, for example (Lucas, 2005). He emphasizes the intellectual skills required to make ethical decisions, in particular to take appropriate ethical actions, as the result of reasoned reflection and self-awareness. Importantly, the notion of 'good enough' actions are embedded in this theory, so that the calculations of utilitarianism and the absolute duties required by deontological approaches are modified by awareness of the difficulty of perfect actions. Because the emphasis is on the character of the decision-maker, here the professional, the focus shifts from external rules to internal values or virtues; it is agent-, not act-based ethics.

> Virtue ethicists … reject both Kantian universalisability and the maximisation of utility as the appropriate ground of good character, and instead draw on other factors in substantiating the appropriate normative conceptions of a good agent.
>
> (Oakley and Cocking, 2001: 15)

A similar distinction is made in applying virtue ethics to the profession of accounting, highlighting the importance of the agent in this approach as opposed to the action-focus of utilitarianism:

> Rather than centering on the reasons for action, virtue ethics attempts to instill certain character traits that lead to taking the right action. In its simplest form, reflection can be seen as consciously thinking about and analyzing what one has done (or is doing). Reflection is also agent-based and it enables us to explore our experiences and come to a new understanding. Reflection is often

initiated when the individual encounters some difficulty in making a decision and attempts to make sense of it.

(Mintz, 2006: 97–8)

However, Appiah (2008) suggests that virtue ethics has been narrowly interpreted as a tool for deciding which acts are virtuous, despite its emphasis on agents rather than acts, leading to its use in quandary ethics or the 'what would Jesus/Ghandi/ Sarah Lund do' approach, a distortion of the original concept of the 'good character'. The influence of virtue ethics on professional discourse is considerable, leading to much examination of concepts such as integrity, transparency and authenticity in contemporary professional practice, with different authors championing particular virtues. For example, Kultgen (1988) decides that care and justice are the most salient virtues to professions (reflecting the work of, respectively, Gilligan, 1982 and Rawls, 1973), and he explores these in depth, arguing that a modified idealism of professionalism offers a buffer against the abuses associated with paternalism. Kultgen delineates the ideal professional, who does not lie, and is diligent, dedicated and passionate about justice: 'The ideal professional is a moral person. She refuses to be an agent in an immoral enterprise or to use immoral means in a legitimate one' (1988: 352). These quotes illustrate one of the problems with virtue ethics: despite the invocation of the 'good enough' practitioner, there is a tendency to idealize and sanctify, which, as the previous chapter suggested, is attractive to professions' self-conceptualization, but not necessarily a reliable basis for ethical behaviour. It also invites disputes as to whether justice or integrity is the greater virtue, which in professional ethics has sometimes led to a sloganeering approach to virtues, so that this year's virtue is transparency, leaving responsibility very much last year's trend. This can be illustrated by Watson's (2010) critique of a major business report on authenticity (Arthur W. Page Society, 2007), which might have been more impressive had there been any exploration of what such a term might mean. As will be seen in analysing codes (below), virtuous words abound in professional ethics, but they are presented as interchangeable and unproblematic, like a series of T-shirts that one can put on and discard at will. Moreover, there is still the sense of the subject as a coherent individual who can, after reflection and reasoning, develop the correct ethical response, when evidence and experience suggest that human behaviour is less consistent or predictable than that (Appiah, 2008). While the shift from external rule-making to internal reflection is helpful to the overall argument of this book, this limited sense of the ethical psychology, together with the core reliance on goodness, is a constraint that may be shifted in taking a Jungian view (see Chapter 8). Virtue ethics is not the only recent addition to professional ethics; others include discourse ethics, feminist ethics and global ethical approaches, which are outlined below.

Discourse ethics, as developed by Habermas, engages with the power dynamics involved in ethical communication, which has under-developed implications for professional ethics. As Christians (2011) points out, this contrasts with the ethics of individualism, and introduces a dialogic form of moral reasoning. Discourse ethics is based in the idea of equal access to ethical debate and decision-making, founded in Habermas's (1989) theory of dialogic communication, which in turn draws on Kantian and critical theory. These principles have been summarized as:

a) participants must have an equal chance to initiate and maintain discourse;
b) participants must have an equal chance to make challenges, explanations, or interpretations;
c) interaction among participants must be free of manipulations, domination, or control; and
d) participants must be equal with respect to power.

(Burleson and Kline, 1979, cited in Day *et al.*, 2001: 408)

Such equality of access would challenge many traditional aspects of professionalism, such as specialist knowledge bases and higher social status; which is both a critique of professional power claims and an example of the unworkability of the approach. Benhabib (1992) explores the tension between the universalizability of discourse ethics, drawing on its Kantian origins, and the generation of norms through discourse, which must meet with the approval of all participants. Again, the discourse is located in reasoning and argument, and requires systems and procedures to ensure equality of access for all parties, a requirement not often found in contemporary professional practice (Curtin and Boynton, 2001). Like other approaches discussed above, there is an emphasis on rational evaluation of choices in a range of different frameworks, a perspective critiqued by Benhabib (1992), among others. While postmodern and critical theory has flourished in many academic fields, including the philosophical grounds of ethics, it has made less impact on professional ethics, as it tends not to lend itself to applied codes or normative instructions. The discourse is one of deconstruction rather than reconstruction, though exceptions are noted below and in the next chapter. One article on ethics and international affairs explains in its opening paragraph:

Postmodern, poststructural, and critical theorists say that there are no universally valid foundations for norms. Whether or not we think that ethics exists in international life, or ought to, these theorists maintain that there are no firm grounds for any particular ethical belief. Rather, they argue, ethics is contextual.

(Crawford, 1998: 121)

By this I understand that we are not talking situationist ethics where the immediate context determines the decision, but rather that ethics is a culturally constructed set of attitudes which fluctuate over time and culture, not a set of discoverable absolutes. It illustrates the is/ought divide, and is a challenge to most ethical approaches that are intrinsically about creating (preferably universal) rules for ideal behaviour, whether of secular or religious origin. Some writers, such as MacIntyre (1984), Bauman (1993) and Cooper (2004) have expressed concern that postmodern approaches to ethical debates have led to anomie and moral drift. Jungian scholar Christopher Hauke (2000) contests this interpretation of postmodernism, finding that the embrace of 'not knowing' provides a refreshing change from the modernist, positivistic approaches to knowledge. Crawford would agree: 'Paradoxically, realising peace and justice in world politics is more likely if one gives up the urge to ground ethics in Enlightenment certainty' (1998: 121). Benhabib (1992) suggests that postmodern approaches critique the instrumentalist use of ethics. Such writers (and not all choose the label 'postmodernist') share a rejection of universal claims to truth, arguing that concepts of reality are socially constructed. Benhabib (1992) also highlights differences between postmodern and feminist approaches to ethics, showing how feminist scholar Carol Gilligan (1982), among others, questioned the dominant view that ethics (particularly virtue ethics) should concern issues of justice, arguing for an ethic of care, rooted in relationship rather than distribution and equity. Feminist scholars particularly challenge the reliance on rationality as the ground for ethical decision-making and the absence of emotional or affective bases for moral judgement (Benhabib, 1992: 49). Gilligan's view opens up space for difference (of all kinds, not only gender), integrating the other, as opposed to presumptions about the similarities between agents. This has led to an emerging and far-reaching ethics of identity (see Appiah, 2005), seeking to understand and reconcile different perspectives, though this has not been applied to professions, despite the work on professional identity outlined in the last chapter. Identity ethics, in turn, has led to increased interest in rights ethics, in which identity is seen as the ground for ethical claims, as embodied in the UN Charter of Human Rights or anti-discrimination policies, for example. Nevertheless, an important aspect of this debate, Benhabib (1992) suggests, is that it is not necessary for all aspects of identity to be understood and assimilated in a system of mutual relationship, as this implies a goal of 'intersubjective transparency'. One of the key insights of postmodern approaches, it seems to me, is that it does not presume a subjective unity, unlike almost all the schools that traditionally inform professional ethics. Far from the coherent, rational and supremely conscious ethicist, 'the postmodern ethical subject is not a unity, does not always know its own wants because the self is heterogeneous' (Benhabib, 1992: 197). This resonates with Hauke's (2000) embrace of multiplicity of self and rejection of a mythical whole – themes that will be revisited in later chapters.

There also seems a connection between these approaches and the broader socio-cultural perspective; as suggested earlier, the circuit of culture (du Gay *et al.*, 1997) describes how meaning is negotiated through a 'circuit of moments' (comprising representation, identity, production, consumption and regulation). Each of these moments is grounded, shaped and altered by its inter-reaction with the other components, emphasizing the fluidity of meaning in cultural contexts. Curtin and Gaither (2007) explore PR ethics from this perspective (see Chapters 2 and 5), placing it under the regulatory heading and reframing ethics as a cultural product. This approach engages with the power dynamics behind the creation of social norms, where inequalities of resources and access to production lead to the domination of one view over another; it also notes that the export of one set of culturally specific codes may fail in another culture. This offers a rich and deep insight into the creation and maintenance of social norms, and how cultural groups who do not have access to the framing processes may evolve their own sets of meanings outside or even in opposition to mainstream regulatory environments.

While I welcome the decoupling of norms from truths and the emphasis on unconscious as well as ideological motives for constructing ethics, there can be something dispiriting about the postmodern refusal to contemplate deeper, universal human meaning, preferring reflections on the fragmented surfaces of things; hence my attraction to hermeneutic ethics in general and Jungian ethics in particular. The latter is explored fully in Chapter 7, but it's worth discussing the inner aspects of hermeneutics here, before considering global ethical approaches. Despite finding very little literature linking professional and hermeneutic ethics, the latter demonstrates how a depth approach to ethics can be understood, philosophically, and offers some resolution between the fragmented ethics of postmodern theory and the normative prescriptions of modernist approaches. Hermeneutics is sometimes called the philosophy of interpretation and has been developed in the past few decades primarily by Riceour (1981) and Gadamer (1989), building on earlier works by Heidegger and others. Gadamer was particularly concerned with the pre-understandings (also termed 'prejudices') a reader brings to the text; the interplay of expectation, realization and adjustment leads to realignments of their frames of interpretation (Jensen, 2002). These adjustments and the interplay between the part of the text and the whole, and the whole text and its context form elements of the circle of hermeneutics, a representation of the dynamics of interpretation. The tensions between different types of hermeneutic ethics are explored by Smith (1997) in his book *Strong Hermeneutics: contingency and moral identity*, in which he distinguishes between weak and strong hermeneutics. The first is advocated by Nietzsche, Rorty and poststructuralists, who argue that any claim to objective knowledge is futile and gave precedence to subjectivity, building on the 'disenchantments' of Copernicus, Darwin and, later, Freud to demonstrate the contingency of the universe and the postmodern dismantling of 'out there' truths. Smith (1997: 17) states that this reframing of all knowledge as interpretive obviates the requirement for any transcendent forces such as 'the true, the real and the good' and is thus incapable of developing an ethic. In contrast, strong hermeneutics, as developed by Gadamer, Riceour and Taylor, seeks not to denigrate reason but to elevate aspects of identity bound in expression:

> it takes seriously the ethic of cognition as an ethic … as one horizon of self-interpretation among others, its status as a cultural injunction is affirmed but it also allowed to admit of truth … For strong hermeneutics, interpretation is the living house of reason not its tomb.
>
> (Smith, 1997: 19)

Thus strong hermeneutics widens the field of ethics to include both rationality and other forms of expressive or experienced identity. Strong hermeneutics admits the whole human being into the discourse, rather than just our brains, an effort requiring high levels of self-understanding. Using Smith's framework one can recast the tension between what Riceour (1981) termed 'the hermeneutics of suspicion' (in which text always means something other than the author intended) and the 'hermeneutics of conversation' (in which the text always means something more than the author intended). The former resonates with concepts from weak hermeneutics in which the emphasis is on deconstruction not reconstruction. The latter seems closer to Gadamer's (1989) dialogic approach – he coins the term *fusion of horizons* to indicate the possibility of finding common ground but also the transience of such discoveries; like horizons, they are always shifting. Strong hermeneutics moves away from the surface of difference towards the shared depth of human experience: ethical knowledge, is not 'out there' but 'in here', as suggested by Heidegger. It is not a set of technical instructions to be applied to all situations, as many ethical codes would imply, but, Gadamer suggests, an aspect of 'being and becoming' (cited in Warnke, 2002: 84). This emphasis on ethics as experiential and connective is a major theme of this book.

Hermeneutic ethics (in its strong version) presumes a universal human experience by which meaning may be shared, if only in passing. One of the struggles in ethical debates is between those who believe universal ethics are possible and those who believe cultural variables make this an impossible, and wrongly framed, ideal. Kantian and other approaches seek such rules or Imperatives, and Cooper (2004: viii) explores both the confusion and opportunities offered by globalization to professions, stressing the need to 'respond to these changes in the knowledge economy with moral agency'. In particular he highlights the absence of shared moral values – of the kind that allow calculations of maximum good or duty in traditional ethics – and shows how Habermas's Moral Point of View recognizes the need for shared procedural (how things are done) and declarative (how symbols and texts work) knowledge. It calls for a continuous self-critical dialogue to help balance perspectives and avoid the 'standard person' problem by which one assumes everyone else (i.e. 'all reasonable men') would respond the same way. Cooper (2004) draws on Habermas' Lifeworld (1996) to demonstrate the role of shared values in collective story-telling and the difficulty of determining such values in a pluralist global culture. He offers a synthesis of discourse and virtue ethics as the basis for professional ethics in a multicultural world. This level of reflexivity is absent from most approaches to professional ethics, which often assume that culturally specific ethics, such as those based in US jurisprudence, can be exported globally – problems already identified in PR's ethical approaches. Feminist critiques have also exposed the gendered assumptions underlying certain aspects of virtue ethics, as suggested above, and postmodern and critical theorists argue that all such attempts are ideological and hegemonic.

I share these reservations but am aware that cultural relativism can lead to a shrug of 'whatever' or divisions over issues such as bribing government officials as a cultural norm. As suggested, strong hermeneutics may offer an avenue out of this impasse, though it is little explored in professional ethics' literature. That may also be a reflection of the dominant concerns of Anglo-American writing on the subject, so this section looks briefly at some Asian approaches to ethics, which raise a completely different set of questions and reinforce my sense that hermeneutic and Jungian approaches offer bridges between Eastern and Western ideas about ethics. Asian ethics are explored by Koehn (2001) – although she warns loudly against lumping together the many approaches found in different Asian cultures and countries – for relevance to global business ethics. She finds relevance in both old approaches (Confucius, 551–479BC) and more recent writing on ethics (Watsuji, 1889–1960), which move beyond rules-based ethics to ethics of self-development and authenticity (respectively). Here the emphasis is on self-awareness and reflexivity, spending time correctly identifying the key issues and deploying virtues and personality, 'refining judgement and overcoming the ego-self' (Koehn, 2001: 17). Confucian ethics emphasizes tradition, the role of the family and the role of leaders, rather than codes: 'By itself a code will not lead to genuine ethical development. People develop only when they attend to the meaning of their actions' (2001: 45). Koehn is clear that the Confucian ideal, *jen** (a word close to virtue, love, exemplary humanity) is not about perfection but is rooted in human imperfection, and is the result of a life-long struggle with the self, in terms very close to Jung's journey of individuation (see Chapter 6). The emphasis here is on awareness or consciousness of one's actions and has some parallel with Aristotle's virtue ethics, discussed earlier. Interestingly, there is no distinction between the public and private domain in Confucian thought, and there are quite different approaches to the concept of profession in Asian ethics, according to Koehn (2001), requiring no separate standard of behaviour of professionals, who are subject to the same ethical standards as all other members of society. This reflects debates considered earlier in the chapter about whether extra-ordinary ethics in professions are even desirable. Kupperman (1999: 26) also draws on Confucian and other Asian approaches to ethics, noting that:

> There is a long and very powerful Western tradition … that pictures ethics as the study of a certain type of choice: one in which good, evil, right, and wrong are at stake. According to this tradition, whether one decides to murder or not, or to lie or not, is typically an ethical matter. How someone spends money, or converses with friends, or has a manner that is cheerful and open rather than sullen and withdrawn is normally not a matter of ethics. Ethics thus focuses on certain special moments. The general tendencies of life are largely ignored, or are considered to lie outside of the subject.

Thus the focus has shifted not only to character but to moral agency in all actions, not just certain specific situations. Again, professional ethics tends to focus on duties and dilemmas associated with the profession (for example, medical, legal and clerical concepts of confidentiality); Asian approaches concern the whole person, not only their professional function, and are located in the whole life, not just the occupational aspects. This can be contrasted with the earlier concern about the focus on quandary ethics in business schools. The influence of Asian thinking on Jung will be explored in later chapters; but the different framework for considering ethics raised here should be noted. The splitting of parts from whole is often seen as consistent with the modernist 'project' in which professions manage some aspects of society, as discussed in the previous chapter. Several ethical scholars suggest that the reintegration of discarded aspects (cf. Weber's 'disenchanted world') is a requirement of a global approach to ethics. For example, the business ethicist Goodpaster (2007) argues for the reintegration of moral purpose into the corporate agenda. The question of where to look for that purpose is deeply explored by Schweiker (2004), who argues that the contemporary culture or *Weltershaung* is 'overhumanised'; that is, over-reliant on human powers to control the environment, regulate behaviour and generally colonize nature through reason, having lost contact with any sense of the sacred. Similar concerns were raised by Durkheim, Weber and Jung a century ago. These later approaches move the argument about ethics into a newer direction, away from the Anglo-American emphasis on reasoning and evaluation towards a greater internal reflexivity that takes in more than abstract thought and cool calculations of either outcomes or duties. Islamic approaches to ethics also differ from western norms, as is illustrated by a brief summary of the key precepts regarding Islamic principles of communication (each of which is the subject of extensive reflection and discussion), which are organized into lists of Dos and Don'ts, including Do not backbite, boast, offend or ridicule others, speak too loudly, utter evil words in public speech, revile the gods of others or prefer one type of audience over another (Hussain, 2009). There are points of similarity with the Christian Ten Commandments, though tolerance for others' gods is novel, as is the centrality of communication ethics to everyday life. The edicts for positive communication include speaking with truth, with knowledge, saying things of high quality, doing justice to the audience, speaking mildly even to sinners, in a moderate tone and pace, communicating with wisdom and 'beautiful preaching' (Hussain, 2009). The details include guidance on using the best argument, making it accessible and suited for the audience, and (how wise) checking all information that comes from dubious sources. How different might the Global Alliance ethical protocols mentioned in Chapter 3 appear if founded on such principles? (See also Vujnovic and Kruckeberg, 2005 for an interesting discussion on Arab models of PR.)

The most interesting attempt to construct a universal ethics for use in business is Koehn's (2001) comparison of certain Asian writers with traditional western ethics. As suggested earlier, she combines the ethics of Confucius and Warsuji with aspects of virtue ethics to navigate a third way between asserting absolute authority of one culturally based ethical view over another and retreating into ethical relativism:

1   the multiplicity of incommensurate human goods serves as a basis for the practice of giving reasons and for virtue;
2   thoughtful human beings (note the plural) are the standard for ethically good actions, but we lack a model for the prudent man or woman; and
3   evil consists not in violating some overarching ethical rule but in pretending that only one good exists.

(Koehn, 2001: 170)

In her fuller explanation of these ideas, it becomes clear that Koehn is moving away from the western emphasis on good versus bad, its use of terms such as evil and tendency to use idealized human models as the basis for ethics. She stresses that ethics has to function in a complex interlocking world of varying cultural perspectives and priorities, and suggests that there may be many ways of evaluating between competing human goods, including enhanced use of practical reasoning, which, like situationist ethics, starts from the particular and ekes out the underlying principles and duties involved. Moreover, like Habermas, Koehn states this can only be achieved dialogically. She notes that individuals are plural, highlighting the heterogeneity of the modern world, unlike Aristotle's 'good man' operating within the consensus on desirable virtues in ancient Greece:

> Virtues do not presume unanimity but disagreement over diverse goods. Good judgement is not a static process of surefootedly moving to the right answer … Good judgement involves stumbling and learning through our mistakes.
>
> (2001: 209)

This reflects some of the discussion (above) from Asian and Islamic traditions, where ethics is a way of being in the world, and raises the debate to a lofty plane of human experience and meaning.

Reflecting on these approaches to professional ethics helps me understand how I made ethical decisions, given that, like most practitioners, I had no formal exposure to ethical theory. I suspect my instincts were primarily Kantian, preferring the absolute to the equivocal, with a strong sense of the wider implications of particular decisions. I wanted to understand or identify the operating principles we were deploying, either in the press office or the trade union campaigns I ran. For example, I remember organizing a local government media event in the mid-1980s to launch a (then) innovative Women's Bus that led to a national outrage about use of taxpayers' money to promote lesbian rights. Despite the fuss, I could never have removed the offending posters. Nowadays, I feel my ethics are hermeneutic, seeking the perspective of the other rather than rushing to judgement. Asian, Islamic and Jungian ethics (see Chapter 7) offer more complex, ambiguous and nuanced responses than the old right/wrong edicts. My question is whether professional ethics might shift its core position somewhat to reflect twenty-first-century issues, which brings me to the role professional bodies might play in changing the ethical climate, should they so choose. The next section considers the role of professional bodies in generating and maintaining ethical approaches and a critique of their most common expression, the code of ethics.

Professional bodies as ethical leaders

Cooper (2004) is clear that professional institutions act as moral agents, citing Goodpaster's (1984) argument that corporations should carry the same moral responsibilities as individuals, given the role they play in shaping ethical cultures. Chapter 3 included an exploration of the role of professional bodies in the establishment of professions; this section considers whether they can be seen as custodians of the profession's ethical standards (as is required by traditional literature and by some legislation, such as the Charter status of the UK's Chartered Institute of Public Relations). There, the development of professional bodies (Oliver and Montgomery, 2005) outlined a progression not dissimilar to theories of moral development (Kohlberg, 1981, 1984; Piaget, 1932), which are examined by Cooper (2004) in his reflections on professional ethics, and Goodpaster (2007) on the moral development of organizations. Rest (1994) also bases ideas about moral development in professions on Piaget and Kohlberg, suggesting the key moral determinants are:

1   Moral sensitivity – (Interpreting the situation)
2   Moral judgment – (Judging which action is morally right/wrong)
3   Moral motivation – (Prioritizing moral values relative to other values)
4   Moral character – (Having courage, persisting, overcoming distractions, implementing skills)

(1994: 23)

Interestingly, these beg the very questions that Durkheim declares ethical theory must address: (a) what is a moral character? (b) what is the nature of moral motivation? (c) what is the nature of the right and the good? And (d) who is the moral judge? (Watts-Miller, 1996: 10). It should also be said that these development models, with their staircase of ascending morality, seem somewhat reductionist. Ethics is seen as situational, and the moral agent with character must exercise a lack of self-interest and good judgement to achieve ethical outcomes. Other literature (e.g. Brown and Trevino, 2006; Needle and Lecker, 1997) looks at ethical leadership by analysing the behaviours of certain business leaders for positive and negative traits, but I do not want to get into discussion of leadership or moral development here. Instead I am asking whether the professional body can create a space in which ethical debate can take place. While Kultgen (1988) points out that professional associations are at the heart of generating codes of ethics and provide the closest available source of moral leadership, he also notes that they are 'scattered objects' and that 'the control they exercise over their members is directed toward maintaining discipline in the project of controlling the market rather than for the public good' (1988: 161). A more rigorous investigate of professions as ethical leaders is offered by Sama and Shoaf (2008: 40) who raise issues close to the heart of this book, albeit with subtly differing conclusions, concerning

> ethical leadership voids that have wreaked havoc on the moral communities their businesses served and were members of, and how moral intelligence at the top might have contributed to better outcomes for all stakeholders.

They use DiNorcia's description of 'non-random collections of groups of people engaged in reciprocal and positive social interaction' (2002, cited in Sama and

Shoaf, 2008: 41), to establish professions as moral communities. Indeed, as they point out, professions not only comprise self-regulating, self-supporting organizations, they also produce mutually agreed codes of conduct that are separate from the law. They then define ethical leadership as founded in

> a model of transformational leadership wherein the vision is one of achieving moral good, and the core values are those of integrity, trust, and moral rectitude. Ethical leaders inspire others in the organization to behave in similarly ethical ways, and they are persuasive in their communities to effect change in the direction of positive moral goals. To the extent that professions are piloted by ethical leaders, there is a greater likelihood that moral intelligence will be promoted in followers and that reciprocal trust will develop in relevant communities to the profession.
>
> (2008: 41)

This view of professions and their capacity for moral transformation is more optimistic than is found in most revisionist writing on professions, where the organization is seen as intent on securing hegemony in its field and sufficient benefits (tangible and non-tangible) for members to ensure its own continued existence. However, Sama and Shoaf (2008: 43) put a heartfelt case for renewed engagement with ethical issues:

> Traditional values of the professions are eroding, leading to breaches of trust, resulting in increasing scrutiny of the professions and their practices, often in the form of regulation. Public recourse is increasingly through litigation. Reinstalling trust and legitimacy requires ethical leadership that embodies moral intelligence and creates moral community through shared values, reciprocity, integrity, transparency, and consistent adherence to principles.

While I do not share their idealism, I am interested in the challenge to professional bodies – in all fields – regarding the recovery of lost public trust and in the face of growing legislative threats. It does seem in their own interests to open a much wider, deeper space for ethical debate than is currently found in most codes of conduct. Much of my argument around professional bodies can be summarized as 'put up or shut up'; it is the moral claims made by codes that invite the challenge to honour the rhetoric or withdraw it altogether. My plea is not for the shared values cited by Sama and Shoaf but for an end to the hypocrisy that underpins (and undermines) most professional ethics as currently constituted; an argument that is clearest in the discussion of codes of ethics.

As was clear from the last chapter, professions require codes of ethics to support the claim for social status, along with the body of knowledge and a national organization. These codes embody the relationship between the occupation and society in general, and most professions or aspiring professions prefer to set store in Codes of Ethics than engage in philosophical debates (Larson, 1977). Abbott says codes of ethics 'are the most concrete cultural form in which professions acknowledge their societal obligations' (Abbott, 1983: 256). He notes that codes tend to be formal objects that play a part in relationships between professional groups, and may lead to the extension or diminution of membership to try and manage unethical colleagues. Freidson (2001) suggests that professional codes fall into three types of obligation: a) obey law/regulations; b) practice competently; and c) reflect values in behaviour, such as care and trust. The first two of these are non-contentious, though hardly constitute an ethic: practitioners who need codes to be reminded to obey the law and do their job can't really be described as professional, given that the same injunctions apply to all citizens and employees. So the notion of professionalism seems to be located in the sense of values, though the issue of how they are to be determined and assessed is problematic. Rowson (2006: 53) summarizes ethical codes as containing four general principles:

1   To seek results that are the most beneficial and least harmful to individuals and to society.
2   To treat individuals justly and fairly by not discriminating between them on irrelevant grounds and by paying attention to their individual needs.
3   To respect people's autonomy as far as possible within a society in which the legitimate interests of all must be considered.
4   To behave with integrity by acting in accord with the stated or implied values, undertakings and objectives of the profession.

Again, this sounds splendid until one stumbles over concepts of 'integrity' and 'values', and it is typical of discussion of codes that virtues are invoked rather than examined. It is these unexamined claims that lead to the use of 'ethics as reputation', in which the code is 'primarily a public relations document' (Kultgen, 1988: 362). This echoes Larson's view that codes tell the public 'what the profession wants to be, not what it is (1977: x), although Davies comments approvingly that 'Probably the most obvious use of a company code of ethics is as part of a public relations exercise' (1997: 98). At a more theoretical level, as was discussed in Chapter 3, new sociology of institutions (NSI) suggests that professional institutions act as entrepreneurs using discourse and rhetoric to influence the social construction of legitimacy. Ethics, codes of conduct and similar claims can be seen as part of this discourse, especially given the lack of rigour or sanctions usually involved (Bartlett *et al.*, 2007). Taking a semiotic perspective, Wernick (1991) shows how a wide range of institutions have learned to deploy signs and symbols for promotional purposes, and it seems reasonable to include professional codes of conduct in this category. The critical scholar Brecher (2010: 353) sees codes as encapsulating the very worst of professionalism and its empty claims to ethics:

of course the transformation of a body of workers into a profession requires the creation of an appropriate code of professional ethics. Furthermore, such codes reflect exactly the ambivalence of professionalization itself: their function is at one and the same time to hold professionals accountable and to protect them from moral accountability. Put crudely, professional ethics instrumentalise moral concern; and in doing so, both take morality out of the picture and depoliticise the object of what might have been moral concern.

There is something shocking in reconceptualizing professional ethics as not only vacuous – a claim made by many critics – but actively pernicious, as undermining rather than enhancing ethical behaviour in professional groups; here their function is protective of the professional, not the client, not society. Banks McDowell (1991: 3) also notes the opposed views of professional ethics from the perspectives of professional and client:

> One [view] widely held, or at least publicly proclaimed, by professionals themselves is that they are conscientious experts devoted to improving the lot of both society and their clients … Another view, found broadly among members of an increasingly cynical public, is that professionals are a rapacious, greedy, often incompetent lot who are frequently overpaid to do more damage than good. My starting point is that both views are accurate, or at least contain some truth. The average professional is a typical human being which means a bundle of contradictions, containing within himself or herself the capacity for genuinely virtuous and altruistic activity, as well as the capacity for mean, selfish, and greedy activity.

This division represents a central argument in the book: no profession can claim to have a grounded ethic if it is not prepared to confront and engage with its mirror image, its shadow self. This is the challenge to professional bodies: to look into the hidden aspects of the group, hidden that is from its members but often all too visible to others. The Jungian approach outlined in the following chapters suggests one path for such a dialogue. A hermeneutic ethic, as outlined earlier, also requires a depth of relationship not often found in writing about professional practice, as Gadamer suggests that; 'ethical advice involves the same level of participation as one's involvement in one's own life. It is not possible to give sound advice unless one takes the situation to be one that affects one's own life and self-understanding' (Warnke, 2002: 86). Given the degree of advice-giving central to many professions from accountants to PR, this is a powerful statement.

However, far from engaging in this deep involvement with clients, most codes of ethics stand as rhetorical proclamations of identity, one of the five 'moments' in the circuit of culture outlined above. Indeed, Curtin and Gaither (2005: 104) suggest that codes can be seen as 'cultural artefacts'. For this reason, I am not covering alternative ethical frameworks such as decision-making processes, like the Potter Box (see McElreath, 1996). These are interesting but tend not to represent the profession in the same way as codes; they are procedural rather than declamatory, lacking the cultural dimension suggested by Curtin and Gaither (2007). So what are the common rhetorical and symbolic contents of codes exactly? Kultgen offers (1988: 74–5) an extensive list of extracts from a wide range of US codes of conduct and it is worth quoting some of them to illustrate dominant themes.

The principal objective of the medical profession is to render service to humanity with full respect for the dignity of man. (American Medical Association)

The continued existence of a free and democratic society depends upon recognition of the concept that justice is based upon the rule of law grounded in respect for the dignity of the individual and his capacity through reason for enlightened self-government. (Law-Association)

The duty of journalists is to serve the truth ... The public's right to know of events of public importance and interest is the overriding mission of the mass media. The purpose of distributing news and enlightened opinion is to serve the general welfare. (Sigma Delta Chi)

Engineers uphold and advance the integrity, honor and dignity of the engineering profession by using their knowledge and skill for the enhancement of human welfare ... Engineers shall hold paramount the safety, health and welfare of the public in the performance of their professional duties. (Engineers' Council for Professional Development)

Psychologists respect the dignity and worth of the individual and strive for the preservation and protection of fundamental human rights. They are committed to increasing knowledge of human behavior and of people's understanding of themselves and others and to the utilization of such knowledge for the promotion of human welfare. (American Psychological Association)

This service is committed to profound faith in the worth, dignity, and great potentiality of the individual human being ... A profession exalts service to the individual and society above personal gain. (American Personnel and Guidance Association)

The distinguishing character of a profession is that its members are dedicated to rendering service to humanity. Financial gain or personal reward must be of secondary consideration. (American Football Coaches Association)

The true professional man places the public's welfare above his own. Such concern for the patient or client is characteristic of a professional calling ... I shall place the welfare and interests of my clients above my own interests. (American Society of Certified Life Underwriters)

From this, one can identify a number of tropes – the invocation of values such as democracy, freedom, service to society, commitment to truth, dignity and the rights of the individual, as well as humanity at large (despite references to 'the professional man'), embodying what is sometimes called the 'service contract' (Cooper, 2004). An image emerges of a champion of human rights, a defender of society, a servant of the greater good, who consistently (it is reiterated above) places the interests of others, including financial interests, above 'his' own. These quotes serve to illustrate Larson's (1977) argument about the ideal-typical professional who is subtly shifted from an abstract ideal to a concrete descriptor, from 'ought' to 'is', creating a (spurious) ground for claiming social benefits.

On the other hand, while some codes stress the abstract ideal, others overemphasize the specific situation, following the trait approach outlined in the last chapter. Indeed, many codes evolved from this school, attempting to offer definitive guidance for a range of situations, e.g. regarding confidentiality, poaching clients, conflicts of interest. Inter-collegiate boundaries are often central to such codes, reflecting the concerns about establishing jurisdiction and control over certain areas of labour:

> the group requires sharp boundaries in order to deny its status to outsiders and to avoid responsibility for their failures. This necessity explains why most codes of professional ethics forbid professionals to deal with outsiders, explicitly limiting collegiality to the accepted membership. The charlatans provide the foil necessary to internal professional unity.
>
> (Abbott, 1983: 868)

In other words, in order to create and maintain a group identity it is necessary for there to be an Other, a concept that will be explored more deeply elsewhere. Many codes reflect ambivalence towards fellow members who must be monitored for unfair competition *and* protected from charges of ethical dereliction. Such codes also imply that they offer a comprehensive set of guidelines for establishing professional standards, in which the code substitutes for genuine reflexivity, leading to a kind of unacknowledged dependency:

> Ethical nostrums designed to address professional practice issues often rest on the bedrock assumption that clarity is the chief question ... The assumption has been that if only practitioners knew what was ethical (or not), if only they had a practicable ethical model to apply, they would be able to choose to operate in an ethical way: and would, in fact, do so.
>
> (Harrison and Galloway, 2005: 1)

This also reflects the criticism earlier in the chapter about the fascination with quandary ethics, focused on specific choices in certain situations – and often reduced to the question of whether to work for oil, arms and tobacco firms, rather than how to relate ethically to other human beings in all our affairs or achieve Aristotle's *eudemonia*, or wellbeing. Such a view is shared by Brecher, as mentioned earlier, who questions the need for extra-ordinary ethics in professions and suggests that codes of conduct become tools of measurement rather than ethics:

> Hence, of course, the existence of *codes* of ethics, as if acting morally well were some sort of add-on to the specific demands of being a nurse, lawyer, doctor, teacher or whatever, rather than something demanded simply by one's being a person. Codification, furthermore, opens the door to measurement and quantification: whether or not a nurse is working 'ethically' all too easily becomes a matter of checking, and *checking off*, against a list of rules, while the rules themselves remain morally and politically unexamined.
>
> (2010: 354, emphasis in original)

Whether based in the ideal or trait approach, recent history provides plentiful evidence of the wholesale disregard for professional codes. As various writers (Harrison and Galloway, 2005; Kultgen, 1988; Parkinson, 2001; Pater and van Gils, 2003) find, members of professional associations pay little attention to their codes, and over the past few years the professional reputations of bankers and politicians (Arthur W. Page Society, 2009), NASA scientists (Robinson, 2002); Roman Catholic priests, medical staff (Kaye, 2006) and others have been exposed as lacking precisely the commitment to client and to society above self. I suggest that one explanation is that an over-idealized version of the professional creates a gulf that the practitioner cannot breach, like the perfect saints whom fallible mortals must always disappoint. As the discussion from PR practitioners in Chapter 2 suggests, members may evolve their own informal codes or find other grounds for conduct. In any event, sanctions against any breaches of codes are rarely invoked (Kultgen, 1988) and as scandals in accounting, banking, medicine, media, sport and clergy have shown, self-regulation has tended to be self-exculpation, reinforcing the sense that codes are promotional rather than regulatory in intent. This exposes the double function of professional bodies: they are between the rock of recruiting and retaining members and the hard place of maintaining status in society. A punitive approach to enforcing ethics alienates the former; a lax attitude, the latter. Nevertheless, the promise to maintain ethical standards is part of the 'deal' guaranteeing professional autonomy. This is what professional bodies protect. To do so they attempt to control the behaviour of their members, though as Kultgen (1988: 136) points out they have limited means for so doing:

> By and large, the mechanisms are not sufficient to enforce a high level of either competence or morality ... Only a minority of professionals belong to professional associations ... Membership is not a condition of practice, so termination of membership is not a severe loss. Expulsion is a threat only to those least likely to suffer it, those who already identify strongly with the profession.

It should also be remembered that professionals may also be subject to trade union and/or employer codes of conduct, as well as their personal belief systems and cultural norms (Coughlan, 2001; Pater and van Gils, 2003). Negotiating between different ethical systems is not covered in this book, but is discussed in the final chapter as a potential direction for future research. Consideration of the individual's role in enacting professional ethics raises a question about who exactly is responsible for living up to the lofty claims listed by Kultgen earlier. Abbott (1983) suggests that the demand for individual conformity with codes of ethics may actually be a substitute for more rigorous regulation (including self-regulation) of the profession as a whole. Thus the individual is held responsible for professional standards while the professional body avoids the

> important, if less charismatic, dilemmas of mediocre practice, overcommitment of time, and maldistribution of effort that many sociologists see as the

basic issues of professional control. In fact, it often tries to deny the existence of corporate professional obligations altogether.

(1983: 879)

Abbott (ibid) calls this 'regressive ethics', which recalls some of the issues discussed in the managerialization of professions in the last chapter, whereby target measurement and performance indicators replace deeper appraisal of professional ethics. In this sense, codes can stand in the way of discussion, either by infantilizing those bound by codes so they are unable to make autonomous ethical decisions or by devolving responsibility from professional body to member, in what Bauman (2008: 62) calls the 'privatisation of ethics'. Bauman (2008: 52) suggests that the shift from societal to consumer ethics has led to an individual struggle with overwhelming choice and inadequate information about consequences:

> The concepts of responsibility and responsible choice which used to reside in the semantic field of ethical duty and moral concern for the Other, have moved or been shifted to the realm of self-fulfilment and calculation of risks.

Responsibility to self has trumped responsibility to the Other, which lay at the heart of traditional ethics (Levinas, 1985, cited in Bauman, 2008: 62–4) and which now forms the core of the consumer 'because you're worth it' myth. Relating this back to professions, the absence of a collective dimension casts practitioners as consumers, making individual choices in their own best interests, while claiming to serve unspecified social functions – a point made clearly by Bivins (1993) regarding PR's absence of a societal concept, as will be explored in the next chapter. In contrast, Messikomer and Cirka (2010: 59) argue that 'For a code to achieve ethical validity, and realize the potential to be a living document, the code development process must be participative, the content must be values-based, and leaders must be authentic ethical managers'. They suggest that a shift 'from dead rule to living dialogue' is only possible with the active participation of those trying to live by its principles.

Conclusion

This chapter has explored various approaches to professional ethics, particularly highlighting the philosophical debates that underpin most of these debates, not always explicitly. While new topics such as virtue ethics, discourse ethics and various postmodern and feminist approaches have developed in recent decades, not all are reflected in discussion of professional ethics, despite the relevance of the issues they raise. Discussion of professional ethics tends rather to concentrate either on idealized versions of the professional or solutions to particular dilemmas – neither approach being well founded in ethical philosophy. There has been recent exploration of professions as ethical leaders, though it seems clear that such roles demand a higher level of reflexivity than can be found in most current codes of conduct. Indeed, Anglo-American codes reflect the ideal-typical approach, while placing responsibility for ethical behaviour on the individual, thus avoiding profession-wide scrutiny of performance, standards and other ethical issues. It would seem that while some approaches to general ethics, such as Asian and virtue ethics, do look at the person (or collective) not just the actions, this is an underdeveloped area and has made little impact on professional ethics. It is hard to avoid the conclusion that professional ethics is primarily a promotional construct, designed to secure and maintain organizational autonomy. There is an absence of engagement with the deeper struggle that comprises genuine professional ethical responsibility.

The next chapter returns to PR as a field to consider the degree to which it has engaged in the debates raised in this and the previous chapter.

References

Abbott, A. (1983) Professional ethics. *The American Journal of Sociology, 88*(5): 855–85.

Appiah, K. (2005) *The Ethics of Identity*. Princeton, NJ and Woodstock: Princeton University Press.

Appiah, K. (2008) *Experiments in Ethics*. Cambridge, MA and London: Harvard University Press.

Arthur W. Page Society (2007) *The authentic enterprise: relationships, values and corporate communications*. Arthur W. Page Society.

Arthur W. Page Society (2009) *The dynamics of public trust in business – emerging opportunities for leaders*. Arthur W. Page Society.

Bartlett, J., Tywoniak, S. and Hatcher, C. (2007) Public relations professional practice and the insitutionalisation of CSR. *Journal of Communication Management, 11*(4): 281–99.

Bauman, Z. (1993) *Postmodern Ethics*. Oxford: Blackwell.

Bauman, Z. (2008) *Does Ethics have a Chance in a World of Consumers?* Cambridge, MA: Harvard University Press.

Benhabib, S. (1992) *Situating the Self: gender, community, and postmodernism in contemporary ethics*. New York, NY: Routledge.

Bivins, T. H. (1993) Public relations, professionalism and the public interest. *Journal of Business Ethics, 12:* 117–26.

Brecher, B. (2010) The politics of professional ethics. *The Journal of Clinical Evaluation in Practice, 16*(2): 351–5.

Brown, M. E. and Trevino, L. K. (2006) Ethical leadership: a review and future directions. *The Leadership Quarterly, 17:* 595–616.

Christians, C. (2011) Journalism ethics in theory and practice. In G. Cheney, S. May and D. Munshi (eds) *The Handbook of Communication Ethics*. New York, NY: Routledge, pp. 190–203.

Cooper, D. E. (2004) *Ethics for Professionals in a Multicultural World*. Upper Saddle River, NJ: Prentice Hall.

Coughlan, R. (2001) An analysis of professional codes of ethics in the hospitality industry. *International Journal of Hospitality Management, 20*(2): 147–62.

Crawford, N. C. (1998) Postmodern ethical conditions and a critical response. *Ethics and International Affairs, 12*(1): 121–40.

Curtin, P. A. and Boynton, L. A. (2001) Ethics in public relations: theory and practice. In R.L. Heath (ed.) *Hanbook of Public Relations*. Thousand Oaks, CA: Sage, pp. 411–22.

Curtin, P. A. and Gaither, T. K. (2005) Privileging identity, difference and power: the circuit of culture as a basis for public relations theory. *Journal of Public Relations Research, 17*(2): 91–115.

Curtin, P. A. and Gaither, T. K. (2007) *International Public Relations: negotiating culture, identity and power.* Thousand Oaks, CA: Sage.

Davies, P. W. F. (1997) *Current Issues in Business Ethics.* London: Routledge.

Day, K. D., Dong, Q. and Robins, C. (2001) Public relations ethics: an overview and discussion of issues for the 21st century. In R.L. Heath (ed.) *Handbook of Public Relations.* Thousand Oaks, CA: Sage, pp. 403–10.

du Gay, P., Hall, S., Janes, L., Mackay, H. and Negus, K. (1997) *Doing Cultural Studies: the story of the Sony Walkman.* London: Sage.

Freedman, B. (1978) A meta-ethics for professional morality. *Ethics, 89*(1): 1–19.

Freidson, E. (2001) *Professionalism: the third logic.* Cambridge: Polity.

Gadamer, H.-G. (1989) *Truth and Method* (2nd rev. edn) New York, NY: Crossroad.

Gewirth, A. (1986) Professional ethics: the separatist thesis. *Ethics, 96*(2): 282–300.

Gilligan, C. (1982) *In a Different Voice: psychological theory and women's development.* Cambridge, MA and London: Harvard University Press.

Goodpaster, K. E. (2007) *Conscience and Corporate Culture.* Malden, MA and Oxford: Blackwell.

Green, B. (ed.) (2009) *Understanding and Researching Professional Practice.* Rotterdam, Netherlands: Sense.

Habermas, J. (1989) *The Structural Transformation of the Public Sphere: an inquiry into a category of bourgeois society.* Cambridge, MA: MIT Press.

Habermas, J. (1996) *Between Facts and Norms: contributions to a discourse theory of law and democracy.* Cambridge, MA: MIT Press.

Harrison, K. and Galloway, C. (2005) Public relations ethics: a simpler (but not simplistic) approach to the complexities. *Prism, 3.* Online. Available at www.praxis.massey.ac.nz, retrieved 14 March, 2007.

Hauke, C. (2000) *Jung and the Postmodern: the interpretation of realities.* London: Routledge.

Hussein, M. Y. (2009) Principles of communication in Islam. In M. Y. Hussein (ed.) *Intercultural Communication in Muslim Societies.* Kuala Lumpur, Malaysia: International Islamic University, pp. 99–104.

Jensen, K. B. (2002) *A Handbook of Media and Communications Research: qualitative and quantitative methodologies.* London: Routledge.

Kaye, R. P. (2006) Regulated (self-)regulation: a new paradigm for controlling the professions. *Public Policy and Administration, 21*(3): 105–19.

Koehn, D. (1994) *The Ground of Professional Ethics.* London: Routledge.

Koehn, D. (2001) *Local Insights, Global Ethics for Business.* Amsterdam: Rodopi.

Kohlberg, L. (1981) *The Philosophy of Moral Development: moral stages and the idea of justice.* San Francisco and London: Harper & Row.

Kohlberg, L. (ed.) (1984) *The Psychology of Moral Development: the nature and validity of moral stages* (1st edn) San Francisco: Harper & Row.

Kultgen, J. (1988) *Ethics and Professionalism.* Philadeplhia: University of Philadelphia Press.

Kupperman, J. J. (1999) *Learning from Asian Philosophy.* New York, NY and Oxford: Oxford University Press.

Larson, M. S. (1977) *The Rise of Professionalism: a sociological analysis.* Berkeley, CA and London: University of California Press.

Lefkowitz. (2003) *Ethics and Values in Industrial-Organisational Psychology.* Mahwah, NJ: Lawrence Erlbaum Associates.

Lucas, P. (2005) Humanising professional ethics. In J. A. R. Strain, Simon (ed.) *The Teaching and Practice of Professional Ethics.* Leicester: Troubador.

McDowell, B. (1991) *Ethical Conduct and the Professional's Dilemma: choosing between service and success.* New York, NY and London: Quorum.

McElreath, M. P. (1996) *Managing Systematic and Ethical Public Relations* (2nd edn) Madison, WI: Brown and Benchmark.

MacIntyre, A. (1984) *After Virtue: a study in moral theory* (2nd edn) Notre Dame, IN: University of Notre Dame Press.

Messikomer, C. M. and Cirka, C. C. (2010) Constructing a code of ethics: an experiential case of a national professional organization. *Journal of Business Ethics, 95:* 55–71.

Mintz, S. M. (2006) Accounting ethics education: integrating reflective learning and virtue ethics. *Journal of Accounting Education, 24*(2–3): 97–117.

Mount, E. (1990) *Professional Ethics in Context: institutions, images, and empathy.* Louisville, KY: Westminster/John Knox Press.

Needle, T. K. and Lecker, M. J. (1997) Psychoethics: a discipline applying psychology to ethics. *Review of Business, 18*(3): 30–4.

Oakley, J. and Cocking, D. (2001) *Virtue Ethics and Professional Roles.* Cambridge: Cambridge University Press.

Oliver, A. L. and Montgomery, K. (2005) Toward the construction of a profession's boundaries: creating a networking agenda. *Human Relations, 58*(9): 1167–84.

Parkinson, M. (2001) The PRSA Code of Professional Standards and Member Code of Ethics: why they are neither professional nor ethical. *Public Relations Quarterly, 46*(3): 27–31.

Pater, A. and van Gils, A. (2003) Stimulating ethical decision-making in a business context: effects of ethical and professional codes. *European Journal of Management, 21*(6): 762–72.

Piaget, J. (1999 [1932]) *The Moral Judgement of the Child.* London: Routledge.

Proulx, C. (1994) On Jung's theory of ethics. *Journal of Analytic Psychology, 39*(1): 101–19.

Rawls, J. (1973) *A Theory of Justice.* Oxford: Oxford University Press.

Rest, J. R. (1994) Background: theory and practice. In J. R. Rest and D. Narvaez (eds) *Moral Development in the Professions: psychology and applied ethics.* Hillsdale, NJ: Lawrence Erlbaum Associates, pp. 1–26.

Riceour, P. (1981) *Hermeneutics and the Human Sciences: essays on language, action and interpretation.* Cambridge: Cambridge University Press.

Robinson, S. (2002) Challenger Flight 51-L. In C. Megone and S. Robinson (eds) *Case Studies in Business Ethics.* London: Routledge, pp. 108–22.

Rowson, R. (2006) *Working Ethics: how to be fair in a culturally complex world.* London: Jessica Kingsley .

Sama, L. M. and Shoaf, V. (2008) Ethical leadership for the professions: fostering a moral community. *Journal of Business Ethics, 78*(1–2): 39–46.

Schweiker, W. (2004) *Theological Ethics and Global Dynamics: in the time of many worlds.* Malden, MA and Oxford: Blackwell.

Sciulli, D. (2005) Continental sociology of professions today: conceptual contributions. *Current Sociology, 53*(6): 915–42.

Smith, N. H. (1997) *Strong Hermeneutics: contingency and moral identity.* London: Routledge.

Vujnovic, M. and Kruckeberg, D. (2005) Imperative for an 'Arab' model of public relations as a framework for diplomatic, corporate and nongovernmental organization relationships. *Public Relations Review, 31*(3): 338–43.

Warnke, G. (2002) Hermeneutics, ethics and politics. In R. J. Dostal (ed.) *The Cambridge Companion to Gadamer.* Cambridge: Cambridge University Press, pp. 79–101.

Watson, T. (2010) Authenticity and the authentic enterprise. *Journal of Communication Management, 14*(3): 189–91.

Watts-Miller, W. (1996) *Durkheim, Morals and Modernity.* London: UCL Press.

Wernick, A. (1991) *Promotional Culture: advertising, ideology and symbolic expression.* London: Sage.

5 Does public relations have professional ethics?

Introduction

An overview of approaches to public relations (PR) ethics was offered in Chapter 2, but the last two chapters have raised a range of issues concerning professionalism and the philosophical underpinnings of professional ethics that add complexity to tensions which are often over-simplified in discussion of PR ethics. For example, they help explain differences between those who see PR as performing an ethical role in society generally and those who see it as undermining democratic values as reflecting sociological divisions between functionalist and revisionist approaches to professionalism. So this chapter delves deeper into the issues raised in Chapter 2 and asks a) whether PR can be considered a profession, according to the definitions offered in Chapter 3 and b) the degree to which PR ethics follows established approaches to professional ethics. This last question involves looking at the philosophical underpinnings of PR ethics, where they can be ascertained and relating back to the general ethical theories explored in Chapter 4. The thread I follow here is the issue of persuasion, which sits uncomfortably at the heart of PR, and attitudes to which determine varying approaches to ethics. For example, excellence approaches that demonize persuasion emphasize PR's ideal symmetrical communication, despite its acknowledged rarity in practice (Grunig, 2001). Rhetorical schools, in contrast, accept persuasion as a fact and work towards generating ethical ways of practising it. Socio-cultural and postmodern scholars take a cooler look, recognizing the reality of persuasion as part of the social construction of meaning, neither good nor bad, and this creates a new space for discussion of PR ethics.

It occurs to me that some readers may be longing for concrete examples at this stage – it would certainly appear that most writing on ethics shifts smartly from abstract debate to case studies. I wonder if there is something in the collective psyche of PR that rushes for solutions rather than staying in the problem for a little longer. Teaching the Chartered Institute of Public Relations diploma to senior practitioners, I was often struck by their resistance to developing strategy when there were glitzy tactics to be drummed up. As a practitioner and then as an academic teaching practitioners, my plaintive cry in the face of all their excited plans was usually 'why?'. We will move towards implications for practice by the end of the book, so impatient readers can jump there, but I hope others will stay with this deeper exploration of important issues in the field of PR. I have resisted the impulse to add case studies or topical examples to this book, not only because they so quickly date, but also because they bring the focus back to specifics and I really want to explore larger themes here. So, the chapter starts with a discussion of PR as a profession, placing it in a sociological context and considering some of the many issues raised in recent years by writers from critical and socio-cultural perspectives. It then looks at how that relationship with society is manifested through approaches to ethics, exploring the roots of ethics in the excellence, rhetorical and other schools, as well as noting developments that have so far been marginalized. In particular, the ethics of persuasion are explored, as this seems a site of deep tension and will be important in understanding a Jungian approach in later chapters. The chapter introduces hermeneutic ethics to PR, speculating on the impact it might have and demonstrating in general terms what depth adds to ethical debates.

Is public relations a profession?

Those scholars who have seriously asked whether PR warrants professional status (e.g. Bivins, 1993; Breit and Demetrious 2010; Pieczka and L'Etang, 2001; Sriramesh and Hornaman, 2006; van Ruler, 2005) have tended to conclude in the negative, as it meets some but not all of the criteria of a profession outlined earlier, given the open entry to this work and the difficulty of imposing ethical and other standards on the membership. L'Etang (2008: 26) goes further, suggesting that 'only when practitioners have a good facility to understand and carry out a variety of research can the occupation move forwards to professional status'. This requirement goes further than traditional definitions of profession, emphasizing the importance of maintaining the body of knowledge and highlighting practitioner resistance to theory found in various investigations (Fawkes and Tench, 2004; van Ruler, 2005), unlike other professional groups such as doctors and lawyers, who must update their knowledge. And of course, unlike medicine or law, anyone can practise PR; as Macnamara (2012) points out, only 3,000 practitioners belonged to the Australian professional body in 2009 out of an estimated 21,000 potential members, a point made earlier by van Ruler (2005) regarding European representation. However, undaunted by the difficulty of controlling practitioners, the field has strenuously sought professional status, because

> that would give credibility and reputation to the industry, increase the accountability and credibility of practitioners, enhance the quality of work produced by practitioners, and give practitioners greater opportunities to contribute to organizational decision making.
>
> (Sriramesh and Hornaman, 2006: 156)

In other words, professional status is good for business. The last point is particularly poignant as it speaks to the longing to be taken seriously in the boardroom and looks to professionalism as offering a path to that table. Locating PR in the dominant coalition has been a key aspect of the excellence project and certainly, in my experience, decision-makers who do not consider the strategic communication aspects of their actions, whether in a corporate or non-governmental organization context, make foolish or futile decisions. Yet there is a strong body of research which suggests that this is largely an unconsummated desire. After half a century of positioning PR as a management function, 84 per cent of senior practitioners throughout Europe cited lack of understanding of communication practice within top management as their main barrier to professionalization (Zerfass *et al.*, 2013). The professional project still has a way to go, it would appear. Sriramesh and Hornaman's survey of literature suggests that for PR to be accepted as a profession (which the majority of their sources say has not yet happened), it must satisfy the following criteria:

1   Maintaining a code of ethics and professional values and norms
2   Commitment to serve in the public interest and be socially responsible
3   Having a body of esoteric, scholarly knowledge
4   Having specialized and standardized education, including graduate study
5   Having technical and research skills
6   Providing a unique service to an organization and the community
7   Membership in professional organizations
8   Having autonomy in organizations to make communication-related decisions.

(2006: 157)

This summary is close to the definitions explored in Chapter 3, though it's not clear which of these hurdles PR fails to leap. Pieczka and L'Etang (2001) believe open access to practice and unenforceable ethics provide obstacles to professional status, noting a tendency to describe what PR professionals *do* (the trait approach), rather than reflect on their wider role, which, they say, is due to 'professionalisation efforts that necessarily rely on an idealistic understanding of the profession' (2001: 229). As they say, most approaches to professionalism in PR rely on a very optimistic view of the profession in society, based on Durkheim and Talcott Parson's benign understanding of professionalism, concepts abandoned by the sociology of professionalism in the 1970s. This is the path that Abbott (2010: 180) says was 'dynamited' 20 years ago, suggesting that those who pursue it are guilty of professional ignorance, to use his taxonomy.

It is worth revisiting Durkheim here, and the distinction he makes between professions and trade and industry (Breit and Demetrious, 2010). The latter type of organizational activity is described as lacking a central body to maintain traditions and uphold ethics, which are therefore undeveloped in the general business community (as opposed to professional groupings). Breit and Demetrious (2010) find that the weak ethics of PR locates it as part of trade and industry rather than the professions. They then interrogate the claims made by PR bodies in New Zealand and Australia against a trait approach to professions (in this case, Volti, 2008) and find a mismatch, with PR failing to meet the criteria for a profession. For example, Breit and Demetrious find thin evidence of a body of knowledge underpinning PR practice in New Zealand and Australia, a view supported by research into UK practitioner attitudes (Tench and Fawkes, 2005) that revealed a resistance to theory and van Ruler's (2005) interrogation of Dutch practitioner attitudes to knowledge. This may also explain problems with self-theorizing (Hutton, 1999, 2001, 2010) and certainly reflects the tensions between practitioners and educators raised in Chapter 2. Heath (2001) argues that practitioners and academics need to establish an international body of knowledge, standards for entry into the field, shared ethical values, professional competencies and a foundation of knowledge to provide practitioners with a reason to depend on universities for education, as in traditional professions such as law and medicine. This raises the role of the professional body in developing and implementing such standards, nationally and globally (see below). This debate is contextualized by van Ruler (2005: 161), who summarizes the literature of professions to produce four models of professions applicable to PR:

a) *knowledge model*, in which professionalisation develops from expertise, with a commitment to both the client and society;
b) *status model*, whereby an organised elite secure power and autonomy;
c) *competition model*, which focuses on the client's demands and evaluation in competition with other professionals; and
d) *personality model*, which is suggested as the development of experts who build a reputation with clients by virtue of expertise and personal charisma.

Van Ruler finds that the knowledge model is strongly represented in US literature, with the competition model endorsed by critical scholars, though she points out that the first is over-reliant on the 'body of knowledge', while the second leads to confused identity – she argues that PR needs a professional 'brand' and to engage more profoundly with deeper discussion of professionalism. For example, van Ruler finds that national professional bodies represent only a small percentage of practitioners, a finding which has not deterred those bodies or other practitioner groups from claiming they are achieving professional recognition. McKie and Munshi (2007: 102) also summarize different versions of PR professionalism:

1 As the ideal behaviour of all involved in the field (that is, behaving professionally has an intertwined moral and operational dimension);
2 As a significant, if elusive, benchmark in the search for parity (in economic and occupational prestige) with more established professions such as law and medicine;
3 As technical competence (beyond amateur level that is usually informed by an appropriate education and relevant research);
4 As an effective management function aligned to dominant coalition objectives (that provides bottom line benefits and/or the furtherance of organisational objectives);
5 As a primary justification for higher status within society (because it fosters communication contributing to mutual understandings between organisations and stakeholders, including society as a whole) and;

6   As the successful outcome of a struggle for territory or jurisdiction in relation to areas of work also claimed by other occupations.

One can see the roots of this matrix in a range of literature; there are connections with Larson's (1977) description of the professional 'project', Abbott's (acknowledged) writing on jurisdiction (1988; 1955), Durkheim (1933) and Parsons (1951) on the contribution of professions to society, with trait approaches and PR-specific literature such as the excellence project. As McKie and Munshi (2007: 102) make clear, these are the concepts of PR as a profession that are prevalent in core texts; for example, the excellence school places PR as a profession with a responsibility to support society, following a version of Durkheim's concept of professions. Like other key concepts, such as ethics or responsibility, these terms are under-investigated and presented as non-problematic, a point also made by van Ruler (2005). The description offered by the major US report into PR education, *The Professional Bond*, illustrates this:

> If you work in public relations, or teach it, you probably have used the word 'profession' from time to time. Indeed, when we define public relations in its broadest sense—as an essential management function that helps an organization and its publics build relationships that enable them to understand and support one another—a case can certainly be made that public relations is a profession.
>
> (PRSA, 2006: 11)

Anne Gregory, the UK academic who has worked most closely with practitioners, describes PR professionalism as 'taking education and training as seriously as other professions … and [joining] the appropriate professional body' (Gregory, 2009: 275). Professional ethics is thus situated in the professional body, although, as the discussion below makes clear, the one does not guarantee the other and neither is presented as problematic. Moloney (2006) characterizes this kind of writing as issuing from scholarly 'supporters' of PR, who act as a kind of promotional agency for the field, a position illustrated by Gregory (2012: 2), who divides PR scholars into 'those scholars who have public relations as a practice at the forefront of their minds and who see the job of academia as being to support, explain, frame and develop the practice and drive it forward' and those who have 'a particular theoretical perspective as their passion and choose public relations as a field in which to explore those perspectives'. This is not my experience: all the academics I have worked with and who I meet at conferences have practitioner backgrounds; it's a feature of an emerging discipline (see also L'Etang, 2005), but many embrace academic opportunities to reflect deeply on their work and its significance, while committed to teaching those who wish to enter the field. Encountering literature helps make sense of past choices and, most importantly, helps develop the kind of insights that will be of value to future generations, not merely reproducing practice but interrogating it so that more thoughtful leaders may emerge. In this way, academics embracing particular theoretical approaches do contribute to the practice, though that is not the primary obligation of academics. A more critical approach to PR professionalism, for example, more robustly based in professionalism studies, would encourage deeper understanding of the field's relationship with neighbouring occupations such as journalism, legal and human resources departments, suitable subjects for the kind of forensic examination offered by Abbott and Freidson into social work and medicine. Where such an approach has been taken, such as Pieczka and L'Etang's (2001) discussion of PR's jurisdiction, the work of professionalism scholars such as Abbott (1988) has generated considerable insights. They suggest that journalism and marketing operate as jurisdictional competitors for the field and this issue is explored further by Hutton (1999, 2001, 2010), who considers that PR's failure to identify its core concept threatens its very survival, given the superior self-theorizing of marketing as a discipline. He cites the loss of jobs from PR to other elements of an organization, such as the legal, human resources and/or marketing departments. Traditionally, there have been tensions between PR and marketing (Hutton 1999, 2001, 2010), and there is certainly an overlap between aspects of social marketing, for example, and the core functions of PR. In this dispute, PR practitioners emphasize their prowess in building relationships with a wide range of internal and external publics rather than customer bases (Bush, 2010), while marketing has emphasized the quantitative research on which it builds proposals (Hutton, 2001). McKie and Munshi (2007: 102) note the 'clear potential for misunderstanding and conflict in such divided core definitions', echoing Hutton's concerns about core concepts, but add that, despite this confusion, 'professionalism comes close to the status of a mantra whose repetition is enough to ensure success for PR in the third millennium' (2007: 103). More recently, McKie and Willis (2012) explore Hutton's (2010) warnings from a complexity perspective, agreeing that advertising and marketing hegemonies have marginalized PR. As with some of the fluid approaches to professions considered in Chapter 3, complexity theory helps delineate the dynamics of PR in a turbulent environment, not to fix it but to recognize that multiplicity and reciprocity are more appropriate values than zero-sum warfare (see also Murphy, 1996, 2000; Murphy and Gilpin, 2013). There is resonance here with the neo-institutional approaches to professionalism outlined by Bartlett *et al.,* (2007), among others, as this also uses a biologically derived framework to explain the behaviour of professions generally and PR in particular, and with L'Etang's (2011a) call for anthropological examination of the field. While most textbooks don't yet reflect these developments, scholars are leaving the old trait approach way behind in seeking to understand PR as an occupational group.

A further problem for PR's claim to professional status was identified by Bivins (1993) two decades ago as the inadequacy of the field's conceptualization of the 'public interest', which it, like other professions, claims to serve, and contradictions between the claim to serve the client and society in general. Like Pieczka and L'Etang (2001), Bivins therefore finds it hard to support the idea of PR as an ethical profession. In particular he highlights the 'additional burden' (1993: 118) on the practitioner of serving both client and society as a whole. As Bivens points out, these tensions are not addressed by Grunig's two-way symmetric model or by the 'entirely insufficient' (1993: 119) Public Relations Society of America (PRSA) code of professional standards. Heath (2006) has argued for PR's role in a 'fully functioning society' and more recently (2010) has suggested that engagement with ideas of society (citing Mead, Buber and PR pioneer John W. Hill) is essential if PR is to develop a sense of its role in democracy, agency and participative decision-making. This matters because the 'mutual understanding' aspect of PR is sometimes offered as its 'social good', the equivalent of justice for law, health for medicine. Others have pointed out that globalization has transformed earlier concepts of publics that underpinned early theory in the field (Valentini *et al.*, 2012) and called for stronger theorizing of society. Maureen Taylor (2010) offers an overview of changing concepts of society in (primarily US) PR scholarship, noting the shift from functionalist approaches that support organizational goals to co-creational theories (including rhetoric, relationship and dialogic theory) where the agency of publics is acknowledged and may be central. The former measures outcomes and results, the latter is more interested in establishing shared meaning (Taylor, 2010: 6–7). Taylor proposes a third, synthetic way that seeks to 'create and co-create the conditions that enact civil society' (2010: 7). She belongs to the rhetorical school, like Heath, and her suggestions are grounded in PR as rhetoric, facilitating dialogic interaction between groups and individuals in society, and stressing choice and rational decision-making. These positions are contested by others, particularly those in the socio-cultural cluster (below), but this is a significant argument for later stages of the book and I will return to it in Chapter 9, when the possibility of civil society as a transcendent function is offered. Bowen (2010) continues the reflection on the nature of PR's social 'good', finding it to be communication, and reframes PR ethics against this backdrop, discussed below.

This recent engagement with societal perspectives is an important shift for the field, as it begins to critique its own practice more deeply, rather than leave the brickbats to outsiders. As suggested earlier, what Edwards and Hodges (2011a) call the socio-cultural turn in PR seems to be gathering momentum, a trend with less enthusiasm for PR's role in society than Taylor or Bowen demonstrate. Two edited books illustrate this development: Edwards and Hodges' (2011b) *Public Relations, Society & Culture* and Ihlen *et al.*'s (2009) *Public Relations and Social Theory.* The former opens up new discussions on PR as an entity in society, as a producer and consumer of meaning, a field that may be examined through a range of sociological and postmodern lenses, together with its agency and scope for social transformation. These are very different topics from those addressed in traditional PR textbooks. For example, Edwards' (2011) chapter on Bourdieu and society explores PR as embedded deep in the fabric of society, 'not a free-floating, neutral occupation, isolated from its social context' (2011: 61). The latter book brings leading social theorists into view, allowing the reader to reconsider PR from a variety of perspectives, including those developed by Weber, Durkheim and Goffman, for example. Here is more evidence of the field looking outside its own borders for theoretical constructs that help explain its position in society, creating a much wider lens for examining practice than that offered by measuring tasks and organizational hierarchies to understand the field.

However, despite all this scholarship, the main debates about PR as a profession still reflect the mantra usage suggested by McKie and Munshi (2007) and evidenced in the Professional Bond quote, rendering technical or sociological definitions redundant. This is also the usage found throughout professional associations at local, national and global level (see the Global Alliance of Public Relations and Communication Management for examples). So, does it matter much if most textbooks and practitioner bodies use 'professional' in the vernacular sense? I think that there are three good reasons for challenging this non-reflexive use of the term:

a)   Engaging with wider literature on professionalism allows deeper questions to be asked about PR as a profession than are currently posed.
b)   Reflection on the role of PR in society represents a move away from the organization-centred analysis that has dominated the past half-century.
c)   Discussion of professionalism reveals the centrality of ethics in that claim, rendering it impossible to talk about professionalism without discussing ethics.

Given the limited engagement with professionalism studies, it is not surprising if the roots of PR ethics are also underexplored. The next section digs deeper into contemporary approaches to PR ethics, to consider the extent to which current debates in professional ethics are reflected.

Underlying philosophies to public relations ethics

In Chapter 2, I set out the four main approaches to PR scholarship as I see it, together with a brief description of their ethical stance; this section reverses that by re-viewing PR ethics from the perspective of ethical philosophy, building on the insights generated in Chapter 4, from traditional to virtue and discourse ethics, ending with comments on socio-cultural and finally hermeneutic ethics. The problem of persuasion for PR ethicists, discussed earlier, is raised here and explored at greater depth towards the end of the chapter.

Traditional approaches to public relations ethics

Most PR textbooks (e.g. Chia and Synnott, 2009; Johnston and Zawawi, 2009; Theaker, 2012) ground discussion of ethics in traditional approaches, offering readers a choice between ethics based either on the consequences of actions as the ground for ethics (Bentham/Mills' utilitarianism) or the duty of professionals to groups such as clients, patients or society generally (Kantian), or even more often, an ad-hoc combination of both. There are problems with both, as suggested in Chapter 4, such as the appearance of impartiality in calculating relative harms and goods issuing from actions (Lucas, 2005) and the inflexibility of Kantian ethics in managing conflicts of ethical duty. There is some scholarly engagement with Kantian approaches, notably from critical scholar Jacquie L'Etang (1992) and excellence supporter Shannon Bowen (2007), who, unsurprisingly, come to differing conclusions. While L'Etang suggests that codes of ethics do not stand up to Kantian principles, Bowen declares that excellence ethics conform closely to Kant's imperatives, finding that 'ethics is a single excellent factor and the common underpinning of all factors that predict excellent public relations' (2007: 275). A Kantian perspective may help explain the aversion to persuasion from the excellence approach, as this can be seen as using others as a means to an end, rather than treating humans as ends in themselves. However, minimizing the extent of persuasion in PR practice does not make PR more ethical, just the descriptions of it more partial. As L'Etang (2011b: 226) has recently commented, PR (and marketing) makes unethical and dualistic use of the rhetoric of exchange, dialogue and understanding, while operating to maximize organizational gains and 'manage' relationships:

> While there is probably little that that can be done about the self-serving motivation that on a Kantian account renders to activities morally worthless, greater transparency with recipients and media might make the exchange more honest.

The excellence perspective on ethics also draws on the systems theory (McElreath, 1996), which underpins this approach, proposing the Potter Box matrix of competing values and saliences as a decision-making tool by working backwards from a situation to identify the core conflicts of interest, relevant principles and so on. This is pragmatic but still located strongly in a traditional combination of duty and consequence. Tilley (2005: 313–15) re-phrases this to suggest a three-tier or pyramid approach to ethical dilemmas:

- *Ethical intent* (input) concerns the planning stages and draws on virtue ethics in its intention to do good
- *Ethical means* in the enactment/outputs of the communication take place within a deontological frame (as legal, obeying codes etc) and
- *Ethical outcomes* can be viewed in their consequences.

This is appealingly neat but skates over philosophical conflicts in these approaches. As Taylor (2010) suggests, the questions raised by functionalist approaches such as excellence concern effective communication to key stakeholders to meet organizational goals more than issues about how society is constructed and PR's role in generating social norms. This and the reliance on codes have stunted the ethical development of the field (Pfau and Wan, 2006).

Virtue ethics

The resurgence of interest in virtue ethics (MacIntyre, 1984) has permeated the rhetorical school of PR, also US-centered (it is rarely taught in the UK or Europe, according to Tench and Fawkes, 2005), hardly surprising as both derive from Aristotelian concepts. For example, Harrison and Galloway's (2005: 14) analysis of PR practitioner roles found that '[v]irtue ethics can explain, in a way that codes-based approaches do not, how "good" people can be led into acting badly because they care for the wrong person or organisation'. As Ihlen (2011: 457) explains, 'Advocates of using rhetoric in public relations have vigorously defended rhetorical practices, including advocacy and persuasion, against the charge of being unethical. It is pointed out that these are not necessarily manipulative per se.' Instead, rhetorical ethical approaches often invoke virtues such as integrity, transparency and honesty as hallmarks of ethical communication (Edgett, 2002; Kent and Taylor, 2002; Pfau and Wan, 2006; Porter, 2010). These indicate the particular virtues to be embraced by ethical practitioners, addressing the personality of the communicator and asking them to reflect on their own motives and behaviours. The communication itself is the object of analysis, and whether the message is for health or arms promotion, the act of persuasion is seen as having at least the potential to be ethical. The concept of the social 'good' is also located in Aristotelian approaches, interpreted in PR as relationship or communication. Bowen (2010) positions communication as the good of PR but does not link it to virtue ethics, instead building an outline of the ideal practitioner who abhors 'dishonesty, vociferous advocacy, spin or manipulation' (2010: 571). The contrasting virtues and vices proposed by Baker (2008) are more clearly located in virtue ethics, with the emphasis on the connection between the two axes. Some discussion of PR ethics from a virtue perspective does seem to reduce to a hierarchy of virtues, as discussed in the previous chapter, with the selection of each particular preferred virtue itself ideological and underexplored. The detailed description of PR's virtues (e.g. Bowen, 2010) can feel relentlessly 'improving' and omits a range of issues and problems. However, the engagement with persuasion by other writers in this school offers a more nuanced assessment of PR than is found in the idealized versions outlined earlier.

Many PR scholars (e.g., Haas, 2001; Day *et al.*, 2001; Pearson, 1989) have engaged with Habermas and discourse ethics, often to support the symmetrical position, given Habermas's rejection of persuasion as inherently unethical (1989). As a result, discourse ethical approaches are associated with excellence rather than relationship management, which might appear a natural 'home'. In other words the emphasis has been on equal access to ethical debate and decision-making, rather than dialogue. Curtin and Boynton (2001) explore how Habermas's discourse ethics has been applied to PR (Leeper, 1996; Pearson, 1989), particularly attempts to construct procedures that will allow everyone taking part to communicate equally. However, as they point out, this rules out advocacy and requires rational application of procedural rules that are more likely to be observed in theory than practice.

All of the approaches discussed so far have their origins in western philosophy and treat ethics as normative and positivist, often with an emphasis on rationality, rules and procedures, especially in their application to professional ethics.

New approaches to public relations ethics

As suggested in the last chapter, in recent decades this position has been challenged by feminist ethics (Benhabib, 1992; Gilligan, 1982), postcolonial (Appiah, 2005) and postmodern perspectives (Bauman, 1993), among others. Moreover, the western domination of ethical thought has been challenged by the introduction of Asian ethical approaches to professional ethics (Koehn, 2001). Some of these ideas have recently made an impact on PR ethics (Curtin and Gaither, 2007; Holtzhausen, 2012), but generally these new(er) directions are rarely reflected in PR textbooks or chapters on ethics. For example, I was surprised at how little was written about hermeneutic approaches to ethics in PR literature, given that both emphasize the creation of shared meaning, as the following quote illustrates:

> The hermeneutic circle may be understood as a model of communication, as it evolves not just in the here and now, but down through history and across cultures. In hermeneutic (and phenomenological) terminology, communication involves a 'fusion of horizons' – a meeting and merging of the expectations that communicators bring with them into the exchange.
>
> (Jensen, 2002: 22)

Hermeneutic philosophy offers a bridge between some of the newer ideas in PR scholarship and the Jungian approach I am proposing. Some academics have made connections between PR and hermeneutics; in particular, Mickey (2003: 118), who argues that 'Hermeneutics offers much as a theoretical source for understanding public relations and placing public relations in a less mechanist or positivist approach'. As explored in Chapter 4, weak hermeneutics can lead to cynicism, but strong hermeneutics looks for commonality and asks the communicator to contemplate their own meaning in depth. The weak hermeneutic perspective offers a profound critique of normative functionalist and instrumental approaches largely found in mainstream PR ethics debates, where ethics is seen in terms of upholding codes, serving society and advancing the profession. A Nietzschean dismissal of these parochial, self-serving and deluded positions is almost irresistible, but strong hermeneutics urges us towards conversation, suggesting hermeneutics as a metatheory that would provide a large enough space for new interpretation of ethical assumptions and greater reflexivity. Warnke (2002) is clear that the claim to understand another does not constitute an ethic; we must presume that the other has something to teach us.

More work has been done recently in postmodern and socio-cultural considerations of PR ethics. For example, Holtzhausen (2012) develops a postmodern approach to PR ethics, in which the central myth of codes is exposed as ideological: 'there can never be a justification for moral codes or sets of ethical rules because they are all socially constructed and therefore serve some hidden purpose in society' (2012: 33). Her postmodern approach usefully rejects 'metanarratives' such as ethical guardian or advocate, embracing instead the contradictions and complexity of contemporary practice. As Holtzhausen says, drawing on Bauman (1993): 'The postmodern rejection of universal ethics thus focuses on the moral responsibility of the individual to the *Other* without an institutionally created ethical framework' (1993: 33). This also echoes Gilligan's (1982) development of a feminist approach to virtue ethics based on the duty of care rather than justice and Buber's (1957) influential I–thou concept. Ethics is thus de-coupled from rules and codes and re-located in the interior of the individual, becoming an aspect of their *identity*.

Traditional debates about PR's identity tend to fix on descriptions of role (e.g. the technician/manager divide), or the relationship with other, proximate, occupational groups, such as marketing (Hutton, 1999, 2001, 2010). Others, such as Neff (2010), focus on how PR is taught and organized, or focus on its role as the generator of organizational identity. These approaches tend towards fixed descriptors, concerning position in the organizational hierarchy, jurisdictional supremacy or communications functions. An exception is found in the 'circuit of culture' (Curtin and Gaither, 2005, 2007), which borrows concepts from cultural and sociological study (du Gay *et al.*, 1997), and describes identity as 'meanings given to a particular object or group through the process of production and consumption' (Curtin and Gaither, 2005: 101). Identity is imagined at the individual, organizational and national levels, and comprises one in a circuit of 'moments' (made up of representation, identity, production, consumption and regulation), offering an approach closer to that found in identity debates in other professions. For example, as suggested in Chapter 3, a review of literature on teachers' professional identity (Beijaard *et al.*, 2004: 108) concludes that: 'Identity development occurs in an intersubjective field and can be best characterised as an ongoing process, a process of interpreting oneself as a certain kind of person and being recognised as such in a given context'. Importantly, Curtin and Gaither (2007: 250–2) establish ethics as an aspect of identity, not a set of actions in certain circumstances: 'identity ethics embraces diversity and pluralism ... the need to embrace conflict, debate and critical inquiry, both for the insights they provide and for the process they facilitate of allowing all to be heard'. They also urge a move away from focus on codes to examine 'what meanings codes have as cultural artifacts ... for example, ethics codes may play quite different roles in different cultures ... [and] ... in constructing the identities of public relations practitioners and the profession' (2005: 104). They reject the focus on the 'public relations practitioner as sole ethical decision-maker in the organization ... [as] typical of the modernist perspective of the powerful individual who can control and direct his environment' (2007: 33).

The role of codes in PR ethics is explored in the next section, which considers the professional body, the generator of both professional identity and the codes that encapsulate that identity. Such institutions represent the relationship between a profession and society, even if they do not have control over all practitioners, and as such must negotiate the tensions between the claims to serve society as a whole, the promotional aspects of the idealized self-image and the collective views of practitioner members. The code of ethics is their primary instrument for establishing a collective statement on the value of ethics to a profession.

Professional bodies and public relations codes of ethics

At the start of this section, it is worth noting that many countries do not have professional bodies for PR practitioners (Sriramesh and Vercic, 2009). A European Delphi Research project in the 1990s found only two thriving associations, in Sweden and the UK, and neither represented the majority of practitioners in their country (van Ruler, 2005). More recently, the Global Alliance has 39 professional associations from across the world under its umbrella, representing 50 countries and 160,000 communication professionals (Global Alliance, 2012). While this is substantial growth in a decade, such bodies cannot claim to represent all practitioners in the field. Partially as a result, but also in common with professional bodies across sectors, as shown in the last chapter, the current state of ethics in PR practice depends heavily on codes of ethics held by the major professional associations. Each association has a code of ethics that provides guidelines for professional conduct and which also demonstrates what should be expected from practitioners. Some codes of ethics are written in terms that forbid a list of certain activities, following the trait approach; others promote ethical principles that need to be followed in the deontological tradition.

> Adherence to a code is a way of ensuring that practitioners meet a minimum standard of practice. They are a valuable safeguard to the community and to clients utilising the services of professional association members. Codes should be supported by education programs for association members which provide examples of good and bad practice, so as to better inform members' ethical practices.
>
> (McCoy, 2009: 123)

As suggested above, such codes are not neutral, value-free statements but ideological tools for generating norms and professional cultures. In the case of PR, it seems that most codes are heavily influenced by the PRSA, which in turn is heavily influenced by the excellence approach, with profound consequences for the field.

> PRSA has adopted 'codes of ethics' which ... seem based on the two-way symmetrical model which focuses on scientific research, two-way communication and 'non-persuasion'. ... Adherence to the codes requires a practitioner to engage in conduct that violates obligations to clients. In short the codes are neither professional nor ethical and until fundamental changes are made those who seek the status of a profession for public relations are doomed to failure.
>
> (Parkinson, 2001: 28)

Parkinson argues that this in turn has influenced models exported around the world: the Global Alliance approach to ethics is broadly similar in tone and content, for example (Breit and Demetrious, 2010). This is obviously testament to its salience, but as Parkinson (2001) points out, it places reputation above professional responsibility. Codes have been studied in the United States (Ki and

Kim, 2010; Parkinson, 2001), Australia and New Zealand (Breit and Demetrious 2010; Harrison and Galloway, 2005), and in a global context (Sriramesh and Vercic, 2009), and similar themes emerge. While Ki and Kim's (2010) claim that codes and value statements can be correlated with higher standards, Pater and Gils (2003) conclude that this is not the case, except where there is supportive training in ethical issues. Interestingly, Ki and Kim (2010) found that practitioners identified professional ethics with key words such as 'expertise, strategic, dedication, hard work, accountability, independence' (2010: 231), which are closer to the vernacular meaning of professionalism as good practice outlined in Chapter 3. This echoes the linkage between professionalism and ethics explored there but does not constitute proof of either. A brief scan of three Anglo-American codes (Global Alliance, the UK's Chartered Institute for Public Relations (CIPR) and the Public Relations Institute of Australia (PRIA)) reveals a number of commonalities, illustrating Parkinson's (2001) point about the global export of one perspective. First, Breit and Demetrious (2010: 27) analyse the Global Alliance website for ethical statements and find that, like so many other codes, the main narrative is promotional:

> Another feature of [Global Alliance] Background statement is its intent to create a dichotomy between legitimate and illegitimate public relations practitioners: 'Many non-professionals say they are in PR but their actions are damaging our reputation as a profession. We need to show our professionalism by means of Global Standards enacted by national associations' (Global Alliance/History 7/28/2009). The significant aspect of this descriptive material is the intense desire of GA to 'show professionalism' in the area. The problems that beset public relations in its struggle to maintain professional status are not new.

However, they do not appear to have consulted other documents on the website, such as the Global Alliance Guiding Principles for the Ethical Practice of Public Relations, which start with the preamble:

> A code of ethics and professional conduct is an individual matter that should be viewed as a guide to make sound values-based decisions. Ethical performance, not principles, is ultimately what counts. No one can dictate precise outcomes for every situation. However, we can apply common values and decision-making processes to arrive at a decision and justify it to others. In making decisions, we should be guided by a higher sense of serving the public as a whole as opposed to specific constituencies on an exclusive basis. Consideration should be given to the protection of privacy of individuals and respect for the spirit as well as the letter of applicable laws.
>
> (Global Alliance, n.d.: 6)

There are three points worth stressing here: a) the emphasis on ethics as a personal matter; (b) the preference for performance over principles (which appears to disregard the idea that performance is usually informed by principle, however unexamined); and c) the exhortation to serve the public over other interests, reinforcing the confusion identified in Parkinson's critique. Similar issues arise in the UK CIPR code, by which members agree to:

> a) maintain the highest standards of professional endeavour, integrity, confidentiality, financial propriety and personal conduct; b) deal honestly and fairly in business with employers, employees, clients, fellow professionals, other professions and the public; c) respect, in their dealings with other people, the legal and regulatory frameworks and codes of all countries where they practise; d) uphold the reputation of, and do nothing that would bring into disrepute, the public relations profession or the Chartered Institute of Public Relations; e) respect and abide by this Code and related Notes of Guidance issued by the Chartered Institute of Public Relations and ensure that others who are accountable to them (e.g. subordinates and sub-contractors) do the same; f) encourage professional training and development among members of the profession in order to raise and maintain professional standards generally.
>
> (CIPR, 2013)

These are almost identical to Friedson's (2001) typology cited above and can be summarized as: be good, be professional and protect the organization. L'Etang (2011b: 230) notes that 'a great deal is left to individual discretion without any guidance ... "transparency and conflicts of interest" appear as a bullet-pointed issue, but there is no guidance about the application of these concepts to practice'. The detailed explication of the code follows the trait approach describing relationships between clients, issues of confidentiality and similar matters, harking back to the early twentieth century, an approach critiqued by Harrison and Galloway (2005). Interestingly, there are clauses about not concealing the identity of clients, which, if observed, would put an end to the 'front organizations' or 'astroturfing' so regularly exposed by websites in the USA and UK.

The PRIA is broadly similar, though more of the clauses relate to business practices regarding fees, misrepresentation and other aspects covered by the trait approach. As Harrison and Galloway (2005) suggest, this implies that practices which are not specified are acceptable, and that codes function as explicit instructions, leading to infantilized responses. Moreover, there is no sanction against those who transgress these edicts: fewer than three or four complaints a year were received by the PRSA, PRIA and Public Relations Institute of South Africa, with slightly more at the CIPR, most of which related to contractual issues between practitioners rather than societal responsibilities (Global Alliance, 2003). Again, this is not uncommon in emerging professions, as Chapter 3 showed, reaffirming the sense that Anglo-American PR codes of ethics are promotional tools, built for reputation not to enhance the field's relationship with society. All the above codes suggest that emphasis on best practice constitutes ethics. They also imply that ethical decisions can be made on the basis of rational evaluation of one's own and others' virtue in a given situation, the most common cited being honesty, fairness and integrity. As suggested earlier there are limits to the virtue ethics approach that are not reflected in these codes; why those virtues and not others, such as Gilligan's (1982) emphasis on care? And why are these virtues presented as unproblematic in phrases such as the Arthur Page Society's 'Tell the Truth' (2009) or the Global Alliance's 'Adhere to the highest standards of accuracy and truth in advancing the interests of clients and employers' (Global Alliance, 2003). The only one which hints that these might be conflicted issues and turns inward comes from the International Association of Business Communicators (IABC), which suggests: 'Be honest not only with others but also and most importantly with yourselves as individuals' (Bowen *et al.*, 2006). The missing element from these edicts then is that of experience, the inner dimension of ethical practice. Curtin and Gaither (2007: 251) stress the 'traitorous identity' necessary to enact ethics in inimical circumstances; offending employers or clients may be required, and as whistle-blowers attest, the price can be high. Recent empirical work (Kang, 2010) explores the experiential aspects of ethical conflicts in PR, through a survey of PRSA members. Over 65 per cent of respondents reported experiencing ethical dissonance, including being forced to be silent and being unable to challenge unethical decisions from above. Some left their organizations; others suffered a range of stress symptoms. It seems the codes were of little use as 'keeping silent is regarded as proper by some public relations practitioners, while others think that it is definitely unethical' (Kang, 2010: 154). One of the prime exacerbating factors was the inability to discuss ethical issues openly with management. Such experiences call for a new approach to PR ethics, moving from external codes to internal guidance.

The ethical 'problem' of persuasion

Throughout this chapter, I've referred to the relationship between PR ethics and persuasion, highlighting the distance between excellence ethics and persuasion, and the approaches embraced by rhetorical scholars and, less theoretically, practitioners. My core argument is that excellent approaches minimize persuasion in order to over-state the idealized versions of the field, and that this impoverishes professional ethics by disregarding the reality of practice. Over the next two chapters I set out one route to generating a meta-narrative of PR that would form the basis for a re-conceptualized ethics, a theme explored in Chapter 9. From this perspective, persuasion becomes the site of a struggle to define PR, the heart of what Cheney and Christianson (2001) call 'contested terrain'. The professional project of PR seems to stumble at persuasion, as it is hard to promote PR as a social good if its main activity, persuasion, is perceived as contaminated by notions of propaganda (Fawkes, 2006). 'As propaganda has become increasingly discredited as an unethical tool for the manipulation of public opinion, new models of supposedly ethical persuasion have been developed ... To notionally distance public relations from propaganda' (Weaver *et al.*, 2006: 13). Fields of persuasion, propaganda, and PR have all been extensively researched and studied – but usually without reference to each other or to the issue of persuasive ethics.

The bulk of persuasion studies (Bettinghaus and Cody, 1994; O'Keefe, 2002; Perloff, 2003; Simons *et al.*, 2001) come from social psychology schools in the USA, which have been concerned with the *process* of persuasion since the 1950s. These say surprising little about the ethics of persuasion and rarely refer to PR, though advertising and public information campaigns often provide useful case studies. Propaganda scholars (such as Pratkanis, 2002) locate propaganda in the shift of persuasive communication from rational argument to emotional triggers. Other scholars of persuasion and propaganda (Jaksa and Pritchard, 1994; Taylor, 2003) propose that propaganda is inherently neutral but, again, there is no discussion of PR. On the other hand the most virulent critics of PR, such as Stauber and Rampton (2004) or Miller and Dinan (2008) (and see also PRWatch.org; Spinwatch.com) assert that it is synonymous with propaganda, citing the frequent creation of 'front organisations', the early writing of Edward Bernays, the role of PR in wartime propaganda and techniques used by corporate interests in peacetime. Core PR texts (Grunig and Hunt, 1984; Seitel, 2004; Wilcox *et al.*, 2003) provide a kind of mirror image to these critical voices: issues of propaganda, past and present, are largely absent from the debate and persuasion is often marginalized in order to emphasize the contribution of PR to the democratic exchange of ideas (Moloney, 2000). Just one illustration of the denial of PR's history is Cutlip *et al.*'s (2000: 159) description of propaganda as 'that dirty word ... Americans have long been deeply suspicious of anything with that label and particularly so since this power device has been used in other countries to gain and hold despotic control'. However,

> the critical theory perspective ... finds no substantive difference between propaganda and public relations ... this is a consequence of a rejection of the notions that propaganda necessarily operates counter to the public interest, and that public relations necessarily works for the public interest.
>
> (Weaver *et al.*, 2006: 21)

Persuasion is thus contaminated by association with propaganda. Despite G. Miller's (1989) famous argument that the similarities between PR and persuasion are 'overwhelming', persuasion is still viewed with distaste, and persuasion is not explored in depth within systems theory approaches. This position is bolstered by Habermas's (1989) concept of the public sphere, which views persuasion as unethical due to the inequalities of interests between persuader and persuadee. However, given the dominance of persuasive messages in the public sphere, Moloney (2000) suggests that the term should be revised to the 'persuasive sphere'. I support this view and that of communicators who seek neither to sanctify nor demonize persuasion: PR is used both to sell arms and raise funds for the victims of war. Persuasion is endemic in our culture and without understanding its role in society and in practice, we cannot collectively evolve a grounded ethic.

Pfau and Wan (2006) suggest that PR has problems with the concept of persuasion because it confuses means and ends: the Grunigian approach mentioned earlier concentrates on means or *processes* – whether they are symmetrical or not

– and deems persuasion unethical because it is asymmetrical. But if we look at the ends or *outcomes* of communication then it is clear how prevalent persuasion is in PR activity.

> Public relations is best viewed as a form of strategic communication, in which persuasion plays an integral role ... Many of the core functions of public relations, such as community relations, media relations, crisis communication and others manifest an implicit if not explicit goal of cultivating or maintaining a positive organizational image.
>
> (Pfau and Wan, 2006: 102)

As outlined above, rhetorical approaches to PR address the role of persuasion in communication, virtue ethics and ideas of democratic debate. Because persuasion is acknowledged, ethical approaches can be proposed. For example, Baker and Martinson (2002) propose five principles for ethical advocacy, called the TARES test, covering 1) Truthfulness 2) Authenticity 3) Respect 4) and 5) Social Responsibility, and Edgett (2002) expands this to ten. These indicate the particular virtues to be embraced by ethical practitioners, addressing the personality of the communicator and asking them to reflect on their own motives and behaviours. Recently, rhetorical scholar Lance Porter (2010) revisited the issue of persuasion in PR, arguing that the dominance of the Grunig models and their distaste for persu–asion has 'vilified' one of the key aspects of modern PR strategy: 'the ultimate outcome of public relations efforts will always remain influencing attitudes and ultimately, behavior. Public relations professionals are paid to advocate ideas and to influence behaviour' (2010: 132).

Another relevant approach to persuasion is offered by the circuit of culture, which restores a wider range of PR practice to legitimacy: 'The dominant normative paradigm has removed propaganda and persuasion from the ranks of legitimate public relations practices, but the circuit demonstrates the need to recognize them as part of the repertoire of legitimate practices' (Curtin and Gaither, 2005: 109).

The conflict between the academic ideal of the ethical guardian and the practitioner identity as an advocate was set out in Chapter 2. The circuit of culture approach suggests that these divergent identities will be processed as divergent ethics, as was suggested earlier. This separation is also explored by Baker (2008), who characterizes this split as between 'principled advocates and pathological partisans', with the former embodying desired virtues and the latter vices. Interestingly, in the light of later Jungian discussion, she calls these 'archetypes' (2008: 235). So the polarity between images and the impact of this division on the field's ethics is not new. However, reframing that argument in the light of intervening chapters highlights the gulf between the self-conceptualization of practitioners as advocates, and the image embedded in US and, by extension, many other national and global codes, of the practitioner as engaged in symmetrical dialogue and social harmony. Moreover, insistence on the 'ethical guardian' role promoted by the excellence project may actually have set ethical debate back, by silencing practitioners who see themselves as advocates not social guardians. The absence of ethical training is raised by scholars and practitioners, but is still framed by discussion of traditional approaches (deontological and consequentialist) rather than engagement with more recent ethical theory (including virtue ethics, feminist, postcolonial and postmodern approaches). At the same time, the reports of practitioner views suggest a rejection of the idealized role of guardian, preferring a very simplistic model of advocate, based in capitalist marketplace approach in which 'the bottom line' trumps all, where ethics is about managing reputation not moral responsibility. It is my view that both sides need to recognize the validity of the opposing argument, abandoning both saintly aspirations and cynical self-justifications.

And this is where Carl Jung comes in, as the next chapters reveal.

Conclusions

This chapter has re-examined PR in the context of professionalism and professional ethics, which were fully explored in previous chapters. This has revealed a vernacular rather than sociologically robust usage of profession as a descriptor, as most scholars agree that PR doesn't meet established criteria. However, looser terms such as community of practice emphasize the field as a collection of practitioners and commentators, which, socio-cultural approaches make clear, has agency in the construction and co-construction of meaning in society. As the focus on PR in society deepens, its role as a profession and its claims to serve society will face increasing scrutiny.

The chapter also found that, just as recent debates in professionalism are barely visible in PR, so current developments in professional ethics have yet to make a wider impact. Revisiting PR ethics revealed a reliance on traditional approaches, with limited engagement in new thinking on these issues. One old idea, hermeneutic ethics, was brought into the discussion to open a new, creative space for ethical dialogue, exchange and connection, a reflexivity that requires self-awareness. In this perspective, ethics is seen more as a process than a series of behaviours, a way of describing relationships with others and with oneself. Most approaches to PR ethics imply a rational evaluation of ethical choices, though newer approaches such as those found in cultural and postmodern ethics reflect a more fluid, nuanced concept of ethical agents. It is these newer ideas that resonate with a Jungian approach, rejecting social convention as a moral arbiter but still seeking some kind of universal meaning. A Jungian ethic argues that dualistic right/wrong, good/bad binaries must be abandoned if ethical self-appraisal is to be honest. Dialectic gives way to dialogic – including internal dialogue with different aspects of the self, recognizing mixed motives and self-delusion in ethical decision-making. Rules will not suffice; one must look inwards not outwards for ethical guidance, suggesting a depth approach for opening deeper dialogue within individuals and, more importantly, the profession as a whole. The next two chapters explore these possibilities, before returning to PR in Chapter 9 to consider the effect such a contribution might make.

References

Abbott, A. (1988) *The System of Professions: an essay on the division of expert labor.* Chicago, IL: University of Chicago Press.

Abbott, A. (1995) Things of boundaries. *Social Research, 62*(4): 857–82.

Abbott, A. (2010) Varieties of ignorance. *American Sociologist, 41:* 174–89.

Appiah, K. (2005) *The Ethics of Identity.* Princeton, NJ and Woodstock: Princeton University Press.

Arthur W. Page Society (2009) *The dynamics of public trust in business – emerging opportunities for leaders.* Arthur W. Page Society.

Baker, S. (2008) The model of the principled advocate and the pathological partisan: a virtue ethics construct of opposing archetypes of public relations and advertising practitioners. *Journal of Mass Media Ethics, 23*(3): 235–53.

Baker, S. and Martinson, D. L. (2002) Out of the red-light district: five principles for ethically proactive public relations. *Public Relations Quarterly, 47*(3): 15–19.

Bartlett, J., Tywoniak, S. and Hatcher, C. (2007) Public relations professional practice and the insitutionalisation of CSR. *Journal of Communication Management, 11*(4): 281–99.

Bauman, Z. (1993) *Postmodern Ethics.* Oxford: Blackwell.

Beijaard, D., Meijer, P. and Verloop, P. (2004) Reconsidering research on teachers' professional identity. *Teaching and Teacher Education, 20:* 107–28.

Benhabib, S. (1992) *Situating the Self: gender, community, and postmodernism in contemporary ethics.* New York, NY: Routledge.

Bettinghaus, E. and Cody, M. J. (1994) *Persuasive Communication.* Fort Worth, TX: Harcourt Brace Jovanovich.

Bivins, T. H. (1993) Public relations, professionalism and the public interest. *Journal of Business Ethics, 12*(2): 117–26.

Bowen, S. A. (2007) The extent of ethics. In E. L. Toth (ed.) *The Future of Excellence in Public Relations and Communication Management.* Mahweh, NJ: Lawrence Erlbaum Associates, pp. 275–97.

Bowen, S. A. (2010) The nature of good in public relations: what should be its normative ethic? In R. L. Heath (ed.) *The SAGE Handbook of Public Relations.* Thousand Oaks, CA: Sage, pp. 569–83.

Bowen, S. A., Heath, R. L., Lee, J., Painter, G., Agraz, F. J., McKie, D. and Toledano, M. (2006) *The Business of Truth: a guide to ethical communication.* San Francisco: International Association of Business Communicators.

Breit, R. and Demetrious, K. (2010) Professionalisation and public relations: an ethical mismatch. *Ethical Space, 7*(4): 20–9.

Buber, M. (1957) *I and Thou.* R. G. Smith, (trans.) New York, NY: Scribner.

Bush, M. (2010) How social media is helping public relations sector not just survive but thrive. *Advertising Age.* Online. Available at http://adage.com/article?article_id=145507

Cheney, G. and Christianson, L. T. (2001) Public relations as contested terrain: a critical response. In R. L. Heath (ed.) *Handbook of Public Relations.* Thousand Oaks, CA: Sage, pp. 167–82.

Chia, J. and Synnott, G. (2009) *An Introduction to Public Relations.* Oxford: Oxford University Press.

CIPR. (2013) Code of Conduct. Online. Available at www.cipr.co.uk/sites/default/files/Code%20of%20Conduct%20-%20agreed%20changes%20November%202013.pdf, retrieved 12 December, 2013.

Curtin, P. A. and Boynton, L. A. (2001) Ethics in public relations: theory and practice. In R.L. Heath (ed.) *Handbook of Public Relations.* Thousand Oaks, CA: Sage, pp. 411–22.

Curtin, P. A. and Gaither, T. K. (2005) Privileging identity, difference and power: the circuit of culture as a basis for public relations theory. *Journal of Public Relations Research, 17*(2): 91–115.

Curtin, P. A. and Gaither, T. K. (2007) *International Public Relations: negotiating culture, identity and power*. Thousand Oaks, CA: Sage.

Cutlip, S. M., Center, A. H. and Broom, G. M. (eds) (2000) *Effective Public Relations* (8th edn) London: Prentice-Hall International.

Day, K. D., Dong, Q. and Robins, C. (2001) Public relations ethics: an overview and discussion of issues for the 21st century. In R. L. Heath (ed.) *Handbook of Public Relations*. Thousand Oaks, CA: Sage, pp. 403–10.

du Gay, P., Hall, S., Janes, L., Mackay, H. and Negus, K. (1997) *Doing Cultural Studies: the story of the Sony Walkman*. London: Sage.

Durkheim, E. (1933) *The Division of Labour in Society*. Glencoe, IL: Free Press.

Edgett, R. (2002) Toward an ethical framework for advocacy. *Journal of Public Relations Research, 14*(1): 1–26.

Edwards, L. (2011) Public relations and society: a Bourdieuvian perspective. In L. Edwards and C. E. M. Hodges (eds) *Public Relations, Society & Culture: theoretical and empirical explorations*. London: Routledge.

Edwards, L. and Hodges, C. E. M. (2011a) Introduction. In L. Edwards and C. E. M. Hodges (eds) *Public Relations, Society & Culture: theoretical and empirical explorations*. London: Routledge, pp. 1–14.

Edwards, L. and Hodges, C. E. M. (eds) (2011b) *Public Relations, Society & Culture: theoretical and empirical explorations* (1st edn) London: Routledge.

Fawkes, J. (2006) Can ethics save public relations from the charge of propaganda? *Ethical Space, 3*(1): 38–42.

Fawkes, J. and Tench, R. (2004) Does employer resistance to theory threaten the future of public relations? A consideration of research findings, comparing UK practitioner, academic and alumni attitudes to public relations education. Paper presented at the 11th International Public Relations Research Symposium, Bled, Slovenia.

Freidson, E. (2001) *Professionalism: the third logic*. Cambridge: Polity.

Gilligan, C. (1982) *In a Different Voice: psychological theory and women's development*. Cambridge, MA and London: Harvard University Press.

Global Alliance. (2003) Global protocol on ethics in public relations. Online. Available at www.globalalliancepr.org/website/sites/default/files/globalalliance/GA_Global_Ethics_Protocol.pdf, retrieved 12 December, 2013.

Global Alliance. (2012) Online. Available at http://melbournemandate.globalalliance pr.org/wp-content/uploads/2012/11/Melbourne-Mandate-Text-final.pdf, retrieved 18 November, 2013.

Global Alliance. (n.d.) Code of Ethics. Online. Available at www.globalalliancepr.org/website/sites/default/files/nolie/Governance/GA%20Code%20of%20Ethics.pdf

Gregory, A. (2009) Ethics and professionalism in public relations. In R. Tench and L. Yeomans (eds) *Exploring Public Relations* (2nd edn) Harlow, Essex: Pearson Education, pp. 273–89.

Gregory, A. (2012) Reviewing public relations research and scholarship in the 21st century. *Public Relations Review, 38*(1): 1–4. doi: http://dx.doi.org/10.1016/j.pubrev.2011.10.003

Grunig, J. E. (2001) Two-way symmetrical public relations: past, present and future. In R.L. Heath (ed.) *Handbook of Public Relations*. Thousands Oaks, CA: Sage, pp. 11–30.

Grunig, J. E. and Hunt, T. (1984) *Managing Public Relations*. New York, NY and London: Holt, Rinehart and Winston.

Haas, T. (2001) Public relations between universality and particularity: towards a moral-philosophical conception of public relations ethics. In R. L. Heath (ed.) *Handbook of Public Relations*. Thousand Oaks, CA: Sage, pp. 423–33.

Habermas, J. (1989) *The Structural Transformation of the Public Sphere: an inquiry into a category of bourgeois society*. Cambridge, MA: MIT Press.

Harrison, K. and Galloway, C. (2005) Public relations ethics: a simpler (but not simplistic) approach to the complexities. *Prism, 3*. Online. Available at www.praxis.massey.ac.nz, retrieved 14 March, 2007.

Heath, R. L. (2001) A rhetorical enactment rationale for public relations: the good organisation communicating well. In R. L. Heath (ed.) *Handbook of Public Relations*. Thousand Oaks, CA: Sage, pp. 31–50.

Heath, R. L. (2006) Onward into more fog: thoughts on public relations' research directions. *Journal of Public Relations Research, 18*(2): 93–114.

Heath, R. L. (2010) Mind, self and society. In R. L. Heath (ed.) *The SAGE Handbook of Public Relations*. Thousand Oaks, CA: Sage, pp. 1–4.

Holtzhausen, D. (2012) *Public Relations as Activism: postmodern approaches to theory and practice*. New York, NY: Routledge.

Hutton, J. G. (1999) The definition, dimensions and domain of public relations. *Public Relations Review, 25*(2): 199–214.

Hutton, J. G. (2001) Defining the relationship between public relations and marketing. In R. L. Heath (ed.) *Handbook of Public Relations*. Thousand Oaks, CA: Sage, pp. 205–14.

Hutton, J. G. (2010) Defining the relationship between public relations and marketing: public relations' most important challenge. In R. L. Heath (ed.) *The SAGE Handbook of Public Relations*. Thousand Oaks, CA: Sage, pp. 509–22.

Ihlen, Ø. (2011) On barnyard scrambles: toward a rhetoric of public relations. *Management Communication Quarterly, 25*(3): 455–73.

Ihlen, Ø., van Ruler, B. and Fredriksson, M. (2009) *Public Relations and Social Theory: key figures and concepts*. New York, NY and London: Routledge.

Jaksa, J. A. and Pritchard, M. S. (1994) *Communication Ethics: methods of analysis*. Belmont, CA: Wadsworth Pub.

Jensen, K. B. (2002) *A Handbook of Media and Communications Research: qualitative and quantitative methodologies*. London: Routledge.

Johnston, J. and Zawawi, C. (2009) *Public Relations: theory and practice*. Crows Nest, NSW, Australia: Allen & Unwin.

Kang, J. -A. (2010) Ethical conflict and job satisfaction of public relations practitioners. *Public Relations Review, 36*(2): 152–6.

Kent, M. L. and Taylor, M. (2002) Toward a dialogic theory of public relations. *Public Relations Review, 14*(28): 21–37.

Ki, E. -J. and Kim, S.-Y. (2010) Ethics statements of public relations firms: what do they say? *Journal of Business Ethics, 91:* 223–36.

Koehn, D. (2001) *Local Insights, Global Ethics for Business*. Amsterdam: Rodopi.

Larson, M. S. (1977) *The Rise of Professionalism: a sociological analysis*. Berkeley, CA and London: University of California Press.

L'Etang, J. (1992) A Kantian approach to codes of ethics. *Journal of Business Ethics, 11*(10): 737–44.

L'Etang, J. (2005) Critical public relations: some reflections. *Public Relations Review, 31*(4): 521–6.

L'Etang, J. (2008) *Public Relations: concepts, practice and critique*. Los Angeles: Sage.

L'Etang, J. (2011a) Imagining public relations anthrolopogy. In L. Edwards and C. E. M. Hodges (eds) *Public Relations, Society & Culture: theoretical and empirical explorations*. London: Routledge, pp. 15–32.

L'Etang, J. (2011b) Public relations and marketing: ethical isues and professional practice in society. In G. Cheney, S. May and D. Munshi (eds) *The Handbook of Communication Ethics*. New York, NY: Routledge, pp. 221–40.

Leeper, K. A. (1996) Public relations ethics and communitarianism, a preliminary investigation. *Public Relations Review, 22*(2): 163–79.

Lucas, P. (2005) Humanising professional ethics. In J. Strain and S. Robinson (eds) *The Teaching and Practice of Professional Ethics*. Leicester: Troubador, pp. 40–50.

McCoy, L. (2009) Ethical practice. In J. Johnston and C. Zawawi (eds) *Public Relations: theory and practice*. Crows Nest, NSW, Australia: Allen & Unwin, pp. 108–35.

McElreath, M. P. (1996) *Managing Systematic and Ethical Public Relations* (2nd edn) Madison, WI: Brown and Benchmark.

MacIntyre, A. (ed.) (1984) *After Virtue: a study in moral theory* (2nd edn) Notre Dame, IN: University of Notre Dame Press.

McKie, D. and Munshi, D. (2007) *Reconfiguring Public Relations: ecology, equity, and enterprise*. London: Routledge.

McKie, D. and Willis, P. (2012) Renegotiating the terms of engagement: public relations, marketing, and contemporary challenges. *Public Relations Review, 38*(5): 846–52. doi: http://dx.doi.org/10.1016/j.pubrev.2012.03.008

Macnamara, J. R. (2012) *Public Relations: theories, practices, critiques* (1st edn) Frenchs Forest, NSW: Pearson Australia.

Mickey, T. J. (2003) *Deconstructing Public Relations: public relations criticism*. Mahwah, NJ and London: Lawrence Erlbaum Associates.

Miller, D. and Dinan, W. (2008) *A Century of Spin: how public relations became the cutting edge of corporate power*. London: Pluto.

Miller, G. (1989) Persuasion and public relations: 2 'P's in a pod? In C. H. Botan and H. Vincent (eds) *Public Relations Theory*. Hillsdale, NJ: Lawrence Erlbaum Associates, pp. 45–81.

Moloney, K. (2000) *Rethinking Public Relations: the spin and the substance*. London: Routledge.

Moloney, K. (2006) *Rethinking Public Relations: PR, propaganda and democracy* (2nd edn) London: Routledge.

Murphy, P. (1996) Chaos theory as a model for managing issues and crises. *Public Relations Review, 22*(2): 95–113.

Murphy, P. (2000) Symmetry, contingency, complexity: accommodating uncertainty in public relations theory. *Public Relations Review, 26*(4): 447–62.

Murphy, P. and Gilpin, D. R. (2013) Complexity theory and the dynamics of reputation. In C. E. Carroll (ed.) *The Handbook of Communication and Corporate Reputation*. John Wiley & Sons, Chichester: West Sussex, pp. 166–82.

Neff, B. D. (2010) Public relations identity: evolving from academic and practitioner partnerships. In R. L. Heath (ed.) *The SAGE Handbook of Public Relations*. Thousand Oaks, CA: Sage, pp. 367–82.

O'Keefe, D. J. (2002) *Persuasion: Theory & Research*. Thousand Oaks, CA: Sage.

Parkinson, M. (2001) The PRSA Code of Professional Standards and Member Code of Ethics: why they are neither professional nor ethical. *Public Relations Quarterly, 46*(3): 27–31.

Parsons, T. (1951) *The Social System*. London: Routledge & Kegan Paul.

Pater, A. and van Gils, A. (2003) Stimulating ethical decision-making in a business context: effects of ethical and professional codes. *European Journal of Management, 21*(6): 762–72.

Pearson, R. (1989) Beyond ethical relativism in public relations: co orientation, rules and the ideal of communication symmetry. In J. E. Grunig and L. A. Grunig (eds) *Public Relations Research Annual, vol 1.* Hillside, NJ: Lawrence Erlbaum Associates, pp. 67–87.

Perloff, R. M. (2003) *The Dynamics of Persuasion Communication and Attitudes in the 21st Century.* Mahwah, NJ: Lawrence Erlbaum Associates.

Pfau, M. and Wan, H. (2006) Persuasion: an intrinsic function in public relations. In C. H. Botan and V. Hazleton (eds) *Public Relations Theory II.* Mahweh, NJ: Lawrence Erlbaum Associates, pp. 101–36.

Pieczka, M. and L'Etang, J. (2001) Public relations and the question of professionalism. In R. L. Heath (ed.) *Handbook of Public Relations.* Thousand Oaks, CA: Sage, pp. 223–35.

Porter, L. (2010) Communicating for the good of the state: a post-symmetrical polemic on persuasion in ethical public relations. *Public Relations Review, 36*(2): 127–33.

Pratkanis, A. R. A. E. (2002) *Age of Propaganda: the everyday use and abuse of persuasion.* New York, NY: W.H. Freeman.

PRSA (2006) *The Professional Bond: public relations education in the 21st century.* New York, NY: Public Relations Society of America.

Seitel, F. P. (ed.) (2004) *The Practice of Public Relations* (9th edn) Harlow: Pearson Education International.

Simons, H. W., Morreale, J. and Gronbeck, B. E. (2001) *Persuasion in Society.* Thousand Oaks, CA: Sage.

Sriramesh, K. and Hornaman, L. (2006) Public relations as a profession: an analysis of curricular content in the United States. *Journal of Creative Communications, 1*(2): 155–72.

Sriramesh, K. and Vercic, D. (eds) (2009) *The Global Public Relations Handbook: theory, research, and practice* (expanded and rev. edn) London: Routledge.

Stauber, J. C. and Rampton, S. (2004) *Toxic Sludge is Good for You: lies, damn lies and the public relations industry.* London: Robinson.

Taylor, M. (2010) Public relations in the enactment of civil society. In R. L. Heath (ed.) *The SAGE Handbook of Public Relations.* Thousand Oaks, CA: Sage, pp. 5–15.

Taylor, P. M. (2003) *Munitions of the Mind: a history of propaganda from the ancient world to the present era.* Manchester and New York, NY: Manchester University Press.

Tench, R. and Fawkes, J. (2005) Mind the gap: exploring different attitudes to public relations education from employers, academics and alumni. Paper presented at the Alan Rawel/CIPR, Lincoln, UK.

Theaker, A. (2012) *The Public Relations Handbook* (4th edn) Abingdon: Routledge.

Tilley, E. (2005) The ethics pyramid: making ethics unavoidable in the public relations process. *Mass Media Ethics, 20*(4): 305–20.

Valentini, C., Kruckeberg, D. and Starck, K. (2012) Public relations and community: a persistent covenant. *Public Relations Review, 38*(5): 873–79.

van Ruler, B. (2005) Professionals are from Venus, scholars are from Mars. *Public Relations Review, 31*(2): 159–73.

Warnke, G. (2002) Hermeneutics, ethics and politics. In R. J. Dostal (ed.) *The Cambridge Companion to Gadamer.* Cambridge: Cambridge University Press, pp. 79–101.

Weaver, C. K., Motion, J. and Roper, J. (2006) From propaganda to discourse (and back again): truth, power the public interest and public relations. In J. L'Etang and M. Pieczka (eds) *Public Relations, Critical Debates and Contemporary Practice*. Mahwah, NJ: Lawrence Erlbaum Associates, pp. 7–21.

Wilcox, D. L., Cameron, G. T., Ault, P. H. and Agee, W. K. (2003) *Public Relations, Strategies and Tactics* (7th edn) Boston, MA: Allyn and Bacon.

Zerfass, A., Vercic, D., Tench, R., Verhoeven, P. and Moreno, A. (2013) European communication monitor annual survey on future trends in communication management and public relations. Online. Available at www.communicationmonitor.eu/

6   Into the psyche

Introduction

For most of my adult life I had a vague awareness but no particular knowledge of Jung's work. I knew that he emphasized the spiritual over the religious (and was interested in spirituality as an antidote to addiction); that he embraced myth as a deep universal narrative (and influenced George Lucas' *Star Wars* films via his follower, Joseph Campbell). I could drop ideas like synchronicity, collective consciousness, persona and shadow into conversation, without ever having read a word of the original. From the late 1980s, I practised a form of meditation that used a Jungian approach to dream work to access material hidden from consciousness both in the individual and collectively, so I was familiar with the process of recognizing the meaning of things I didn't really understand, in my own and other's images, much as I responded to Yeats or Tarkovsky; a deep sense-making that resisted articulation. Over time I began to understand that one cannot permanently lock out the knife-wielding stranger who lurches into a dream or ignore the wounded creatures who ask for help; they are aspects of the self looking to make connections, and they'll be back. It's important to stress that none of this was an intellectual activity – while I read Freud as a teenager and spent several extremely fruitful years in neo-Freudian therapy, I had no real interest in researching Jungian concepts until I astonished myself one afternoon having coffee with the splendid public relations (PR) professor, David McKie, in a San Francisco conference centre: all PhDs are autobiographical, he said, what do you really want to do? A Jungian analysis of PR I replied, despite having just submitted a detailed proposal on persuasion ethics. And here we are. In the end, the thesis was a Jungian approach to professional ethics, with PR as an illustrative case study. This book has returned the focus to PR.

So I started reading Jung himself, with the contested autobiography, *Memories, Dreams, Reflections* (1963), before entering what turned out to be a vast scholarship of disagreement and interpretation – not helped by the fact that Jung's collected works run to over 20 volumes[1] and that he never consolidated his core concepts, but re-visited and re-phrased them over his long life (1875–1961), frequently diverging from earlier versions. As this chapter demonstrates, there are multiple perspectives on some of his key contributions: the relationship between the ego and the self; the relationship between the self and the transcendent function (whether God or some other overarching field); the ontology of archetypes, for example. I have summarized the key conflicts and left to one side all those concerning Jungian analytic therapy as that is outside the scope and purpose of this book: I am interested in bringing Jung's ideas to the socio-cultural debates in PR, and also in adding a further dimension of depth, both through a Jungian and a more generalized hermeneutic engagement. So my presentation of the Jungian psyche is directed to the goal of exploring issues of self and identity at individual and, particularly, group or professional level. The application of Jungian ideas to organizations and groups of various descriptions is introduced to pave the way for re-conceptualizing professions in Chapter 8. The next chapter shows how these elements might combine to create a new idea of ethics. Another key insight generated by a Jungian approach is the fragmented nature of the self, the multiplicity of voices and impulses that must be negotiated in everyday life, particularly the necessity of owning one's own shame, past and present; the alternative, as I knew too well, is to act it out. And here I return to my relationship with Jungian ideas; both in discussion and then in the readings, I discovered a closer representation of the contradictory messiness of being than I'd encountered elsewhere; it helped me understand the process by which I had evolved from a damaged and barely functioning young woman with no inner communication systems (I relied on my eczema to tell me how I felt) to a reasonably self-aware mature adult. So while I have read a great deal into the Jungian literature, presented to three Jungian conferences and published in a Jungian journal (Fawkes, 2010), the real insight into these ideas is rooted in experience.

The chapter starts with the intellectual context for Jung's ideas, followed by an overview of Jungian scholarship, before discussing his concepts of psyche and their interrelationship within a transcendent framework. It concludes with consideration of Jungian attitudes to the individual and to society.

Jung's concepts in context

Jungian concepts permeate the culture through talk of introverts and extraverts, archetypes, collective unconscious, shadow dynamics, animus/anima, self and other terms taken from his extensive writings. Yet many believe that his contribution to thought was undervalued by academics in the twentieth century (Proulx, 1994), leaving the 'cause' to proselytisers (Bishop, 1999b). Storr (1999) notes that Jung's ideas are more likely to be cited by philosophers and literary scholars than by psychiatrists, given the dominance of neuroscience in that field. This is echoed by Jones (2007), who notes that despite postmodern reassessment of psychology, particularly the move away from the natural science paradigm, Jung is still missing from mainstream psychology. She argues that, regardless of this marginalization, Jung's central ideas are increasingly pertinent to the confusion arising from the past decades of postmodernism, both in psychology and in the culture generally. There has been a resurgence in interest in his philosophy and psychology in recent years (Bishop, 1999b; Jones, 2007; Samuels, 1993), and it is suggested that his time may be coming: 'If twentieth-century philosophers have devoted most of their attention, in psychology, to Freud, some are starting to realise the usefulness of examining Jung's ideas from a philosophical perspective' (Proulx, 1994: 101).

Jung's work forms the basis of analytical psychology, also called depth psychology, as practised throughout the world (Samuels, 1985) and has deeply influenced cultural studies, especially literature, film and the study of genre. His study of personality types has been modified into the Myers-Briggs index, which is used in appraisals throughout business. Jung was a keen scholar of philosophy as well as one of the founders of psychiatry, and his philosophical ideas are seen in a tradition of sense-making that goes back to Plato (Casement, 2001; Kugler, 1997) and forward to postmodernism (Hauke, 2000; Jones, 2007; Salman, 1997). Jung himself denied being a philosopher (1949/1990: 11) though others place him in the tradition of Kant, Schopenhauer and Nietzsche (Bishop, 1999a; Huskinson, 2004; Kugler, 1997), each of whom influenced his ideas deeply. Hauke (2006) sets Jung's thinking about the unconscious in the tradition of the German Romantic movement, including Schopenhauer's descriptions of Will as a hidden driving force barely accessible to ordinary consciousness, a notion that was termed the unconscious in the mid-nineteenth century. Carus (1846, cited in Hauke, 2006: 57) even distinguished three levels of the unconscious, clearly prefiguring Jung's analysis. Jung refers to the influence of Nietzsche throughout his work and the links are explored in depth by Bishop (1999b) and Huskinson (2004b). Both Jung and Nietzsche were influenced by Schopenhauer's notion of 'will', though they took this idea in different directions. The key connections worth mentioning here are the rejection of bourgeois morality, the engagement with the self, its conception as a totality and the recognition of deeper forces underlying the material universe. Interestingly, Nietzsche also uses the term archetype: 'Jung's reading of Nietzsche laid the foundations for one of the most influential concepts of Jungian psychology, the archetype, with its emphasis on the power of the Unconscious as the source of the creative impulse' (Bishop, 1999b: 211), though Stevens attributes the origins of this concept to Plato, Kant and Schopenhauer (see below).

Another key theme in Jung's work is the union of opposites: 'Life is born only of the spark of opposites' (Jung, CW7/78), which is also found in many literatures, most notably in Taoist teaching and in the European tradition of Hegel. Here again, Nietzsche's influence is apparent, as Huskinson (2004) points out, though she notes that where Nietzsche proposes a dyadic pair of opposites between which one must choose, Jung envisages a triadic structure of opposite pairs contained or conjoined (but still distinct) in a union, *coniunctio oppositorium*. As Huskinson comments:

> The interplay of opposites is crucial to Jungian psychology ... Opposition is a necessary condition for the psyche as the very conflict and tension initiated by antithetical forces creates the energy needed by the psyche to generate its momentum and dynamism.
>
> (2004: 35)

The point is that there is intellectual precedence for many of Jung's ideas, though the application of these ideas in human psychology distinguishes Jung from other philosophers. He himself usually resisted that description, preferring to see himself as an empirical scientist: 'it is only as an empiricist, and never as a philosopher, that I have been concerned with depth psychology' (Jung, 1949/1990: 11) – a claim that doesn't always stand up. While also Jung refused to see himself as an artist (Stein, 1998), his engagement with the world often resembles that of a poet or other creative thinkers, as Susan Rowland (2010) explores in her book, *C.G. Jung in the Humanities: taking the soul's path*.

Several reasons are usually offered as to why Jung is not more often cited in philosophical or psychological literature: his alleged failure to challenge Nazism, his mysticism and, related to the latter, his idiosyncratic methodology. I do not intend to focus on biographical issues but as Jung's ambivalence towards the rise of Nazism in Germany continues to be a source of concern to modern scholars, it should be briefly addressed. Jung's anti-Semitism and racial prejudices are considered by several scholars (Casement, 2001; Grossman, 1999; Kirsch, 2004; Rowland, 2010), the consensus being that he was at best naïve, at worst wilfully ignorant of the effect of his comments. Samuels (1993) is clear that Jung's views were a cause of public dispute in the 1930s, so the defence of ignorance may not hold. This aspect of his life shocked me when I started reading, as it was not part of the image I previously held and indeed I met people who flatly denied the possibility of Jung being anything other than saintly. Samuels suggests that Jung's contradictions need to be held, rather than explained or rationalized: 'The shadows around Jung are going to linger, for they want us to pay psychological attention to them' (1993: 294). There was also the matter of his affairs with patients (Robinson, 2005), as depicted in Cronenberg's film *A Dangerous Method* (2012). There are historical disputes here, and I am not an apologist, but I remind myself that teacher–student relationships were common in my undergraduate days, if unthinkable now. Mattoon (2005) considers his long-term impact, positive and negative, on the feminist movement, concluding that while his statements about women are often disparaging, his emphasis on the importance of balancing masculine and feminine qualities in both men and women has been significant. The relationship between Jungian ideas and wider social issues is explored more fully below, but in relation to their relevance to contemporary debates, not historical or biographical issues.

As to the 'charge' of mysticism, another ground for rejecting Jung's approach, this was partly attributable to his methodology and his, then unorthodox, practice of engaging directly with the unconscious through dream work, word association, imagination and other techniques (Stevens, 2002). As can be seen elsewhere in this chapter there is a commitment to psychic wholeness within a transcendent framework, a view that unsurprisingly disqualifies him from the natural scientific paradigm but, in a post-Cartesian world this may be to his credit. Rowland (2010) considers Western science to consist of three main paradigms, the Aristotelian, Newtonian and holistic, with Jung obviously belonging in the latter, along with recent development in chaos and complexity theory. Jung explored such ideas, arising with the introduction of quantum physics, with the physicist Pauli over a hundred years ago (Mattoon, 2005; Rowland, 2010; Stevens, 2006), but they are only just entering mainstream thinking, not least because they are often counter-intuitive, or at least counter-Newtonian.

> The theory of an acausal connecting principle made Jung intensely alert to the findings of the new physics, which posited a relationship between observer and observed, and which exploded the old mechanistic understanding of matter in preference for a new, dynamic, interactive view of material reality.
>
> (Tacey, 1998: 225)

Jung himself suggested that 'since psyche and matter ... are in continuous contact with one another, it is not only possible but fairly probable that psyche and matter are two different aspects of one and the same thing' (CW8/418). However, it is also true that some supporters of Jung have tended to obscure or simplify the nature of his ideas (hence Samuels' coinage of 'post-Jungians', to encompass later, more critical, reflection on Jung's work – see below). Tacey (1997) contrasts the fanatical loyalty to Jung amongst his undergraduate students with the indifference of the academy to Jung's ideas. Nevertheless, there is a sense, as the Proulx quote above suggests, that while Freud dominated the past century, Jung has much more in common with postmodern approaches to experience, within limits, as will be explored below. 'One way forward would be to relate the post-Jungian discourse to the postmodern interest in the "Other" which carries the possibility of a mutually fulfilling spiritual exploration' (Casement, 1998: 2). This suggestion is taken up by Jones (2007) in her exploration of Jung's ideas from a postmodern perspective, comparing his concepts of self and other to those posited by, for example, Gergen, Harre, and Bruner. She concludes that Jung and postmodernists share a range of concerns about the self and the construction of meaning, the use of symbols and relationship to reality but they are 'back to back' (2007: 129), facing in opposite directions, with Jung focused inwards on the self as a spiritual entity, and the others reaching towards sociological conclusions. Like Jones, I hope to offer some connective tissue between these domains, bringing the inner workings into the social field of professions.

In summary, there is a wide-ranging discussion about Jung's contribution to modern thought and how his concepts might be related to current concerns and debates in a range of fields, even if psychology and moral philosophy scholars are less engaged than others.

The next section looks at groupings within Jungian practice and scholarship.

Approaches to Jung

Jungian analyst and scholar, Andrew Samuels (1985, 1997) argues that there is no particular body of Jungian theory but a range of ideas, often challenged and revised by Jung himself, published in a long life-time of lectures, books and articles, which are given different emphasis by different interpreters. Samuels (1985: 15–16) gathers these into three loose schools, which can be summarized as:

- Classical – closest to the original work of Jung, based at the Zurich CG Jung Institute and including writers such as Murray Stein;
- Analytical – drawing on the developmental work of Klein and others, largely based in London and including writers like Samuels himself; and
- Archetypal – working through play and active imagination, and influenced by Hillman and others, primarily in the USA.

These differences reflect emphases in therapeutic practice as well as theoretical divergences.

> 'In contrast to the "developmental" school, the "classical" school defines development not so much by years of age or even by psychological stages, as by the individual's attainment of that conscious Self which is his or hers alone to realise'.
>
> (Hart, 1997: 89)

Samuels has subsequently (1998) suggested that the archetypal school has faded or been absorbed into other approaches but that a Jungian fundamentalism has emerged at one end of the spectrum while alliances, even mergers, with Freudian psychoanalysis have taken place at the other. Many therapists use a combination of all of these approaches (Mattoon, 2005). Samuels (1985: 15–16) further distinguishes between Jungians and those post-Jungians who have critiqued, developed and extended some of his ideas. As Casement (1998: 1) describes it:

> The term 'post-Jungian' is used here not simply to refer to those who have come after Jung, but to differentiate 'post-Jungians' from 'Jungians'. Post-Jungians are committed to developing further the original insights of Jung himself and include those who have moved away from a total emphasis on psychic reality to an approach that also takes into account the reality of the outer world.

Stein (1998) disputes this typology of Jung's ideas and resists such internal divisions, suggesting that his work should be seen like that of an artist, as embodying a lifetime's struggle with key concerns. There is clearly tension here between those who wish to introduce Jungian ideas to debates in other disciplines and those who are more protective of the original oeuvre. Given that this book seeks, as do other post-Jungians, to build bridges between the therapeutic value of Jung's writings and practices and the wider world, and to incorporate more recent discussion of his ideas, it essentially takes a post-Jungian approach. But it also points in the opposite direction, asking the 'outer world' to reconsider and embrace the inner. Perhaps this is post-post-Jungian.

There are also differences in approach defined by the therapeutic techniques preferred. The clinical tools developed by Jung and his followers are outside the scope of this book but are summarised by Mattoon (2005) as analysis, dream work, active imagination (using sandplay and other creative techniques to engage with dream and other images from the psyche), transference and counter-transference (the projection of unacknowledged contents from the psyche onto the therapist and vice versa), but as Mattoon (2005: 101) points out: 'The uniqueness of Jungian therapy is less a set of techniques than an attitude towards the psyche, which is partly conscious and partly unconscious … The therapist is more knowledgeable than the client, but the wisdom is in the psyches of both'. She cites Adler's description of the four stages of Jungian analysis and their relation to other approaches as:

> (1) confession or *catharsis*, a process that occurs in all psychotherapy; (2) elucidation or *interpretation*, the major stage in Freudian analysis; (3) *education,* adaptation to social demands and needs [Adlerian] … ; and (4) transformation or *individuation*, in which the client discovers and develops an individual pattern of life … the most specifically Jungian.
>
> (Adler, 1967, cited in Mattoon, 2005: 107, emphasis in original)

These methods are not solely confined to clinical practice: they are relevant to Jung's ground for developing broader ideas from his own and patients' experiences to more general theories. His work with the unconscious, in mental institutions at the turn of the last century, led him to conceptualize the scope of the psyche and its functions, recognizing that the ego cannot see beyond its own borders. The above-mentioned techniques are thus tools for individual therapy but also means of gaining insight into the unconscious.

The next section takes an overview of the Jungian concepts of psyche, its development and component parts. It should be noted that the above schools dispute some interpretations or draw different distinctions between elements. These intra-disciplinary debates are somewhat compressed in the following summary.

The development of the psyche

Hester Solomon (1997) is clear that Jung's primary concern was with the structures of the psyche rather than their development, particularly in infancy. She suggests that there was an almost tacit agreement that Freud would focus on infantile psychology while Jung tackled the second half of life, though some Jungians, like Solomon herself, have since focused on the early years. As a result, there is no precise schema for moral development along the lines of Piaget or Kohlberg, though Solomon describes how Jungian analysts (especially in the London-based development school) have adapted approaches for dealing with early life issues and object relations in patients, particularly drawing on the work of Klein, Bion, Winicott and Bowlby. Nevertheless, other writers do see Jung as describing stages of moral development. Stein (2006), for example, emphasizes Jung's role in considering development over the full lifespan rather than just infancy and childhood. Stein (2006: 199ff) combines Jung's outline of a lifespan with that of his protégé, Erich Neumann, producing an arc in three phases that can be summarized as:

1   Containment/nurturance (Neumann used the term matriarchal) which encompasses the early stages of childhood as the psyche is engaged in

post-partum growth and the emergence of a distinction between personal self and other. Issues of care and emotional stability are relevant here, and their absence may encourage the kind of defensive splitting and projecting ego defences that need help to adjust later in life. While the mother is seen as the primary nurturing figure, others can of course take this function and institutions, such as schools or church may also be involved.

2   Adapting/adjusting (which Neumann called patriarchal), in which the individual takes a place in wider society. This is seen as embodying the masculine aspects of the psyche – the functions of differentiation and adaptation – though again the biological father is not a requirement. Issues of competition, performance and responsibility rise in priority.

3   Centring/integrating stage (or individual in Neumann's terminology) which will be explored in more detail below. This is the subject ... of the second half of life when the 'unlived' aspects of the first half demand a response. This may mean leaving social roles behind in order to discover one's underlying psychic needs. This stage is about identifying shadow materials, owning projections and learning to live in balance with opposing forces.

Stein comments that this timeline is loose but can be helpful in determining what kind of help a new patient most requires; unconditional support and containment, or encouragement to engage with external reality. A Jungian approach encourages balance between inner and outer attention. The first two stages describe the growth to adulthood, through the recognition of the role of others and the creation of a social function. These stages are not prescriptive, but generally the individual emerges from the first into the second and may or may not move towards the integrative stage in the second half of life (which Jung placed at around 35 years of age, though the timing of these stages varies from individual to individual and between cultures and epochs). Robinson (2005: 77) refers to Jung's description of the second half of life as involving the 'problem of opposites':

What defines the second half of life is the presence of a psychological maturity in which the biological, collective demands have been dutifully fulfilled such that the 'cultural task' of the conscious development of one's individual personality can, properly, morally, now be the orienting principle of one's life.

In contemporary Anglo-American culture there is a long-drawn-out adolescence that seems to extend into middle age; the desire for bourgeois trappings is postponed or rejected, so that the mid-life crisis follows a period of stagnancy: Jung anticipated this, noting that 'the wine of youth does not always clear with advancing years' (CW8/774). My own anxiety at 25 was that I was unable to emerge from a destructive, teenage way of life and lacked any of the tools for becoming an adult (it was not a popular goal among London bohemians of the 1960s and 1970s). While I remained out of sync with more stable contemporaries,

I spent the next period alternately conducting revolutionary campaigns and acquiring job status, property and qualifications, even if I had to wait for the long-term relationship. First an identity had to be constructed; then I could learn to let it all go. Jung himself describes this as:

> Something in us wishes to remain a child, to be unconscious or, at most, conscious only of the ego… to do nothing or else indulge our own craving for pleasure or power … here the individual is faced with the necessity of recognizing and accepting what is different and strange as part of his own life, as a kind of 'also-I'.
>
> (CW7/764)

There are other Jungian approaches to development theory, particularly from the London-based developmental school, with particular interest in neuroscientific discoveries on the evolution of identity, a developing field of neuropsychobiology (Knox, 2003; Wilkinson, 2006), but these aspects are not explored here.

Jungian structure of the psyche

There are contradictions between different parts of Jung's writing: he revised some lectures and articles but left others to stand as testimony to his evolving ideas, and he never wrote a definitive summary of his thoughts. Moreover, the different schools of Jungian thinkers and therapists also emphasize different aspects of his writing. These caveats aside, he can be said to perceive the psyche as consisting of a) personal consciousness (with the ego at the centre); b) the personal unconscious; and c) the collective unconscious (CW8/321). Personal consciousness includes everything of which the individual is aware, with the ego acting as the main organizer for managing external and internal stimuli; personal unconscious includes forgotten and repressed material and peripheral, low-interest contents; and the collective unconscious contains the possibilities of representations common to all people (archetypes), which may surface differently according to the particular cultures and epoch, and which form the basic structure underpinning the individual psyche. These elements are seen as compensatory; that is, the more the personal conscious refuses to deal with unwelcome thoughts or insights, the more powerful the unconscious becomes. The relationship between these elements can be antago-nistic but resolving the opposing forces in the psyche can also be a source of joy and fulfilment. Jung considered the unconscious, both personal and collective, as a more benign presence than did his one-time mentor, Freud: 'Consciousness grows out of an unconscious psyche which is older than it' (CW9i/502). Jung (CW8/382) describes the personal unconscious as consisting of:

> everything of which I know, but of which I am not at the moment thinking; everything of which I was once conscious but have now forgotten; everything perceived by my sense, but not noted by my conscious mind; everything which, involuntarily and without paying attention to it, I feel, think, remember,

want and do; all the future things that are taking shape in me and will sometime come to consciousness: all this is the content of the unconscious.

Jung sees the ego as the centre of consciousness but the personal unconscious may contain material (some of it in the shadow, see below) that is wiser than the ego. The psyche is envisaged as a self-regulatory (homeostatic) system, comprising entities of opposites (see below for discussion of archetypes) within the conscious and unconscious that continually negotiate to generate a fluid meaning, or personal mythology, to the individual. The self was sometimes described as the centre of the person, sometimes as the totality (Samuels, 1985: 91), but in any event is greater than the ego, which is closer to will or driver in Jung's schema. The unconscious is perceived as potentially beneficial, a source of insight and healing. His concept of compensation suggests that the conscious and unconscious can be seen to balance each other, with material hidden in the unconscious compensating for consciously held attitudes.

Underneath the personal unconscious lies what Jung called the collective unconscious, the water table, as it were, underpinning humanity. This where the archetypal domain resides, the source of humanity's shaping fables, which both reflect and influence understanding of individual and collective experience. It is outside of time and can be accessed through dreams and symbols. The work of popular writers such as Joseph Campbell has spread this view through books like *The Hero with a Thousand Faces* (Campbell, 1949), which promoted the idea of a universal human mythology.

> In addition to our immediate consciousness [...] there exists a second psychic system of a collective, universal and impersonal nature that is identical in all individuals. This collective unconscious does not develop individually but is inherited. It consists of pre-existent forms, the archetypes, which can only become conscious secondarily and which give definite form to certain psychic contents.
>
> (Jung, CW9i/90)

As suggested earlier, there are schools of Jungian studies, mainly following scholar and analyst James Hillman, which treat the archetypal realm as having an external reality and others, such as Samuels, who which see it as metaphorical, operating in the imaginary plane (see further discussion, below).

The next section looks at some (not all) of the components of the psyche: the ego, persona, shadow and their container, the self. The chapter then discusses how these functions may be integrated during a lifetime, before considering the relationship between the individual and society from a Jungian perspective. The ground is thus laid for exploring in the next chapter how these ideas might form the basis for an ethic.

Archetypes and complexes

Jung discovered through early word-association investigations with patients that certain issues or blockages arose repeatedly, which he termed first complexes and later archetypes. He then realized that while the distribution varied from patient to patient, themes and images recurred consistently, suggesting the existence of a body of powerful symbolic forces or *complexes* that help organize the unconscious (Stein, 1998). In this schema, clusters of feelings and thoughts aggregate (Jung uses the term 'constellate') to form a complex that may focus on the mother or mother-substitutes, for example. This complex is outside the ego's control and may erupt in unexpected devotion or hostility (depending on the content of the complex) when meeting a matriarchal figure. Indeed the ego may switch from devotion to resentment, as complexes are, like so much in the Jungian landscape, two-faced, containing their opposites. Building relationships with or awareness of these forces, through word association, play, and drawing, analysis releases the helpful aspects of the unconscious and encourages greater creative use of the individual's potential. There is a further discussion of complexes as manifesting in groups later in the chapter.

The idea of individual complexes developed into the concept of archetypes introduced above, which are organized in binary opposites in what can be either a creative or destructive tension. Take for example, the opposing archetypes of persona and shadow, the former containing conscious, 'approved' elements of the personality, the latter the repository for all that is feared or despised in the individual. Note, the shadow is not necessarily comprised of 'bad' elements: it is the unlived, unintegrated qualities that create disturbance; labelling such aspects good or bad exacerbates this. The other powerful pairing identified by Jung is the anima/animus division, which is said to represent the masculine characteristics in a woman and the feminine characteristics in a man (Samuels, 1985: 31). A wide range of archetypes was described, including the Divine Child, the Hero, the Wise Old Man/Woman, the Trickster and other characters recognizable from religious texts as well as mythologies (Jung read extensively in these areas and was deeply influenced by writings from alchemy and Gnosticism), though Jung is clear their origins precede any of these texts.

Jungians and post-Jungians exhibit a range of responses to the ontology of archetypes, as suggested earlier; particularly between those who value an objective dimension of the psyche and those who see it from a subjective perspective. Hillman (1975) considered the archetype to be the central feature of analytical psychology, and Tacey (1998: 225) summarizes this position:

> The entire thrust of Jung's research was to extend the psyche temporally and spatially into culture, history and physicality. After his separation from the Freudian School, Jung moved away from the psychologistic worldview, which wanted to reduce everything to human subjectivity. Jung became more impressed by the objective dimension of psychic experience: although we feel psyche is 'inside' us, psyche reveals itself as a cosmos in its own right. Jung greatly valued ancient philosophical traditions because of their keen perception of the objectivity of the soul.

This last point is potent: Eastern and other traditions which embrace a mutli-layered reality undoubtedly influenced Jung and help frame Jungian ethics (see next chapter). Of course this is difficult for Western culture and Jung did not argue for whole-scale abandonment of Enlightenment ideas (unlikely, given his affinity with Kant). The more metaphorical approach is illustrated by Samuels' (1985: 27) description of archetypes:

> (a) archetypal structures and patterns are the crystallisation of experiences over time, (b) they constellate experience in accordance with innate schemata and act as an imprimatur of subsequent experience, (c) images deriving from archetypal structures involve us in a search for correspondence in the environment.

As suggested above, this view of archetypes is what Tacey might call 'psychologistic', with all explanations attributable to personal conscious and unconscious history and culture. But according to Samuels (1985), post-Jungian scholars and clinicians have moved away from precise labelling of archetypes to using them as descriptors of the 'perspective' employed by an individual patient, the characters or forces they use to make sense of their own world. It is the combinations and interactions of archetypes that form the particular dynamics of each individual's drama. Stevens (2006: 84) suggests that archetypes can be clustered into four groups: events – such as birth, death, marriage; figures – such as Mother, Trickster, Hero; symbols – like sun, water, snake; and motifs – like the apocalypse, creation. Stevens emphasizes that archetypes represent the commonalities in human experience, unlike many other approaches that look at differences between people. They are important because they represent the capacity for experience shared by humans, but do not determine who will experience what. They can be imagined as templates, suggesting potential not actual content. As well as considering the antecedents of this concept in Plato, Kant and Schopenhauer, Stevens also shows how developments in evolutionary psychology offer support for such structures; the connections between neuroscience, cognitive science, theory of mind, linguistics and quantum physics are discussed by various Jungian scholars (Hauke, 2005; Knox, 2003; Mattoon, 2005; Rowland, 2010; Wilkinson, 2006), though these are not pursued here. Stein (1998) states that the most powerful archetypes are those of persona/shadow and animus/anima, and Solomon (2000: 199) describes the concept of the shadow as 'central to Jung's understanding of the self as an ethical entity'; this book concentrates on shadow dynamics rather than other archetypal struggles.

The ego

The ego is often conflated with persona (see below) in everyday use and there are different interpretations of Jung's writing on this subject. For example, Hart (1997: 89) describes the classical school's 'spirit of dialogue between the conscious and unconscious … [which] therefore regards the ego as uniquely indispensable to the whole process, in contrast to the archetypal school, for which the ego is one of many autonomous archetypal entities'. Colman sees the ego as 'mid-wife' for the entry of the self into the world of ego-consciousness, so that the ego, 'despite its absurd littleness in the face of cosmic infinity, is also seen to be at the centre of the process of (2006: 160), though this suggests that the metaphorical midwife, mother and baby are all separate entities, when others see them as aspects of the self. Generally, Jung saw the ego as the central organizing principle for the conscious self, and distinguished an efficient well-functioning ego from a weak ego system (Stein, 1998). A weak ego is more likely to identify with the persona and project shadow material onto others; a well-functioning ego has the capacity to recognize the shadow as its own, see its place in the wider psyche and so facilitate the realization of the self into consciousness. Jung defines the ego as forming: 'as it were, the centre of the field of consciousness; and, in so far as this comprises the empirical personality, the ego is the subject of all personal acts of consciousness' (CW9ii/1). Hauke (2000: 150) summarizes Jung's conception of the ego–self relationship as follows: 'The relationship between the ego – the centre of consciousness – and the unconscious self – the centre and totality of the psyche – is not one where the ego takes charge but one in which the ego is to the self as the "moved is to the mover"'.

I recognize this movement in myself: it took over a decade to build a functioning ego, capable of discriminating between impulses, acknowledging doubts and acting in my own self-interest. The experience of a weak ego was of being continually overwhelmed, paralysed by choices, contradictions and the simple challenges of everyday life. I was pathologically late, unable to calculate the time it took to get from a to b, even routine journeys like to work, and so confused about my core identity that I would change outfits several times, no matter how late I was. The weak ego, in my experience, also manifested absurd levels of grandiosity, enraged when the universe failed to reorganize itself around my needs. I arrived everywhere late, angry and badly dressed.

Jungian ideas on ego development involve the useful friction between the baby's inner needs and the outer environment until the child recognizes its differentiation from the unconscious and material worlds (Mattoon, 2005; Stein, 1998). The theme of struggle is thus set from infancy, though this is seen as natural and healthy rather than problematic. It is from these early struggles between the innate and the exterior that the particular alignment of the individual ego emerges, along the axes which Jung describes in *Psychological Types* (CW6) and which are the basis for personality tests such as the Myers-Briggs Index. The two categories are attitude and function, both consisting of axes of opposites. The former is the familiar introversion–extraversion dimension; the latter are characterized as sensation–intuition or thinking–feeling axes (laid out as a quadrant). The intention of this typology is not to categorize people, though this is sometimes lost in later applications (Mattoon, 2005), but to understand which elements of the ego are most developed (superior) and which may need encouragement to grow (inferior). Beebe (1992) calls sensation/intuition/thinking and feeling 'compass points' by which one may navigate. Again, Jung's sense of the psyche as homeostatic applies here: there is the sense of the greater potential that all human beings embody but which many need effort and assistance to realize. It is interesting to note that the ego is required to relinquish some control in assimilating shadow material and ceding authority to the self (see below), a challenging task to any entity. As will be seen in the discussion of individuation, it has to experience a Copernican revolution in accepting that it is not only *not* the totality of the psyche but not even its centre.

Persona

Jung described the public face of the individual as the 'persona', drawing on the Greek masks of ancient drama. Jung called persona 'a complicated system of relations between individual consciousness and society ... a kind of mask designed ... to make a definite impression upon others and ... to conceal the true nature of the individual' (CW7/305–9*)*. He described the two sources of the persona as 'on the one hand the expectations and demands of society and on the other ... the social aims and aspirations of the individual' (CW6/798). As the ego gravitates to the public 'approved' view, unconscious activity starts to compensate. The idea of compensation is central to Jung's concept of how the psyche operates. Mattoon (2005) provides the example of the professional persona as particularly resistant to change, as an individual over-identifies with their work role (she cites Miller's Willy Loman as an example). 'The difficulty in changing the persona is proportional to the stake one has in the roles one plays in family, work situation and community at large' (2005: 18). However, the persona should not be viewed as a negative aspect of the psyche; it is essential to the acquisition of social skills and status, and the first half of life is generally spent developing a 'public' self. (My concern with clothes reflects this: I didn't know whether to present myself as vamp, cowhand, schoolgirl or matron.) It also evolves over time, adjusting to changing circumstances and status; what Stein (1998: 119) calls a 'competent' ego will accommodate these adjustments, negotiating a path between social expectations and inner needs. The persona can be seen as engaged with object relations, navigating the individual's relationship with their society. The two pitfalls, Stein (1998: 119) points out, are over-identification with the persona–objects relationship, a sense that who one is in the world is the entirety of one's existence, and its opposite, over-attention to the inner world, so that the needs of others lack salience. Stein suggests that the adult persona often reflects the personality type outlined above but points out that in any event, introvert or extravert, 'the persona needs to both relate to objects and protect the subject'. When these functions deteriorate, fail to adapt to new situations or are not developed, help may be required. That help may be hidden in the shadow.

Shadow

The shadow comprises those elements of the personal unconscious that are not considered acceptable to consciousness (CW9ii/14). They are not necessarily 'bad', simply rejected, as a workaholic might reject relaxation, for example. But because they are outside the control of the ego they may be less socially accept-able (or conformist) than other traits (Stein, 1998). Such repression/ rejection may have been required by family, educational or other societal demands. Not only is the ego unaware of this shadow personality, it can uncon-sciously project rejected aspects on to others, making them 'carry' the unlived elements (Storr, 1999: xv). To continue the example, the compulsive worker may perceive his/her colleagues as lightweights whom he/she both despises and envies. I have certainly been there. It is worth repeating that while the shadow comprises those elements that the individual has rejected from consciousness as threatening the preservation of a certain version of him/herself, it is not necessarily malign. After nearly a decade of political activity, I had to acknowledge that the sainted martyr may be noble but is not particularly lovable. Maintaining that self-image cost connections with friends and self; abandoning it at the end of the 1980s enabled me to return to art classes without feeling I was letting down the entire British working class. This is typical of shadow material: it contains creativity, the unlived desire to draw, make music, make mistakes. On the other hand, some people may over-identify with their shadow dimensions, making a habit of behaving anti-socially, elevating greed or bullying to a modus operandi (Casement, 2006). Fictional characters from Gordon Gekko to the *Wire's* Omar Little illustrate the charismatic qualities that can attach to those who live out this archetypal aspect. Their unlived qualities may include compassion, tenderness, vulnerability. Whitmont (1969/1991: 16) notes that the individual who over-identifies with the shadow, becoming a 'bad boy' for example, may find a softer aspect in their unlived shadow. I have a friend who spent his formative years in a gang of serious, nasty football hooligans; but his arms were tattooed with intricate roses and lilies, and he has had to learn to express this kindness. Casement (2006) stresses that the shadow itself contains a positive and negative aspect. It also operates at three levels: personal conscious, personal unconscious and collective unconscious (reflecting the three layers of conscious-ness outlined earlier). Whitmont (1969/1991: 15) describes the shadow as consisting of

> complexes, of personal qualities resting on behaviour patterns which are a
> definite 'dark' part of the personality structure. In most instances they are
> readily observable by others. Only we ourselves cannot see them. The shadow
> qualities are usually in glaring contrast to the ego's ideals and wistful efforts.
> The sensitive altruist may have a brutal egotist somewhere inside himself; the
> shadow of the courageous figure may be a whining coward; the everloving
> sweetheart may harbour a bitter shrew.

It is worth noting this contrast between the ego's ideals and the shadow, though the emphasis on darkness seems at odds with most Jungian writing about the shadow. The tension between these polarities, or between the outer appearance and the inner reality, has a tendency to become acute in approaching the second half of life

(Jung's particular arena of interest). This is discussed more fully in describing individuation. At this point help may be required in shifting habits of thought and action and embracing the possibilities offered by reviewing and owning that which has been ignored or rejected earlier. The motivation for doing this may be the growing sense that the persona or mask is increasingly false, that a (psychologically uncomfortable) gap has emerged between the public and private personalities. Stein (1998) points out the difficulty, alluded to above, of asking the ego to detect its own shadow and I am still astonished by how many expect self-diagnosis to be effective. Perhaps it is a side effect of the over-reliance on human intelligence that prevents us from seeking help. The Jungian methods outlined earlier are routes to the unconscious, which contains the solutions to problems raised by uncontrolled shadow activity, such as outbursts of rage or violence in usually peaceable and people-pleasing types. The Jungian analyst and writer, June Singer (1995), illustrates this dynamic with the story of a hard-working head teacher who broke into cars to steal worthless items at intervals, behaviour of which he was barely conscious until arrested. Looking back, I suspect I relegated my body to the shadow; indeed I distinctly remembering deciding to 'live in the library' of my head at the age of eight or nine, when my childhood eczema was very severe and my body a site of constant pain. I didn't really return for three decades, when I woke from major surgery to hear an inner voice cry: *now* will you listen to me? So I did. It should also be stressed that it is not possible to raise the entirety of the shadow to consciousness – some aspects belong in the collective unconscious and to the archetype, and moreover it is a lifetime's work to deal with those aspects that may be accessible to consciousness. 'The serious problems of life are never fully solved... The meaning and purpose seems to lie not in its solution but in our working at it incessantly' (CW8/771). The process of raising those aspects of the shadow capable of assimilation is called individuation.

Individuation and the self

This section outlines the process of individuation in bringing the psyche to consciousness of the self. Its ethical implications are explored in more detail in the next chapter; the following aims to round up the central themes of Jungian approaches to the psyche. As can be seen from earlier descriptions of some of the components of the Jungian psyche, the individual can be conceived of as a multiplicity of sub-personalities (Stein, 1998). The internal pressures that arise when persona drifts away from the core personality or shadow material starts 'leaking' into the outer world can become intolerable. This is where the core principle of Jung's therapy starts: the journey of integration. This process can only be sketched here, with particular attention to the integration of persona and shadow (marginalizing the other aspects, such as animus and anima, whose integration is essential to individuation). The realization of the whole self, the totality of the psyche, is the goal of Jungian therapy, according to Hart (1997: 91), who describes 'wholeness' as 'the fullest possible consciousness of all that comprises one's own personality, and it is approached in the steady, honest and demanding self-discipline that Jung called individuation'. Others challenge this conceptualization, as can be seen below. But taking this approach, the stages on this path start with integrating disowned or invisible (to the ego) elements of the psyche. As Stein (1998: 122) puts it, 'integration hinges on self-acceptance, on fully accepting those parts of oneself that do not belong in the persona image, which is itself usually an image of an ideal or at least of a cultural norm'. This process necessitates what Hauke (2000: 169) calls the 'dual struggle of the subject with, on the one hand, the "inner world" of the unconscious in all its infantile, personal and collective aspects and, on the other hand, the struggle with the "outer world" of collective society'. The difficulty of this struggle should not be underestimated. Jung describes individuation as:

> becoming a single, homogeneous being, and, in so far as 'individuality' embraces our innermost, last, and incomparable uniqueness, it also implies becoming one's own Self. We could therefore translate individuation as 'coming to Selfhood' or 'Self-realization'... The Self is our life's goal, for it is the most complete expression of that fateful combination we call individuality.
>
> (CW7/266 and 404)

It is clear that for Jung, the realization of the self is the *telos*, or purpose of human life, and Beebe (1998: 58) echoes this:

> In Jungian work it has come to mean the will of the psychological individual to become conscious and, though assuredly not perfect, psychologically whole; that is, with no part of the self split off in the unconscious, inaccessible even to dialogue with the ego. Our image for this goal of undissociated wholeness is the philosopher's stone of the alchemists.

The quote from Beebe does illustrate some of the problems in writing about Jungian ideas as he uses 'self' to encompass primarily conscious elements, though others (e.g. Hauke, 2006) suggest that the shadow cannot be wholly raised to consciousness – and, of course, many uses of the Jungian 'self' encompass the unconscious, so it must remain mysterious to the ego. However, there is so much material that *can* be brought to consciousness that the rest of the iceberg can rest under the surface. The urgency concerns those aspects of self that are actually required for living a whole life and which are capable of being integrated into one's consciousness – as long as one is prepared to live with contradictions and inconsistencies.

The issue of psychic wholeness is contentious to postmodernists: Tacey (1998) argues that it is incompatible with postmodernist approaches; Hauke, a Jungian postmodernist, proves the point by rejecting the normative tendencies inherent in the 'fantasy of wholeness' (2005: 81) and argues that 'The bias towards wholeness results in a pathologising of sub-personalities as part-objects which are regarded as insufficient or a sign of immaturity' (2000: 64). He claims that Samuels

(1993) supports this resistance, and these quotes illustrate the difficulty of applying Jungian theory to another field when a core concept such as 'wholeness' is deeply contested. Returning to Jung, one finds that his concepts allow for more fluidity than the critics permit: the idea of wholeness is not homogeneity but homeostasis, a kind of dynamic balance, described by Jung as

> a process not of dissolution but of construction, in which thesis and antithesis both play their part. In this way it becomes a new content that governs the whole attitude, putting an end to the division and forcing the energy of the opposite into a common channel. The standstill is overcome and life can flow on with renewed power towards new goals.
>
> (CW6/827)

These ideas are not new: in addition to the philosophers mentioned earlier, Jung drew on a range of long-neglected literature to develop his ideas of individuation. For example, learning to hold opposing forces in one field (*coniunctio oppositorium*), so central to Jung's thinking, has origins in Gnosticism, Taoism and alchemy, as well as Hegel's dialectics (Casement, 2006; Papadopoulos, 2006; Stein, 2006). Jung was deeply influenced by aspects of Eastern philosophy, such as Taoism: 'The meanings of *tao* are as follows: way, method, principle, natural force or life force, the regulated processes of nature, the idea of the world, the prime cause of all phenomena, the right, the good, the moral order (CW6 cited in Beebe, 1992: 28).

Jung also used the *I Ching* as a methodology, and wrote extensively on the influence of Chinese and other Asian philosophies, one of the critical texts being *The Secret of the Golden Flower;* he wrote the introduction to Wilhelm's translation (Wilhelm and Jung, 1962). I am not addressing the influence of Gnosticism or alchemy here, though the latter plays a central role in forming Jung's concept of transformation, in which impure aspects (*nigredo)* are integrated to create a new substance, giving rise to the concept of working with the shadow (Casement, 2006). Alchemy provides a narrative structure for this inner work and its metaphors are used throughout his writing, particularly in personal works such as the recently published *Red Book* (Jung and Shamdasani, 2009). Jung's clinical methods not only drew on the *I Ching* but also on a range of tools designed to allow the unconscious to surface, such as analysis, dream work, active imagination, transference and counter-transference (Mattoon, 2005), and influenced both his practice and his approach to psychic change.

The multiple meanings of the Jungian concept of self are explored by Colman (2000, 2006) comparing the different schools of Jungian thought and contrasting the Jungian sense of the 'Self' from the everyday use of 'I, myself, me', which Jung terms the personal self. The Jungian self is sometimes capitalized to denote the difference, but this is used inconsistently by Jung and Jungian writers, and this book uses lower case, except in direct quotations. This section aims to elucidate the difference between the Jungian and ordinary uses of the word. Colman contrasts the personal self with 'that which transcends consciousness, that which is greater than what I take to be my "self" (2000: 3). He describes three approaches to the self commonly found in Jungian and post-Jungian thought: the self as the totality of the psyche; the self as an archetype; the self as a personification of the unconscious; and offers his own contribution: the self as the *process* of the psyche. The first of these posits that the self cannot be fully present in consciousness, because the self includes the unconscious, personal and collective. And while personal elements have the potential to be raised to consciousness, collective aspects, in particular archetypal entities cannot be fully known: 'We do not know the archetypes – we only know the multiple representations of them in consciousness' (Colman, 2000: 5). Colman emphasizes that this approach to self evokes the unknowability of God, rendering all symbolic representations futile, and likens it to mystical experiences described by thinkers such as Meister Eckhart, in which there is no longer conscious and unconscious, subject or object, the dualities merged in the eternal. The second approach, the self as archetype, is also found in Jung's writing, though, as Colman points out, it is not easy to reconcile the sense of the self as the whole with its role as an archetype within the totality. Nevertheless, symbolic representations of the self can be found in dreams, for example, and Colman suggests that this may be more common in 'fragmented individuals' (2000: 8), for whom images of wholeness may have a galvanising effect. The idea of the self as a personification of the unconscious can be seen in the metaphor of the king as the nation, though as Colman points out, the problem persists of part and whole, namely that the king is still a member, however exalted, of the nation he rules. Colman resolves some of these paradoxes by proposing the self as *process*, 'an organising principle within the psyche but ... better thought of as the organising principle of the psyche' (2000: 14). In a later work, he adds that this approach removes the contradiction

> between the self as an organising principle (archetype) and the self as a totality as there is no need to distinguish between the organisation/system and that which is organising it ... the self-organisation of the totality of psychic functioning ... includes the capacity to create meaning and pattern, allowing us to organise elements of our experience into archetypal imagery and behaviour.
>
> (2006: 170)

The idea of self as process is echoed by Mathers, who states that 'Self is neither a unity nor a deity: it is process not a thing – a 'becoming' rather than an 'is' (2000: 224). Bishop (1999b: 227) would seem to support this view, suggesting that the chief characteristic of the Jungian self is

> its capacity for creation and self-transformation, a striving for an ever more complete union of the two great opposites, consciousness and the Unconscious. In the process of creating the Self, the libido (conceived by Jung as a stream of psychic energy) descends into the depths of the Collective Unconscious (the great psychic M/Other), dying unto the conscious world as

it introverts, to reemerge stronger, bolder, more creative, born anew: like a god which dies and is reborn.

However, the phrase 'creating the Self' implies something that can be constructed or improved, rather than accessed or realized, illustrating the enormous difficulty of discussing these issues. Colman (2006), like Jones (2007), recognizes the resonance between social constructionist views of the self and the Jungian persona. Jones explores the relationship between Jungian psychology and postmodernist approaches, finding their views of the self almost mutually exclusive: 'Whereas Hermans' description of the self seems blind to the domain that James called the spiritual self, Jung's description of the self could be viewed as located solely in that domain (and is blind to the social) (2007: 91).

This illustrates both the possibilities and problems of linking Jung to socio-cultural perspectives: his ideas combine both a postmodern fragmented and fluid individual self with a deep hermeneutic collective connection with humanity. Jones (2007) also notes the indebtedness of Jung's concepts of self to William James (1905), who defines the material, social and spiritual self, and speaks of the relationship between selves, though this again evokes the confusion of self as content, part or whole, as discussed above. Brooke (2009) conducts a review of the many approaches to the Jungian self, placing them in a phenomenological setting and concluding that there are similarities between Jung's sense of self or psyche and what Heidegger called the 'life world':

> If the self is the totality of the psyche and the psyche is the lifeworld, then it seems we must understand the self as always and irreducibly situated in and related to the world. The self is situated within psyche's landscape of material things, events, rituals, myths, stories, memories, phantasies, and dream images, bound together in *language* and *time*.
>
> (2009: 604)

These quotes illustrate the complexity of the ideas congregating around the concept of self, even within Jungian writing, let alone in other fields of psychology and sociology. There are sufficient contradictions to fill a library and they cannot be resolved here, though it is worth remembering some of the issues raised in earlier chapters about the inner and outer 'world views'. There is a sense that a Jungian idea of self is wholly in the inner worlds, while social constructionist approaches, for example, stress the external. Or rather, given Brooke's view, above, that Jung's life world is seen from the inside out, that of sociologists from the outside in. The tension between the individual and society is explored more fully below, but this section concludes with a reminder that the essential framework or container for the realized self lies in the transcendent, which, as Tacey makes clear, makes possible:

> the regulation of the opposites, the balancing of inner and outer demands, and the compensatory mechanisms of psychic life. The Self disallows extremism

of any kind, and, through the agency of the 'transcendent function', works actively to undermine extremism before it becomes chronic and established.

(1998: 230)

For some writers, the realization of the self is synonymous with realization of God and it is impossible to talk about self without talking about the transcendent, though as Colman points out: 'that is not to say that all such representations appear in the form of "God", nor that "God" and "the self" are the same thing' (2000: 5). He cites Jung's claim that religious symbolism of wholeness is parallel to the goal of individuation (CW11/414) and that any symbol that is greater than the individual may be a symbol of the total self (CW11/232). This echoes Jung's statement that 'The Self is not only the centre but also the whole circumference which embraces both conscious and unconscious' (CW12/44). In a later work Colman (2006) cites Jung's statement that 'the symbolism of psychic wholeness coincides with the God-image, but it can never prove that the God-image is God himself or that the self takes the place of God' (CW9ii/308). This transcendent function is considered next.

The transcendent function

A key aspect of Jung's approach is his view of psychology as teleological, rather than morbid or pathological. Papadopoulos (2006) contrasts this approach with that of Freud, who, he suggests, is reductive, using symptoms to track back to problems, where Jung sees them as pointing forward, to solutions. 'Teleology refers to the approach that considers phenomena in terms of their *telos* … being the goal, end, purpose and fulfillment' (2006: 29). He finds four distinct uses of teleology in Jung's writing:

- Therapeutic teleology – referring to clinical practice
- Methodological teleology – referring to its use in scientific investigations
- Human teleology – referring to human drive for psychological development
- Natural teleology – referring to the laws of nature.

(2006: 30)

It is the latter two aspects which are of interest here, in that they imply an innate drive to fulfilment which goes beyond 'self-improvement' to the unfolding of the entirety of the human psyche within a transcendent framework. As suggested earlier, the tension between religious and secular interpretations of Jung run through debates between Jungians, post-Jungians and others who argue about whether Jungian psychology requires the acceptance of a deity or whether the self can be seen as a generic spiritual or even purely psychological entity. Jung (CW9i) suggests that faith describes the organized social aspects of observance (he also calls this confession) while religion is closer to the personal direct experience, although common usage might well reverse these terms. The latter experience is located in the psyche but that does not, he says, mean it is nothing. Indeed Jung suggests that a more psychological approach to myth might revitalize churches suffering from the over-rationalization of current times. Although this aspect is described as the transcendent function, his idea of self as God is closer to immanence, the God-within, than transcendence, the God-above, as the following quote illustrates:

> This 'something' is strange to us and yet so near, wholly ourselves and yet unknowable, a virtual centre of so mysterious a constitution that it can claim anything—kinship with beasts and gods, with crystals and with stars— without moving us to wonder, without even exciting our disapprobation… I have called this centre the *Self*. Intellectually the Self is no more than a psychological concept, a construct that serves to express an unknowable essence which we cannot grasp as such, since by definition it transcends our powers of comprehension. It might equally well be called the 'God within us'.
>
> (CW7/398–9)

There is ambivalence here: the term 'psychological concept' implies something knowable, yet Jung's Self is also mysterious and unknowable. Perhaps recent attempts to reduce the psyche entirely to electrical impulses have compounded the contradiction. For example, Bishop (1999b: 227) argues for a more secular interpretation:

> Clearly, the concept of the Self does not so much reject as replace the notion of divine transcendence with the much less clear notion of psychological transcendence. In the psychic economy that Jung proposes, the archetype of the Self replaces the concept of God.

This seems to suggest a narcissistic fascination and some (see below) do make this accusation; to me the transcendent function is precisely the opposite of solipsism as it requires the individual to place themselves in a larger, collective framework. Brooke's understanding of psyche and self helps resolve these apparent divisions:

> The terms psyche and self would seem to be almost interchangeable. Their expanse and dimensions are the same. The term self seems to be useful in emphasizing that the primordial occurrence of gathering which Jung calls the psyche is potentially someone's. It is out of that gathering now called the self that we are constituted and come into being as the persons we are.
>
> (2009: 604–5)

The representation of this transcendent principle is sometimes characterized by a Christ/Buddha archetype that embodies the concept of the fullest human potential and is closest to a 'God' archetype. This is intended as an image of wholeness, of maximum potential, not necessarily as a religious symbol. Jung suggests that Christ cannot stand alone as an analogy for the Self as the image embodies only the good (CW9ii/79–98). The Taoist yin–yang symbol is also often used to represent the self, in that it embodies the totality of human experience and potential, good and evil, light and dark. Huskinson (2004: 36) comments on the transcendent as the unifying container of opposites:

> The transcendent function is a twofold process: the spontaneous emergence of a unifying symbol unites opposing elements; and from this union, it establishes a new conscious attitude, one that is more integrated and enriched with those elements that were hitherto unconscious ... The transcendent function enables the personality to move from a one-sided attitude to a new, more complete, one ... The development of the personality is therefore advanced when the opposites of conscious and unconscious complement one another. The conscious attitude requires compensation from the unconscious attitude if it is to flourish, but this does not mean that the unconscious attitude is privileged over consciousness.

Whatever the characterization, or the symbolism of the transcendent, what is crucial is the concept of the ego's relative insignificance within a greater whole. This was the key concern of Jung's correspondence with the founder of Alcoholics Anonymous, where he suggested that alcoholism

> involves a spiritual thirst for a sense of wholeness – the true secret of its numinous power and the reason why a person can be led into an addiction. He understood intuitively that only a radical conversion to something equally satisfying to the individual at a deep level can promote recovery.
>
> (Adenbrooke, n.d.)

Like many mystic traditions, the de-centering of the ego from the centre and sum of the universe is the first step in any spiritual awareness. For the ego to surrender, it must find *something*, a group, an idea, a deity, greater than itself. This allows the possibility for society as an overarching entity, explored in Chapter 3. The relationship between the individual and society and the operation of group complexes are explored in the next chapter. There, individuation, the process of raising shadow into consciousness, is suggested as a basis for an ethic, drawing on a range of ethical approaches that stress wholeness rather than rightness.

Conclusions

This chapter has located Jungian ideas in an intellectual context, demonstrating the breadth and depth of his thinking and influences. It also summariszed the main schools of Jungian thought, stressing the different interpretations offered by Jungians and post-Jungians and the impossibility of offering a definitive summary of Jung's concepts. Nevertheless, key features such as persona, ego and shadow were described and placed in the context of the self, a highly contested concept, and the transcendent function.

This discussion stressed the multiple aspects of the whole, in which parts may see themselves as autonomous until brought into contact with the unconscious, at which point they may shift their internal relationships. For this to begin the individual needs to re-envision him or herself as part of a greater whole, whether that is seen as divine or humanist. Over time, this can lead to individuation or self-realization, the goal of human development, in Jung's view. The difficulties of this journey and its possibilities as an ethical foundation are explored in the next chapter.

Note

1   All references to Jung cite the *Collected Works* and the relevant paragraph, not page.

References

Adenbrooke, M. (n.d.) Jung and the labyrinth of addiction. Online. Available at www.thesap. org.uk/jung-and-addiction, retrieved 25 January, 2012.

Beebe, J. (1992) *Integrity in Depth*. College Station, TX: Texas A&M University.

Beebe, J. (1998) Towards a Jungian analysis of character. In A. Casement (ed.) *Post-Jungians Today: key papers in analytical psychology*. London: Routledge, pp. 53–66.

Bishop, P. (1999a) C. G. Jung and F. Nietzsche: Dionysos and analytical psychology. In P. Bishop (ed.) *Jung in Contexts: a reader*. London and New York, NY: Routledge, pp. 205–41.

Bishop, P. (ed.) (1999b) *Jung in Contexts: a reader*. London and New York, NY: Routledge.

Brooke, R. (2009) *Jung and Phenomenology*. Pittsburgh, PA: Trivium Publications.

Campbell, J. (1949) *The Hero with a Thousand Faces*. New York, NY: Pantheon.

Casement, A. (1998) *Post-Jungians Today: key papers in contemporary analytical psychology*. London: Routledge.

Casement, A. (2001) *Carl Gustav Jung*. London: Sage.

Casement, A. (2006) The shadow. In R. K. Papadopoulos (ed.) *The Handbook of Jungian Psychology*. Hove, East Sussex: Routledge, pp. 94–112.

Colman, W. (2000) Models of the self in Jungian thought. In E. Christopher and H. M. Solomon (eds) *Jungian Thought in the Modern World*. London: Free Association, pp. 3–19.

Colman, W. (2006) The self. In R. K. Papadopoulos (ed.) *The Handbook of Jungian Psychology*. Hove, East Sussex: Routledge, pp. 153–74.

Cronenberg, D. T. (2012) A dangerous method. Culver City, CA: Sony Pictures Home Entertainment.

Fawkes, J. (2010) The shadow of excellence: a Jungian approach to public relations ethics. *Review of Communication, 10*(3): 211–27.

Grossman, S. (1999) C. G. Jung and national socialism. In P. Bishop (ed.) *Jung in Contexts: a reader*. London: Routledge, pp. 92–121.

Hart, D. L. (1997) The classical Jungian school. In P. Young-Eisendrath and T. Dawson (eds) *The Cambridge Companion to Jung*. Cambridge: Cambridge University Press, pp. 89–100.

Hauke, C. (2000) *Jung and the Postmodern: the interpretation of realities*. London: Routledge.

Hauke, C. (2005) *Human Being Human: culture and the soul*. London: Routledge.

Hauke, C. (2006) The unconscious: personal and collective. In R. K. Papadopoulos (ed.) *The Handbook of Jungian Pyschology*. Hove, East Sussex: Routledge, pp. 54–73.

Hillman, J. (ed.) (1975) *Re-Visioning Psychology* (1st edn) New York, NY: Harper & Row.

Huskinson, L. (2004) *Nietzsche and Jung: the whole self in the union of opposites*. Hove, East Sussex: Brunner-Routledge.

James, W. (1905) *Varieties of Religious Experience: a study in human nature*. London: Longmans.

Jones, R. A. (2007) *Jung, Psychology, Postmodernity*. Hove, East Sussex: Routledge.

Jung, C. G. *Aion*, Vol. 9ii, *Collected Works* (eds Read, H., Adler, G. A. and Fordham, M.; trans. R. F. C. Hull). London: Routledge & Kegan Paul.

Jung, C. G. *The Archetypes and the Collective Unconscious*, Vol. 9i, *Collected Works*, (ed. Read, H., Adler, G. A. and Fordham, M.; trans. R. F. C. Hull). London: Routledge & Kegan Paul.

Jung, C. G. (1949/1990) Foreword. Neumann, E. *Depth Psychology and a New Ethic*. Boston: Shambala Press. pp 11–18.

Jung, C. G., *Psychology and Alchemy*, Vol. 12, *Collected Works*, (eds Read, H., Adler, G. A. and Fordham, M.; trans. R. F. C. Hull). London: Routledge & Kegan Paul.

Jung, C. G. *The Structure and Dynamics of the Psyche*, Vol. 8, *Collected Works* (eds Read, H., Adler, G. A. and Fordham, M.; trans. R. F. C. Hull). London: Routledge & Kegan Paul.

Jung, C. G. *Two Essays on Analytical Psychology*, Vol. 7, *Collected Works* (eds Read, H., Adler, G. A. and Fordham, M.; trans. R. F. C. Hull). London: Routledge & Kegan Paul.

Jung, C. G. *The Structure and Dynamics of the Psyche*, Vol. 8, *Collected Works* (eds Read, H., Adler, G. A. and Fordham, M.; trans. R. F. C. Hull). London: Routledge & Kegan Paul.

Jung, C. G. *Psychological Types*, Vol. 6, *Collected Works* (eds Read, H., Adler, G. A. and Fordham, M.; trans. R. F. C. Hull). London: Routledge & Kegan Paul.

Jung, C. G. *Psychology and Alchemy*, Vol. 12, *Collected Works* (eds Read, H., Adler, G.A. and Fordham, M.; trans. R. F. C. Hull). London: Routledge & Kegan Paul.

Jung, C. G. Jaffe, A. and Winston, C. (1963) *Memories, Dreams, Reflections*. London: Collins and Routledge & Kegan Paul.

Jung, C. G. and Shamdasani, S. (2009) *The Red Book = Liber Novus*. New York: W.W. Norton & Co.

Kirsch, T. B. (2004) Cultural complexes in the history of Jung, Freud and their followers. In T. Singer and S. L. Kimbles (eds) *The Cultural Complex: contemporary Jungian perspectives on psyche and society*. New York, NY: Brunner-Routledge.

Knox, J. (2003) *Archetype, Attachment, Analysis: Jungian psychology and the emergent mind*. Hove, East Sussex: Brunner-Routledge.

Kugler, P. (1997) Psychic imaging: a bridge between subject and object. In T. Dawson and P. Young-Eisendrath (eds) *The Cambridge Companion to Jung*. Cambridge: Cambridge University Press, pp. 71–118.

Mathers, D. (2000) Spirits and spirituality. In E. Christopher and H. M. Solomon (eds) *Jungian Thought in the Modern World*. London: Free Association, pp. 217–32.

Mattoon, M. A. (2005) *Jung and the Human Psyche: an understandable introduction*. London: Routledge.

Papadopoulos, R. K. (2006) *The Handbook of Jungian Psychology: theory, practice and applications*. London: Routledge.

Proulx, C. (1994) On Jung's theory of ethics. *Journal of Analytic Psychology, 39*(1): 101–19.

Robinson, D. W. (2005) *Conscience and Jung's moral vision: from Id to Thou*. New York, NY: Paulist Press.

Rowland, S. (2010) *C.G. Jung in the Humanities: taking the soul's path*. New Orleans, LA: Spring Journal Books.

Salman, S. (1997) The creative psyche: Jung's major contribution. In P. Young-Eisendrath and T. Dawson (eds) *The Cambridge Companion to Jung*. Cambridge: Cambridge University Press, pp. 52–70.

Samuels, A. (1985) *Jung and the Post-Jungians*. London: Routledge and Kegan Paul.

Samuels, A. (1993) *The Political Psyche*. London: Routledge.

Samuels, A. (1997) Introduction: Jung and the post-Jungians. In P. Young-Eisendrath and T. Dawson (eds) *The Cambridge Companion to Jung*. Cambridge: Cambridge University Press, pp. 1–16.

Samuels, A. (1998) Will the post-Jungians survive? In A. Casement (ed.) *Post-Jungians Today: key papers in contemporary analytical psychology*. London: Routledge, pp. 15–32.

Singer, J. (1995) *Boundaries of the Soul: the practice of Jung's psychology*. Sturminster Newton: Prism Press.

Solomon, H. M. (1997) The developmental school. In P. Young-Eisendrath and T. Dawson (eds) *Cambridge Companion to Jung*. Cambridge: Cambridge University Press, pp. 119–40.

Solomon, H. M. (2000) The ethical self. In E. Christopher, H. Solomon and E. Christopher (eds) *Jungian Thought in the Modern World*. London: Free Association Books, pp. 191–216.

Stein, M. (1998) *Jung's Map of the Soul: an introduction*. Chicago, IL: Open Court.

Stein, M. (2006) Individuation. In R. K. Papadopoulos (ed.) *The Handbook of Jungian Psychology: theory, practice and applications*. London: Routledge, pp. 196–214.

Stevens, A. (ed.) (2002) *Archetype Revisited: an updated natural history of the self* (2nd edn) London: Brunner-Routledge.

Stevens, A. (2006) The archetypes. In R. K. Papadopoulos (ed.) *The Handbook of Jungian Psychology*. Hove, East Sussex: Routledge, pp. 74–93.

Storr, A. (1999) Foreword. In P. Bishop (ed.) *Jung in Contexts: a reader*. London: Routledge, pp. xi–xvii

Tacey, D. (1997) Jung in the academy: devotions and resistances. *Journal of Analytic Psychology, 42*(2): 269–83.

Tacey, D. (1998) Twisting and turning with James Hillman: from anima to world soul, from academia to pop. In A. Casement (ed.) *Post-Jungians Today: key papers in contemporary analytical psychology*. London: Routledge, pp. 215–34.

Whitmont, E. C. (1969/1991) The evolution of the shadow. In C. Zweig and J. Abrams (eds) *Meeting the Shadow*. New York, NY: Tarcher: Penguin, pp. 12–19.

Wilhelm, R. and Jung, C. G. (eds) (1962) *The Secret of the Golden Flower: a Chinese book of life* (4th rev. edn) New York, NY: Harvest/HBJ.

Wilkinson, M. (2006) *Coming into Mind: the mind–brain relationship: a Jungian clinical perspective*. London: Routledge.

7   Towards a Jungian ethic

Introduction

One of the many insights that struck me when reading Jungian literature, and that resonated with my own experience, was the premise that the parts of the self are multiple, and in particular that an ethical impulse cannot be assumed or prescribed when those parts all want to go off in different directions. The metaphor that helped me as I started engaging with my own messy psyche was that of a committee – I had plenty of practice chairing difficult groups and when I looked around my own consciousness I saw revolutionaries, appeasers, party-goers and recluses, all different ages, even genders. The hardest to acknowledge were the sad children; the part I most identified with had long ago locked herself in a library and didn't want to come out. Who could blame her – everyone else was shouting. So Jung's naming of parts reflected a process I had already stumbled upon – with help, of course. That before one can engage with other people in a manner that is reasonably decent and respectful of the other (law-abiding and socially acceptable were never personal criteria), it is necessary to acknowledge all the elements that wish to behave in precisely the opposite direction. I recognize that in using my own experience, there is a danger of over-personalizing these observations, but over 35 years of working on this stuff I have noticed that such conflicts are found every day in perfectly 'normal' society and workplaces, not restricted to the dysfunctional. In literature, in meetings with practitioners (including public relations (PR) representatives of oil companies at a Chartered Institute of Public Relations event in Aberdeen), in conversations with students and colleagues, both at my own universities and at conferences, and in the process of publishing papers on these themes, I have found a recognition that the monolithic edicts about correct ethical behaviour do not always speak to practitioners or academics. There is a willingness to engage with something, anything, different. This chapter suggests how individuation – outlined in the previous chapter – offers insights and even a template for an ethical *process*. It builds on findings from Jung, Jungian and post-Jungian writers, and from earlier chapters, to suggest that wholeness can be a richer foundation for ethics than idealized and partial self-images; that facing the shadow is the first and most significant step in this journey; and that this process is available to groups as well as individuals. This chapter sets out the relationship between individuation, integration and ethics.

As the last chapter demonstrated, Jung saw the integration of the different aspects of the self as the central goal of depth psychology. By this he clearly does not mean a completed task or a permanent state of psychic equilibrium – the archetypal aspects of the Jungian psyche are not susceptible to fantasies of control or finality. The challenge is to understand that one's own individual psyche comprises conscious and unconscious material, and that in the unconscious realm lies shadow material, aspects of the personality that are not acknowledged or recognized as one's own, and often, projected as 'problems' onto other people or groups. As I began to make inner relationships with some of the most troublesome parts of myself, other energies emerged: I went back to life drawing, took writing classes, reclaimed something creative that had become lost in the turmoil. In hindsight, this is very Jungian, a classic example of what can be released when the inner elements become more harmonious.

The core texts that underpin this chapter are Neumann's (1949/1990) *Depth Psychology and a New Ethic*, along with Beebe's (1992) *Integrity in Depth*, Robinson (2005) on Jung's moral conscience and Solomon (2000, 2001) on Jungian ethics in the analytic relationship. Christina Becker's (2004) *The Heart of the Matter: individuation as an ethical process* was brought to my attention recently and covers very similar ground, though she, like Solomon, takes her insights back into the therapeutic field, and mine are intended for application to the fields of professions generally and PR in particular. There is also a smattering of journal articles and related arguments about Jung's place in wider philosophical debates on ethics and moral philosophy. These all demonstrate the applicability of Jungian ideas to ethics, with varying emphasis on ethical relationships in the counselling room (Solomon, 2000, 2001; Becker, 2004), individual ethical behaviour (Beebe, 1992; Robinson, 2005) and moral development as a philosophical debate (Amir, 2005; Proulx, 1994), while Neumann looks to the implications of a Jungian ethic for a changing world order. Most of the cited authors comment on the paucity of writing about Jung and ethics, despite the natural correlation between integration and integrity (as highlighted by Beebe, 1992). Robinson (2005: 15) suggests several reasons for this omission: primarily the absence of an articulated or systematic exposition on ethics in Jung's writings, apart from two short essays, 'Good and evil in analytical psychology' and 'A psychological view of conscience' (CW10)[1]. (Jung also wrote the foreword to Neumann's (1949/1990) *Depth Psychology and a New Ethic*, as Proulx 1994, not Robinson, 2005, points out.) He did not set out a list of desirable characteristics, for example, as in virtue ethics, or attempt to generate moral codes like a Kantian, though he was closely concerned with universal moral values. Indeed, Jung states in the foreword to Neumann, 'it is only as an empiricist, and never as a philosopher, that I have been concerned with depth psychology, and cannot boast of ever having tried my hand at formulating ethical principles' (1949/1990: 11). Nevertheless, Jung refers to ethical issues and moral development throughout his work, especially in regard to the shadow, and all of the above writers place individuation at the heart of their consideration of ethics.

It may be, as Robinson (2005) also suggests, that Jung's 'psycho-cartography', the kind of mapping set out in the last chapter, is so alluring that most writers are still exploring the scope and nature of his thinking about the human interior. As the necessity of working with the shadow is suggested as the first step in developing an ethical attitude, the lack of attention to Jung as an ethicist does seem remarkable. There is of course a great deal in Jung and those who study his writing about the nature of Good and Evil (such as his famous/infamous *Answer to Job*), some of which is mentioned in this chapter, though it does not focus on theological debates. The literature also gives considerable attention to the ethics of psychotherapy, a difficult subject for many Jungian analysts, not least because of Jung's sexual relations with several female patients, as Robinson (2005) points out. While psychologists may have been reluctant to enter philosophical territory (though Amir, 2005, suggests they have commandeered it) the emerging field of moral psychology, which synthesizes both fields, may be the rightful home of this discussion. Beebe (1998: 54) describes moral psychology as reviving 'moral philosophy from its nearly moribund state … with a new insistence on psychological realism in philosophical discourse about morality'. While the terminology is not clear (this approach is also sometimes seen as critical psychology) and is not relevant here, it is interesting to note that the borders between philosophy and psychology are as permeable as earlier chapters found between sociology and psychology. Again, I am seeking to expand socio-cultural approaches to include Jungian insights, here regarding ethics.

Jungian concepts of morality and ethics

As with so much in Jungian psychology, even the terms 'morality' and 'ethics' are contested. Solomon (2000) and Robinson (2005) both highlight Jung's distinction between morality and ethics; he saw the former as belonging to the collective social norms (as in *mores*) where the ethical struggle involves separating from received wisdom in order to form a deeper ethical attitude. Codes are thus expressions of the dominant historical and cultural forces, the 'shoulds' and 'oughts' based in 'moral reaction'; Jung seems to see society as innately conservative and repressive (though this may be a biographical rather than a sociological observation). According to Samuels (1985: 61) 'Jung thought that ethics and morality are innate but that the individual has to free himself from the collective norms to experience this'. Like Nietzsche, Jung rejects the 'performance' of morals and refers back to classical ethics and Gnosticism, in which morality was intrinsic rather than extrinsic (CW10/ 167–70). Jung distinguishes between morality and ethics, suggesting that the former relies on rules and codes, while the latter is 'reflective … subject to conscious scrutiny' and is engaged when 'a fundamental conflict arises between two possible modes of moral behaviour' (CW10/855). Solomon develops this into the notion of the 'ethical attitude', achieved 'through judgement, discernment and conscious struggle, often between conflicting rights or duties' (Solomon, 2001: 191). Samuels (1989: 197), however, suggests that Jung's use of the term 'ethic' to indicate personal or inner conscience is idiosyncratic, as 'ethics' is often used in philosophy to mean the wider discussion of moral codes; however, he agrees that the distinction between social norms and personal values is important. Samuels

(1989) offers an alternative distinction between moral imagination and original morality, the former a dialogic, almost experimental, way of looking at morality; the latter offering a more grounded but less reflective perspective. Samuels (1989:199) also illustrates how social morality can be used to fuel shadow dynamics:

> If we ask ourselves what it is that enables such shadow projections to occur and be effective, we have to posit some hypothetical force such as original morality. For *something* enables me to take the superior position in relation to you, leaving you smelling of my shit. It's the judgmental flavour of shadow projections that gives them their power and this may be laid at the door of original morality. In its isolated, 'pure' form, original morality has helped to create our divided world, slouching towards apocalypse.

This helps elucidate Jung's view of the pernicious aspects of social *mores*, reflected in his views about society (below). The emphasis is on ethics as struggle, as an approach wrestled from competing impulses, something social morality absolutely avoids.

> Jung distinguishes the moral code from the conscience. The moral code is a human institution, while conscience is the reaction of the unconscious ... in the case of the ethical conscience, the unconscious places one in a dilemma where one is forced to choose between incompatible duties. In this case, Jung believes one's moral duty is to suffer the conflict to the end, without trying to escape, in the hope that it will activate the transcendent function.
>
> (Proulx, 1994: 114–15)

Here the futility of decision boxes and purely rational ethics is exposed: instead of leaping to 'fix' an ethical problem, Jung asks us to stay with it, to savour it in all its complexity. As Proulx (1994: 110) makes clear, real ethical decisions cluster around the *conflict* between received wisdom and personal ethics, a painful configuration:

> He did not put faith in any set of moral rules which could be valid in all cases. 'We do not reach a solution in principle as to how we should always act. To want one is wrong' (Jung 1959: 462). In fact, he expected one to experience the ethical problem at the exact moment when his/her prevailing set of rules proved to be lacking. In his mind, ethics always resulted from conflicts of duties. His notion of conscience, and his distinction between what is moral and what is ethical, contain the theoretical basis he needed to explain this particular view of ethics.

Proulx criticises this reliance on conflict as the catalyst for ethics, but it seems she has interpreted conflict as 'moral catastrophe', though these unpleasant connotations are largely absent from Jung's concepts of holding opposing forces in balance. To be 'in' the conflict is to be caught in dualism, taking sides; the skill lies in stepping outside the war zone without losing contact with feelings, intuition, senses or intellect in order to comprehend the range of impulses or forces. A Jungian approach encourages familiarity with one's psychic landscape, so that contradictions and conflicts are no longer overwhelming. Again, this requires a move away from the right/wrong absolutism of much traditional Western, particularly Christian, ethical assumptions.

Becker (2004) and D.W. Robinson (2005) both explore Jung's ideas of conscience, which he saw as one's own inner 'voice of God'. Robinson finds that 'Jung's theory of conscience, despite complexities in his own presentation and distorted readings of him by advocates and detractors alike, is sound and significant' (2005: 6). Robinson characterizes western approaches to conscience as either 'traditional' or 'profane': the former is attributed to the word of God, that is, placing personal inclination in the wider moral order; while the latter is 'severed from its sacred roots' (2005: 12), located in family, culture and social norms, as subjective and relativist. Robinson suggests that Jung's approach is superior 'for addressing the needs of the current moral climate' (2005: 13). Becker addresses similar issues, identifying the key schism between those moral philosophers who hold that human beings have an innate ethical response and those who believe that only institutions of justice and law can impose ethical standards (2004: 27). She also cites Edward O. Wilson's (1998) discussion of ethics either as human constructs (the empirical approach) or located in some transcendental relationship to consciousness, the former appealing to the mind, the latter to the heart. While the transcendental is clearly central to a Jungian ethic, Robinson (2005: 91) notes that this is complicated by other aspects of Jungian thought:

> the task of distinguishing between psychological observation from ethical evaluation is complicated by the fact that for Jung the realm of ethical values was in a complex – in fact inseparable from – relationship with the psychic sphere ... Psyche is thus both *means* and, often, the *end* for the realization of moral goods.

Robinson suggests that Jung's consultation with the inner voice – a process that may not yield instant results – allows a third way to emerge between the rational processes of decision-making and the emotional drives of desire and self-interest. This *experience* of ethics can be contrasted with the emphasis on rational evaluation of choices that is the hallmark of most post-Enlightenment ethics (see Chapter 4); it is a new contribution to western thinking, with Eastern origins, as is explored below. Beebe (1992: 23) also highlights the importance of the feeling aspect of consciousness and Jung's novel distinction between feeling and emotion:

> This recognition that feeling-understanding is as rational in its aim and design as thinking-understanding was a landmark in the history of thought, a break with tradition, because philosophy had always confused feeling with emotion,

denying it the status of reason and mistaking it, in a misapplied compliment to the feeling function, for the affective influence of the irrational.

This ability to combine thought and feeling allows the conflict of duties to which Proulx refers above not only to be withstood but to provide a space for reflection and growth. The discussion below on working with shadow attests both to the discomforts and rewards which this process involves, at the heart of a Jungian ethic.

It is worth touching on relational ethics, which is explored by Solomon from the Jungian developmental school (sketched in Chapter 6), which draws on Klein, Bion and Winnicott's theories on object-relations to emphasize that the self is not ethical in a vacuum; it requires internal relations with shadow and other aspects of personality as well as external relations with other humans and society as a whole. As Solomon (2001:446). puts it 'the teleological project of the self to acquire wholeness requires the withdrawal of projections and the integration of their contents'. This idea has resonance with Buber's (1957) emphasis on the I–Thou relationship (in which the other is a moral subject) as the cornerstone of ethics, though Bauman (1993) critiques this as depending on commonality of situation and therefore contingent on circumstances. Robinson (2005) notes that Jung strongly rejected Buber's position as reliant on a shared and particularly Christian view of God as a unifying force, without due recognition of cultural and religious differences. Robinson places the Jungian conscience as moving between the extremes of the objectification of human experience on the one hand, leading to alienation and reductionism, and subjectivism on the other, in which the individualised experience ceases to search for commonality with others. Jung's idea of other is closer to an element of oneself, a reflection of some aspect of the human potential, and so, not contingent on circumstances, though circumstances may raise these issues into consciousness. There is a danger here, as Beebe (1998: 56) points out, that this view of the other can come to seem narcissistic, as if the external world is mere projection, but as Solomon says, and as was considered in the previous chapter, the withdrawal of projections involves a move *away* from a narcissistic relation with the world towards one in which self and others are seen with more compassion in all their confusion and complexity. It is a continuing ethical struggle that involves closeness, separation and differentiation between self and others (Solomon, 2001: 452). As also suggested in the previous chapter, Jung's sense of the development of the psyche is seen as whole-life process and it is the ethical implications of this which the next section explores, echoing Solomon's statement that 'a Jungian approach to understanding how the self may achieve an ethical attitude can be located within the context of the unfolding of the self over the stages of an entire life' (2000: 198).

Individuation as an ethical process

This journey is described by many writers (Stein, 1997; 1998; Stevens, 2002; Storr, 1999) and was outlined in the last chapter. Here Lydia Amir, a philosopher, considers individuation as an ethical process, summarizing Jung's (CW16) description of individuation as a process of four stages:

1   An acknowledgement of precisely the fallibility, vulnerability, and dependence that is an integral part of the strange openness we experience in our emotional lives and a source of the power which the relevant passions can exert over us. It is only by giving up, in the first instance, our pretensions to rational control that we open the way for a deeper, transformed, self-understanding.

2   ...To acknowledge the shortcomings of the human condition (shortcomings from the perspective of an ideal of pure rational control) need not lead to self-abasement or despair ... This is the beginning of true morality, a morality which is free from sentimentality and illusion ...

3   ...The process of moral reconstruction ... this stage involves an appeal to the patient's desire to resume control over his moral destiny.

4   The fourth and 'final' stage of the transformational process can never represent some ultimate phase where the human psyche has 'arrived' at an equilibrium state ... The process of transformation is not the imposition of an externally devised 'cure', but rather the realization of a dynamic, two-way process.

(Amir, 2005: 45–6)

Amir sees this process as a foundation for ethics, noting the move away from rationality as the arbiter of the 'good', which

gives up many of the traditional assumptions about the straightforward authority of reason in determining the good life. But for all that, its continuity with the traditional ethical project is shown by the fact that it offers a way of pursuing the ancient question 'how should I live' in a manner consistent with the equally ancient injunction 'know thyself'.

(2005: 46)

Individuation has been described as a recurring 'night sea journey' (Jacobi, 1967) and a 'labyrinthine spiral' (Whitmont, 1978), with the ego moving through phases towards wholeness. Hart, who studied with Jung, describes individuation as 'a spiritual undertaking ... the conscious response to ... an innate and powerful drive toward spiritual realisation and ultimate meaning' (1997: 99). This places Jung as a teleological thinker, who looks forward to some kind of realization and considers ethical development over a whole human life not just the pre-adult stages (Papadopoulos, 2006; Solomon, 2000).

If human beings have an innate capacity to behave both individually and in groups in recognisably ethical ways ... then we can say that embedded in the human psyche are templates or deep structures that correspond to moral intent, shaping thoughts, feelings and our ethical behaviour accordingly.

(Solomon, 2000: 199)

Central to this ethical development, as Solomon points out, is the struggle between the shadow and the persona, which is explored more fully below. It is important to remember the limitations of this journey: Beebe (1998) alerts the romantic (analyst as well as analysand) to the danger of fantasising that the shadow can be finally integrated let alone vanquished – it is a constant and, like other archetypes, is connected through the individual to the collective and unchanging unconscious. This is echoed by Hauke's admonitions on the 'fantasy of wholeness' (2005: 81) as the unconscious cannot be made wholly conscious. Nevertheless, these writers agree that reclaiming projections and building a relationship with the shadow in the psyche is the first step in developing an ethical attitude. Not that this task should be underestimated. Hart (1997) describes working with a middle-aged man who experienced himself as a victim of others' abuse and neglect so was appalled to find himself overwhelmed by the urge to kill an innocent stranger, an event followed by a dream that illustrated both the dangerous animal within and the calm, regulating self that kept it under control. The man was able to acknowledge his fear of his own aggression, which he had previously blamed on other people, and to realize that a power within had the 'capacity to contain and control psychic life' (Hart, 1997: 99). As Samuels (1985: 65) points out, 'There is a compelling moral aspect to integration of the shadow: to unblock personal and communal relationship and also to admit the inadmissible, yet human'. Jung (CW9ii/13–14) says,

> the Shadow is a moral problem that challenges the whole ego-personality, for no one can become conscious of the shadow without considerable moral effort. To become conscious of it involves recognising the dark aspect of the personality as present and real. This act is the essential condition for self-knowledge and it therefore, as a rule, meets with considerable resistance.

As Jung suggests, the acceptance of one's own humanity has a cataclysmic effect on relations with others, who suddenly become human amongst humans where once they would have merely been Wrong. In comprehending one's own flaws, Jung (CW10/104) argues that one comes to understand the frailty of human morality in oneself and the other, generating compassion, modesty, love of neighbour and other ethical responses. This is the cornerstone of a new ethic. One moment of revelation in my thirties was realising how rude I'd been to the colleague walking towards me, but instead of berating me he asked how I was. I mumbled something about the incident and he commented on how tired I seemed. In a Joycean epiphany I realized he had been kinder to me than I would ever have been to him – and, importantly, than I would ever have been to myself. He demonstrated an ethical attitude I could barely comprehend, for all my commitment to doing (being) right.

The next section examines working with the shadow more closely, as the first step towards ethical responsibility.

Working with the shadow

Samuels (1998) and others emphasize the withdrawal of projections and engagement with the shadow as the primary means of 'owning' oneself, and this is the most common description of the task of individuation. There are also other requirements involving building relations with a full range of archetypes, especially anima (in men) and animus (in women), which are not explored here. Leading Jungian analyst and scholar John Beebe (1992), however, explains individuation in terms of building internal relations with all the compass points of Jung's psychological types (see previous chapter). Here, the underdeveloped function-attitudes can be seen as shadow or compensatory aspects for the more publically accepted or persona qualities. Jung describes how superior and inferior function-attitudes will have emerged over time; the task of individuation is to connect with the normally disregarded functions and attitudes or with their shadow aspects.

> I have spent many years pursuing the implications of this theory, and I am sure Jung means that a psychologically developed individual will have a differentiated self-knowledge that includes all four kinds of intelligence—a feeling, a thinking, an intuitive, and a sensation awareness.
>
> (Beebe, 1992: 17)

These two positions are not mutually exclusive, but merely reflect different emphases: after all, the 'inferior' or underdeveloped dimensions of the psychological type are likely to hold the shadow aspects, the dominant or 'superior' aspects will be lodged in the persona, as Stevens (2001) elucidates. Both stress that the purpose is the integration of neglected aspects of the self to realize its wholeness, consciously. And both involve the conjunction of opposites, a central theme of Jung's approach to the psyche, as discussed in the previous chapter. To reverse my core argument: if wholeness is a foundation for ethics, then partial, idealized self-images cannot be.

But, as Whitmont (1969/1991: 15) points out: 'Recognition of the shadow can bring about very marked effects on the conscious personality. The very notion that the other person's evil could be pointing at oneself carries shock effects of varying degrees, depending on the strength of one's ethical and moral convictions'.

Refusal to face the shadow can lead, Whitmont suggests, to acute isolation: 'instead of a real relation to the surrounding world there is only an illusory one, for we relate not to the world as it is but to the "evil wicked world" which our shadow projection shows us' (1969/1991: 17). Of course, this may still appear preferable to psychic change. Stevens (2001: 66) helps explain why:

> Not only do we repress the shadow in the personal unconscious, but we deny its existence in ourselves, and project it out on to others. This is done quite unconsciously: we are not aware that we do it. It is an act of ego-preservation which enables us to deny our own 'badness' and to attribute it to others, whom we then hold responsible for it. It explains the ubiquitous practice of

scapegoating and underlies all kinds of prejudice against people belonging to identifiable groups other than our own.

Nevertheless, for those willing to look into the darkness, the rewards are considerable, as the shadow also contains that which can release the individual from the constraints of their ego drives. 'It is not until we have truly been shocked into seeing ourselves as we really are, instead of as we wish or hopefully assume we are, that we can take the first step towards individuality', comments Whitmont (1969/1991: 16). Beebe (1992: 35) offers insight to the experience of working with his shadow:

> The decision to approach the shadow involves anxiety, doubt, shame, and a desire to repair the relationship with an other whose needs I have somehow missed. My recognition of the need to look at shadow starts with a painfulness, a stoppage, an absence of the sense of well-being, and an agitation from within to feel okay again. Or I can be feeling too good, and suddenly realise that I am secretly afraid. I think these are symptoms of integrity.

Stevens (2001: 67) also outlines the difficulties and rewards of working with the shadow, highlighting the moral and societal implications:

> The most demanding part of a Jungian analysis occurs when the analysand (the person undergoing analysis) begins to confront his own shadow. That this should be difficult is not surprising since the whole shadow complex is tinged with feelings of guilt and unworthiness, and with fears of rejection should its true nature be discovered or exposed. However painful the process may be, it is necessary to persevere because much Self potential and instinctive energy is locked away in the shadow and therefore unavailable to the total personality ... To own one's shadow is to become responsible for it, so that one's morality is less blind and less compulsive, and ethical choices become possible. Shadow consciousness is important not only for personal development, therefore, but as a basis for greater social harmony and international understanding.

This stresses the connection between working with the shadow and developing ethical modes of being, Like the other authors cited, I am arguing for engagement with the shadow in individuals and in groups – such as professions – as the foundation for depth ethics, an 'ethical attitude' as Solomon (2000: 198) calls it. As the next chapter explores, this offers an alternative ethical pathway to the promotional reliance on codes and compliance.

Many Jungian writers suggest means of access to the shadow but these are nearly all aimed at individuals; the implications for collectives will be considered later. One writer (Miller, 1989/1991) suggests a range of tactics for accessing the shadow, such as soliciting feedback from others, examining projections, slips, faux pas, and use of humour as well as consulting dreams and daydreams. He, like many others, some of whom are explored below, is clear that this is a process that can be undertaken outside the therapeutic relationship. Some, like Hede (2007), take the concepts of shadow dynamics into workplaces and organizations so as to better understand and engage with forces operating in society generally, as well as within individuals. Hede (2007) draws on both Jung and Goleman's (2004) work on emotional intelligence to suggest some mechanisms for managing shadow projections in the workplace, such as identifying common emotional triggers and constructing protocols for managing emotional reactivity. Groups are encouraged to take responsibility for their inner-awareness and resist becoming overwhelmed by shadow material. This will be considered again later in the context of professions. The next three sections look at the rewards of integrating shadow elements, bringing the opposites together in a new wholeness, at the individual (micro), societal (macro) and finally professional (meso) levels.

Wholeness, opposites and integrity – micro-level ethics

Much of the earlier discussion in this chapter has been about bringing unconscious materials to consciousness. Central to this process is the union of opposites, as was discussed briefly in the previous chapter, and is illustrated by the desire to generate dialogue between persona and shadow. When this approach is applied to moral issues, the challenge to western thought becomes obvious. Jung, like Nietzsche, rejected the either/or, good/bad morality of the church:

> We must beware of thinking of good and evil as absolute opposites. The criterion of ethical action can no longer consist in the simple view that good has the force of a categorical imperative, while so-called evil can resolutely be shunned. Recognition of the reality of evil necessarily relativises the good, and the evil likewise, converting both into halves of the paradoxical whole.
>
> (Jung *et al.*, 1963: 361)

Amir (2005: 46) criticizes Jung for basing his ethics on Aristotle and Nietzsche rather than a wider range of theorists, concluding that 'while a philosopher is able to present various normative theories of morality with their pros and cons, the Jungian psychoanalyst is committed, for no good reasons, to a non-pluralistic view of morality'. Yet this suggests that Jung was rigidly applying these theories rather than drawing on their insights to construct an ethic founded in the (expanded) consciousness of the individual psyche, therefore infinitely plural. A Jungian ethic cannot be prescriptive: he is clear that what might be ethically appropriate for one person would be damaging for another. Proulx comments that Jung rejected western culture's preference for objective criteria by which to judge the ethics of actions, arguing that any answer to the ethical problem could only be subjectively valid, and that it should 'stress a person's convictions, not his/her actions' (1994: 105). However, she notes that this raises the issue of subjectivism:

> The fear of the consequences of moral subjectivism makes it difficult for a lot of thinkers to examine seriously the hypothesis that a moral judgement is only the subjective judgement of an individual, a judgement that can make no claim to universal validity.
>
> (Proulx, 1994: 106)

But, for Jung, the purpose of understanding one's own shadow is not to treat all actions as morally equal but to step outside the narrow considerations of ego and persona to envision the greater potential for behaving according to higher/deeper principles. An ethical subjectivism located in the ego is likely to produce radically different behaviour than one based in the self, and Proulx seems not to make that distinction. One outcome of this process, according to Beebe (1992: 35), is integrity: 'What *can* individuate out of a person's character is integrity, that accountability for the impact of the self upon others which makes the work on the rest of character – recognizing it, allowing for it, compensating for it, training it – possible.

This integrity emerges directly from the process of individuation, linking ethics with recognition of the shadow:

> An initial stage is denial that there is shadow … a turning-point stage is the acceptance of shadow; a final stage is a sense of restored wholeness once the 'full disclosure' of the shadow has been integrated. I believe this to be a dialectic of integrity, proceeding through the shadow.
>
> (Beebe, 1992: 61)

Beebe also links integrity to moral responsibility: 'It is the function of integrity to remember our obligation to this other, and anxiety reminds us that we have an obligation to the obligation' (1992: 33–4). Later, he adds: 'Integrity is the paradoxical combination of vulnerability and confidence that makes work on character possible' (1998: 61).

The process of individuation involves a shift away from the ego-centred, will-driven aspects of personality to expand into a more profound relationship with oneself and others that offers a basis for an ethical 'style of living'. Here, Solomon is describing the therapeutic relationship, but it has wider implications: 'The ethical attitude develops, personally and professionally, through the self progressing from a narcissistic mode of relating' (2000: 204). What is crucial to this process is that it takes place within a transcendent framework, namely within a context that is greater and more significant than the personal ego and which allows the psyche to see itself from a new perspective. As was seen in the last chapter, it is also the container of opposites, a forum not for the *removal* of opposition but where conflict can be held. In the context of ethics, Jung also sees this as the source of conscience:

> There is scarcely any psychic phenomenon that shows the polarity of the psyche in a clearer light than conscience. Its undoubted dynamism, in order to

be understood at all, can only be explained in terms of energy, that is, as a potential based on opposites. Conscience brings these ever-present and necessary opposites to conscious perception.

(CW 10, cited in Robinson, 2005: 158).

The next section places Jungian ethics in a broader philosophical context, exploring his sources and antecedents; the next chapter relates these ideas forward to approaches to professional ethics.

Amir (2005) conducts a very interesting survey of different psychological approaches (Freudian, Jungian, humanistic, and developmental psychology) to identify problems with their underlying moral philosophy. She argues that psychological concepts of mental health and dysfunction or balance have replaced older terms of morality such as virtues and vices, but that these concepts lack philosophical depth, and those applying them in practice lack philosophical qualifications for the task. Amir (2005) concedes that, while she finds Jung's choice of ethical theorists arbitrary (she claims they were Aristotle and Nietzsche, though others would disagree), his approach to morality is sensitive and non-reductive, and, importantly, that depth psychology has insights that are relevant outside the therapeutic relationship, to reach the 'wider territory of philosophical ethics' (2005: 46). Another philosopher scrutinizing psychological theory is Proulx (1994), who places Jung's ethics in the counter-enlightenment position set out by Nietzsche, by his rejection of rationality as the primary instrument for assessing ethics. She therefore claims that Jung takes a position against Kant, though he described himself as a Kantian (Douglas, 1997). For example, his youthful reading of Kant's *ding-in-such*, thing-in-itself, left him 'thunderstruck' (Jarrett, 1999: 194) and influenced his concepts on the timeless reality of archetypes. Douglas (1997) notes that, despite radically different approaches to phenomena, Kant emphasizes, as does Jung, the necessity of a transcendent framework for moral and ethical struggle. Others have also commented on the connection between Jung's archetypes and Kant's sense of innate or *a priori* dispositions (Amir, 2005). Proulx's and Amir's contributions as ethical philosophers are unusual in engaging with Jungian ideas; most of the literature on ethics excludes Jung and, as Solomon (2000; 2001) and Robinson (2005) have noted, there is surprisingly little engagement with ethical literature from Jungians. Beebe (1998: 54) critiques depth psychology for its reluctance to engage with the wider debates of moral psychology, which he finds highly pertinent to the theory and practice of Jungian analysis:

Moral psychology has rebounded with a new insistence on psychological realism in philosophical discourse about morality. It inquires of literature, history, psychoanalysis, sociology, feminism, and ethnic studies what people are really like, examining differing notions of good and exploring diverse lures to self-deception. It has taken up anew the effort to examine what might foster a healthier moral development in a world that calls out to be treated more justly, more fairly, and more carefully.

One of the interesting aspects of a Jungian approach to ethics is that it moves away from ethics as an 'ought' by rejecting the good/bad dualism of traditional Western approaches, suggesting the possibility of non-normative ethics. In many ways, Jung's approach to ethics, implicit and explicit, is closer to classical Asian responses, including Taoist and Zen ethical attitudes. These linkages are not of course surprising given Jung's extensive reading in Asian literature, his involvement with the first publication in the West of the *I Ching* and other interests, outlined earlier, in Hinduism and Tao. His book *Psychological Types* (CW6) 'reveals extensive knowledge of Hindu and Taoist primary and secondary texts and incorporates their understanding about the interplay of opposites' (Douglas, 1997: 28). The parallels between Eastern approaches to the development of the self and the Jungian concept of individuation as part of a second-half of life journey can be seen in the following quote from Kupperman's (1999: 18) *Learning from Asian Philosophy*:

> The notion of a reflective phase of development that leads to a second nature is absolutely central to most classical Asian philosophies, as represented in such works as ... the Upanishads, the Bhagavad Gita, most early Buddhist texts, and the Analects of Confucius. A good example, portrayed in mythic terms, is found in the Katha Upanishad (Upanishads, 55–66). Nachiketas, dissatisfied with his father's attitudes, is consigned to the kingdom of death, where it is revealed to him (before he returns to life) that the inner nature of the individual is identical with the divine reality of the entire universe. This revelation makes death seem quite different and calls for a different orientation in one's life. Nachiketas is then on his way toward becoming a different person.

(Interestingly, despite the closeness of theme between Kupperman's thesis on Asian approaches to ethics and the psychology of the self, there is no mention of Jung in the index; Aristotle and Confucius are the preferred philosophers here.) It is this 'different person' who embodies the ethical relationship with self and others, a transformation effected through the process of integrating aspects of the shadow (metaphorically represented in this and other stories as the descent into the underworld) and re-merging with a new relationship between the conscious and unconscious. As Jung puts it in his forward to Neumann (1949/1990), the ethical relates to how one '[brings] the conscious and the unconscious into responsible relationship' (1949/1990: 15). Kupperman (1993: 3) argues that the formation of the self is seen as an ethical problem in many Asian traditions (noting that it receives little attention in the west), as is the issue of the fluidity of the self, the 'problem of how it can be consistent with a stable persona'. Most of the ethical approaches outlined in Chapter 4 make assumptions about the coherence and consistency of the ethical decision-maker, whatever his/her ethical approach, the exceptions being feminist and postmodern ethicists (see next chapter). For Jung, the fluidity and realization of the self is central to becoming an ethical being, as the quote above suggests. Moreover, Loy's (1999) chapter on Asian and Jungian ethics describes

Taoist and Buddhist ethics as shifting from the vertical axis, where hierarchy reflects status and power, to a horizontal axis 'all being citizens of the great commonwealth that is the natural world' (1999: 87). This shift from the vertical whereby ethical responsibility is shifted up or down hierarchies to the horizontal helps illustrate the arguments in this book. The horizontal axis offers a kind of transcendence without a deity, as is found in Taoist and Buddhist ethics, embracing all aspects of creation.

The next question is: can this ethical development take place in groups?

The Jungian individual and society – macro-level ethics

Jung's emphasis on the internal working of the psyche has led to criticisms that he failed to engage with wider social issues or even to place individuals in a social context, except in encouraging them to separate from the social norms. Singer and Kimbles (2004: 4) note that Jung tended to set the individual against the group, rather than exploring the internal dynamics of the group, perhaps reflecting his own introversion:

> Living in 'the collective' is most easily seen by Jungians as monstrous and magically destructive. In the Jungian tradition (as in the more general Western tradition), the individual has been given the heroic task of slaying the group's devouring hold on him or her.

As Singer and Kimbles suggest, Jung's writing about society tends to use pejorative terms such as 'common herd', 'mass man' (CW10/148–96) and so on. Jung is concerned with the individual above all: 'The great events of world history are ... profoundly unimportant ... the essential thing is the life of the individual' (CW10/315). Gatherings are often seen as traumatic: 'The change of character that is brought about by the uprush of collective forces is amazing. A gentle and reasonable being can be transformed into a maniac or a savage beast' (Jung, 1938:16). But this is not an entirely anti-social view, as Jung's belief is that the unexamined unconscious is then projected outwards, leading to confrontation, war and catastrophe (Tacey, 2006:61). As Jung puts it in *Psychological Types*:

> It is obvious that a social group consisting of stunted individuals cannot be a healthy and viable institution ... As the individual is not just a single, separate being, but by his very existence presupposes a collective relationship, it follows that the process of individuation must lead to more intense and broader collective relationships and not to isolation.
>
> (CW6/758)

As Proulx (1994: 103) writes, 'Jung was interested in developing a new *Weltanschauung*, a new global picture of the world that could replace the old medieval one that had collapsed in the last few centuries'. However, she is critical of a tendency to moral elitism, with individuation reserved for the morally superior, a point shared by Robinson (2005), though he stresses that the choices are in the hands of individuals not elite groups. While individuation will not be attractive to or suitable for all (especially those with weak egos who become overwhelmed if shadow material is raised precipitously), it is *available* to all as a fundamental human process. The connection to Alcoholics Anonymous, noted earlier, also suggests that this is a process that can be enacted regardless of class or education, given sufficient motivation or, indeed, desperation.

Another criticism, voiced by Stevens (1990), suggests that Jung's concept of individuation is too closely bound in his own experience and too detached from social concerns. Post-Jungian writing is not so constrained and the question of Jung's relationship to societal dynamics is explored by many writers, including Jones (2007), who contrasts Jung's view of society with that of G.H. Mead (1934). Jones (2007: 92) suggests that Jungian engagement with society is primarily through projection: 'We need other people in order to see our own self – but we need them, instrumentally'. Her view is reinforced by Jung's statement that

> [i]ndividuation means precisely the better and more complete fulfilment of the collective qualities of the human being, since adequate consideration of the peculiarity of the individual is more conducive to a better social performance than when the peculiarity is neglected or suppressed.
>
> (CW 7/267)

While this indicates a sense of the individual in society, the latter plays the role of audience rather than co-creator. Unlike Mead's view, we do not learn who we are from those around us but from engagement with inner aspects of the self. This has bearings on the sense of an ethic, explored below, where the 'other' is often seen as central to ethical understanding. Although many note that Jung's schema is intended to be consistent across micro and macrocosms and that he applies archetypal concepts to groups and nations in his writing, Jones considers there to be a false premise in extrapolating from individual to group dynamics. Andrew Samuels (1993), who has been particularly influential in his writing on the applicability of Jung's ideas to political, social and economic matters, finds another problem in treating political issues as clinical matters, without challenging the external context or causes of alienation. He also critiques the use of the developmental metaphor from the individual to the collective, with its implications of linear progress, and it is worth remembering here the dangers of substituting a Jungian positivism for the somewhat discredited modernist concept. A further danger in individuation as a social or ethical driver is raised by Beebe (1998: 56), who warns that the emphasis on individuation in depth psychology can lead to self-absorption: 'Jungian work sometimes tilts the moral balance between self and other in such a way that the self comes to seem more important than the other. This is sometimes spoken of as the narcissistic use of psychotherapy.'

As always with writing about Jung, there are many voices. While conscious of the pitfalls outlined above, I am drawn to those who see Jung as always looking for the commonalities in human experience, the connective tissues, placing him in the hermeneutic tradition of Heidegger and Riceour (Brooke, 2009; Hauke, 2005). Just as the goal of individuation in the person is connectivity, so it is in groups, as Hauke (2005) suggests. Beneath the sociology of difference lies something shared, residing in the collective unconscious and rising from time to time, place to place, person to person, group to group, to demonstrate universal human themes, shaped by personal and cultural variations, many of which Jung wrote about in his travels in Europe and Africa. Like his contemporaries Weber and Durkheim, Jung expresses concern at Western social and political movements and trends, particularly the loss of collective values and the fragmentation and rationalization that dominated much of the last century, and urges greater engagement with collective issues. The next section looks at these global issues from a Jungian perspective before returning to groups and cultural dynamics in organizations.

This wider, deeper, view of the contribution of a Jungian ethic to the world is endorsed by Jung's former protégé Erich Neumann, who wrote *Depth Psychology and a New Ethic* in 1949 in Israel, where he had moved in the aftermath of the Holocaust. The book was written at speed and with passion, and has a cool introduction by Jung, who stresses the importance of confrontation with the unconscious as an ethical issue:

> The problem is indeed a vital one. This may explain why the question of a new ethic is of such serious and urgent concern to the author, who argues his case with a boldness and passion well matched by his penetrating insight and thoughtfulness.
>
> (1949/1990: 18)

Robinson's (2005) critique of the book may explain Jung's apparent caution in endorsing the book, as he finds that Neumann simplifies the role of conscience and its individuated 'Voice' in the collective, without considering how such a collective might produce far-from-ethical results. Neumann describes the old ethic as requiring either the repression, through denial and projection, or the suppression, through self-denial and sacrifice, of the personal and collective shadow. He ascribes the first response to the 'masses'; the second to an ascetic 'elite'. In either event, the effect is a division between actual behaviour and declared standards; indeed the higher the bar is raised, the greater the danger of this split leading to collective scapegoating of others, as occurred in Nazi Germany: 'The old ethic demands suppression and sacrifice and … does not consider the condition of the psyche or whole personality, but contents itself with the ethical attitude of the conscious mind … (which) encourages an illusory form of ethics' (Neumann, 1949/1990: 74).

Neumann's 'new ethic' is based on Jungian acceptance of the separated sections of the psyche as one's own, both individually and collectively: the aim is not to be good but to be psychologically autonomous. 'The new ethic rejects the hegemony of a partial structure of the personality and postulates the total personality as the basis for ethical conduct' (Neumann, 1949/1990: 92). There is also discussion of how such a shift might occur, and here there are problems, such as the reliance on 'superior individuals' who will effect their own inner changes and lead the 'inferior' masses. A hierarchical approach to individual development runs through the book and this may explain the hostile reception it received on publication, according to Yandell (1990). It is interesting that while Neumann's other works (e.g. *The Great Mother*, 1955 and *The Origins and History of Consciousness*, 1954) continue to play a major part in Jungian and post-Jungian studies, this book has received little attention in recent writing on Jungian ethics, with the exception of Becker (2004). Despite its problems, Neumann helps elucidate an ethic based on wholeness rather than partial, idealized goodness; particularly regarding the collective projection or scapegoating of sections of society. Neumann was obviously referring to the Holocaust, but the demonization of groups of people such as Muslims or children, as well as persistent anti-Semitism, is clearly of current concern. It is also interesting that Neumann (1949/1990: 113) highlighted the ethical dangers of self-delusion: 'It may actually appear as if the principle of deception has taken the place occupied by evil in the old ethic ... the principle of truth in new ethics is bound up with the authenticity of the relationship between the ego and the unconscious'.

Given that I am suggesting that professional ethics are based on self-delusion, Neumann's ethical relationship with the unconscious is highly relevant. Neumann also demonstrates that Jungian ethics have resonance far beyond the therapeutic relationship. While Neumann's attempt to introduce a Jungian ethic to world politics was not successful in the mid-twentieth century, either in global events (or academe, given the paucity of references to Jungian thought in post-war ethical discussion), there is renewed interest in alternative approaches (not to be confused with New Age approaches, which continue the polarity of good/bad, and emphasize self-development rather than collective ethical engagement). In the following, Tacey is not responding to Neumann, but his comments help explain past resistance to Jungian ideas in contemporary culture:

> our entire age is now virtually 'allergic' to the idea of wholeness and balance, reading any attempt at unity as an undesirable 'imposition' of order. I believe we have to educate ourselves out of this postmodern complex, and re-experience the liberating and healing contribution of wholeness, by experiencing anew the powerful symbols of wholeness which are now almost banned from our postmodern vocabulary. Today we are still reacting against the oppressive unities of old, still rebelling against the religions and philo-sophies that grew corrupt under their own political weight and social power. In that sense we are not postmodern at all, but only most-modern, excited by fragmentation, plurality, bits and gaps. But the psyche or soul is not controlled by the laws of fashion, and it may be demanding a new experience of unity which our age is still unable to respond to.
>
> (Tacey, 1998: 231)

While other writers (Hauke, for example) would disagree with Tacey's character-ization of postmodernism, it seems to me that there is now a willingness, driven by the exhaustion of all other avenues, to embrace new idea, such as complexity, and that a Jungian ethic has something to offer twenty-first-century confusion, both in the field of professional ethics and beyond.

These linkages are not of course surprising given Jung's extensive reading in Asian literature, his involvement with the first publication in the West of the *I-Ching* and other interests, outlined earlier, in Hinduism and Tao, and they strengthen the case for a Jungian ethic making a contribution to discussion on global ethics. For example, Jung also criticizes the tendency of European culture to claim god-like qualities to itself: 'We have withdrawn gods from mountains and trees and animals but keep them in our newspapers and culture, convinced we know that some people are bad' (CW11/6–9), a quote which contains echoes of Weber's disenchantment and Durkheim's loss of the sacred in everyday life. These concerns are taken up by, among others, Schweiker (2004) in his book on global ethics, in which he explores the idea that humanity takes too much credit for its achievements and demonstrates not enough humility at its shortcomings. Jung's struggle to develop an inner ethic from the individual and collective psyche has much to offer, even if it is only sketched here. The general, socio-cultural implications of these ideas are considered in Chapters 8 and 10, with the intervening chapter examining PR ethics through this Jungian lens.

The cultural complex – meso-level ethics

So far this chapter has looked at Jungian ethics from an individual (micro) and global (macro) perspective; it now returns to the meso level of organizations, where professions can be located, as was established in earlier chapters. Here, the concept of the cultural complex is introduced to explain how individuation might manifest in groups, such as professions. Joseph Henderson (1990) is the writer most associated with exploring aspects of the Jungian collective, and his ideas have been extended by Singer and Kimbles (2004), who identify complexes within groups and organizations, operating between the level of the individual and the collective:

> As personal complexes emerge out of the level of the personal unconscious in their interaction with deeper levels of the psyche and early parental/familial relationships, cultural complexes can be thought of arising out the cultural unconscious as it interacts with both the archetypal and personal realms of the psyche and the broader outer world arena of schools, communities, media, and all the other forms of cultural and group life. As such, cultural complexes can be thought of as forming the essential components of an inner sociology. But this inner sociology does not claim to be objective or scientific in its description of different groups and classes of people.
>
> (2004: 4)

Singer and Kimbles claim that cultural complexes, like individual complexes, are 'repetitive, autonomous, resist consciousness, and collect experience that confirms their historical point of view' (2004: 6). This helps explain how organizational cultures develop and resist change, and the concept has gained currency in recent years, to understand the behaviours of large groups from organizations to nations, as will be explored more fully in the next chapter. I suggest that this is the key element of a Jungian socio-cultural approach and warrants further discussion here, as the concept plays a central part in imagining individuation as a new ethical foundation for professions.

As Singer and Kimbles (2004: 237) put it:

> A potential way of understanding the process of individuation in the group is to think of it as the gradual working through and integration of the group's core cultural complexes over its lifetime – which may be generation upon generation.

Such an approach explains how a group may develop defensive systems, such as 'false fronts', analogous to those found in individuals, strategies for deflecting self-awareness through denial and blame, for example (Singer, 2004). This response is evident in almost all groups suddenly under public spotlight, from church leaders defending the protection of abusers over the abused to politicians aggrieved when their long-standing expenses scams are revealed. The Leveson Inquiry into British journalism has seen the press squirming to defend its traditional role as upholder of truth in the face of political dissembling while answering charges of corruption and invasion of privacy. Perhaps they are not to be unduly blamed; it is as hard for groups as for individuals to acknowledge their own, previously hidden shadow materials:

> This dialectic is not an easy path for collectives. Neither has our collective psychology made it easy for individuals to take the path of embracing shame. Only recently, in fact, has psychology itself 'embraced shame' as a topic for sustained inquiry.
>
> (Beebe, 1992: 61)

So the observations made earlier about the difficulty of this path are amplified in collective defence mechanisms. Similar analyses have been made of organizations (e.g. Hede, 2007), suggesting that the division between persona and shadow in individuals is reflected in divisions between 'overt self' and shadow self in groups, which extend beyond the individual to influence group dynamics in the workplace. The relationship between these aspects is moderated by what Hede (2007: 27) terms the 'inner observer', though it is not clear why he does not use the terms 'persona', 'ego', 'shadow' and 'self', as these are the dynamics under scrutiny. Hede (2007: 27) goes on to describe how

> [i]n emotionally competent individuals, their inner observer gains consciousness over their shadow self and keeps it in a dormant state by maintaining awareness of its ever-present reality and its potential for engulfment of the overt self. For many people, however, their inner observer is unaware of and unable to manage their shadow self which when triggered, can erupt with emotional reactivity so as to engulf their overt self.

Hede uses Goleman's (2004) work on emotional intelligence (EI), to create a matrix of 'emotional competencies ... which have a bearing on managing the shadow group' (Hede, 2007: 35). These competences comprise self-awareness, self-management, social awareness and relationship management, and require high levels of EI, self-monitoring, and management of one's own and others' emotions to raise consciousness of shadow dynamics within a group. While the implication that shadow aspects of the group can be 'managed' to keep them dormant is somewhat at odds with Jungian thinking, it is interesting to see such ideas in management literature. Another example is the claim that organizational individuation constitutes a new theory of organizational culture (Feldman, 2004). This occurs at a social level and involves the integration of the 'other', as viewed both in terms of 'ethnicity, gender, and cultural/social background' and as the disavowed elements of the group (Feldman, 2004: 251). Feldman uses the work of Kimbles (2000) and Bion (1959) to analyse group dynamics, particularly Bion's distinction between the task-orientated, rational work group and the implicit bonds of shame, blame, denial and projection that congregate under this surface. Although Feldman does not directly address ethical issues, they are implicit in his approach, again illustrating how Jungian theory offers insights into organizations. Jungian psychology is also operationalized as a tool for addressing and healing organizational issues by Corlett and Pearson (2003), offering guidance for, among others, 'managerial leaders who are open to new ideas for improving the effectiveness of their organizations, democratizing the workplace and re-energizing their work processes' (2003: xv) by deploying what they call Jungian Organizational Theory. While Corlett and Pearson use psychological types as their main diagnostic instrument, Neville (2010) explores organizations through Jungian archetypes. Using Greek mythology as a typology, generating classifications such as the Eros organization, the Heracles organization and so on. This approach draws on cultural and organizational commentators Hofstede (1991) and Handy (1976, 1979), noting that the latter used four Greek gods (Zeus, Apollo, Dionysus and Athena) to classify organizations. Matthews (2002) even suggests that 'competition' can be considered as an archetype operating in organizations and capitalism generally, though none of the other archetypes suggested by Jung are abstract nouns. Interestingly, given the links found between Jung and contemporary writers, Matthews locates his reasoning in the similarities between Jungian and complexity theory.

While these examples illustrate the richness of Jung's ideas applied to organizations, none of the cited writers have looked at professions from this perspective, and in many ways it is Jungian analyst Guggenbühl-Craig (1972/1991) who comes closest to my argument in his analysis of the shadow side of healing professions, particularly physicians, priests and, of course, analysts. He describes how infatuation with images of healing or saving others can fuel darker figures, before discussing the shadow dynamics of the consulting room:

> The shadow of the false prophet accompanies the pastor or priest all his life. Sometimes it emerges into the outside world as a narrow sectarian or as a hated demagogue within the church's organisation. Sometimes it resides

within. The noble images of physician and clergyman are forever accompanied by the shadow figures of quack and false prophet.

(1972/1991: 111)

These examples illustrate the themes of cultural complexes, which, as Kimbles (2004: 186) points out,

> tend to be bipolar, so that when they are activated the group ego or the individual ego of a group member becomes identified with one part of the unconscious cultural complex, while the other part is projected out onto the suitable hook of another group or one of its members.

The possibility is thus created that professions may operate in such a dynamic, creating idealized self-images and projecting their shadow material onto others. The role of cultural complexes in professions is explored in the next chapter, but this introduction serves to illustrate that the ethical outcome that results from the individuation process is available to groups as well as individuals.

Conclusions

This chapter has explored Jungian and post-Jungian writing on ethics, morality, conscience and integrity to establish the basics of an ethic. It has shown how individuation can form the framework for an ethic, in which the task is to raise shadow elements to consciousness, so that the individual or group is aware of (at least some of) the impulses that may be determining behaviour. Jung sees this as a moral challenge, particularly in taking ownership of individual and collective characteristics and behaviours that were previously rejected or denied. This act alters the ethical relationship to others because they are no longer being made to carry projected shadow materials. Jungians also consider that the act of accepting the shadow is in itself transformative and that many long-standing issues fall away or come into perspective in the process of working with the shadow. While the full process of individuation involves building a relationship with all the key archetypal aspects of the self, for the purposes of this book, the act of engaging with shadow material is seen as the first step in the process of developing depth ethics for professions.

Note

1   All references to Jung cite the *Collected Works* and the relevant paragraph, not page.

References

Amir, L. B. (2005) Morality, psychology, philosophy. *Philosophical Practice, 1*(1): 43–57.
Bauman, Z. (1993) *Postmodern Ethics*. Oxford: Blackwell.
Becker, C. (2004) *The Heart of the Matter: individuation as an ethical process*. Brooklyn, NY: Chiron.

Beebe, J. (1992) *Integrity in Depth*. College Station, TX: Texas A&M University.

Beebe, J. (1998) Towards a Jungian analysis of character. In A. Casement (ed.) *Post-Jungians Today: key papers in analytical psychology*. London: Routledge, pp. 53–66

Bion, W. R. (1959) *Experiences in Groups, and Other Papers*. New York, NY: Basic Books.

Brooke, R. (2009) *Jung and Phenomenology*. Pittsburgh, PA: Trivium Publications.

Buber, M. (1957) *I and Thou*. R. G. Smith (trans.) New York, NY: Scribner.

Corlett, J. G. and Pearson, C. (2003) *Mapping the Organizational Psyche: a Jungian theory of organizational dynamics and change*. Gainesville, FL: Center for Applications of Psychological Type.

Douglas, C. (1997) The historical context of analytical psychology. In P. Young-Eisendrath and T. Dawson (eds) *The Cambridge Companion to Jung*. Cambridge: Cambridge University Press, pp. 17–34.

Feldman, B. (2004) Towards a theory of organizational culture: integrating the 'other' from a post-Jungian perspective. In T. Singer and S. L. Kimbles (eds) *The Cultural Complex: contemporary Jungian perspectives on psyche and society*. New York, NY: Brunner-Routledge, pp. 251–61.

Goleman, D. (2004) *Emotional Intelligence: why it can matter more than IQ*. London: Bloomsbury.

Guggenbuhl-Craig, A. (1972/1991) Quacks, charlatans and false prophets. In C. Zweig and J. Abrams (eds) *Meeting the Shadow: the hidden power of the dark side of human nature*. New York, NY: Tarcher/Penguin, pp. 110–16.

Handy, C. B. (1976) *Understanding Organizations*. Harmondsworth: Penguin Education.

Handy, C. B. (1979) *Gods of Management: how they work, and why they will fail*. London: Pan Books.

Hart, D. L. (1997) The classical Jungian school. In P. Young-Eisendrath and T. Dawson (eds) *The Cambridge Companion to Jung*. Cambridge: Cambridge University Press, pp. 89–100.

Hauke, C. (2005) *Human Being Human: culture and the soul*. London: Routledge.

Hede, A. (2007) The shadow group: towards an explanation of interpersonal conflict in work groups. *Journal of Managerial Psychology, 22*(1): 25–39.

Henderson, J. L. (1990) *Shadow and Self: selected papers in analytical psychology*. Wilmette, IL: Chiron.

Hofstede, G. (1991) *Cultures and Organizations: software of the mind*. London: McGraw-Hill.

Jacobi, J. (1967) *The Way of Individuation*. New York, NY: Meridian.

Jarrett, J. (1999) Schopenhauer and Jung. In P. Bishop (ed.) *Jung in Contexts: a reader*. London: Routledge, pp. 193–204.

Jones, R. A. (2007) *Jung, Psychology, Postmodernity*. Hove, East Sussex: Routledge.

Jung, C. G. *Civilisation in Transition*, Vol. 10, *Collected Works* (eds Read, H., Adler, G. A. and Fordham, M.; trans. R. F. C. Hull). London: Routledge & Kegan Paul.

Jung, C. G. *Aion*, Vol. 9ii, *Collected Works* (eds Read, H., Adler, G.A. and Fordham, M.; trans. R. F. C. Hull). London: Routledge & Kegan Paul.

Jung, C. G. '*The Practice of Psychotherapy*, Vol. 16, *Collected Works* (eds Read, H., Adler, G. A. and Fordham, M.; trans. R. F. C. Hull). London: Routledge & Kegan Paul.

Jung, C. G. *Psychological Types*, Vol. 6, *Collected Works* (eds Read, H., Adler, G. A. and Fordham, M.; trans. R. F. C. Hull). London: Routledge & Kegan Paul.

Jung, C. G. *Psychology and religion*, Vol. 11, *Collected Works* (eds Read, H., Adler, G. A. and Fordham, M.; trans. R. F. C. Hull). London: Routledge & Kegan Paul.

Jung, C. G. *Two Essays on Analytical Psychology,* Vol. 7, *Collected Works* (eds Read, H., Adler, G.A. and Fordham, M.; trans. R. F. C. Hull). London: Routledge & Kegan Paul.

Jung, C. G., Jaffe, A. and Winston, C. (1963) *Memories, Dreams, Reflections.* London: Collins; Routledge & Kegan Paul.

Kimbles, S. L. (2000) The cultural complex and the myth of invisibility. In T. Singer (ed.) *The Vision Thing: myth, politics and psyche in the world.* London and New York, NY: Routledge, pp. 157–69.

Kimbles, S. L. (2004) A cultural complex operating in the overlap of clinical and cultural space. In T. Singer and S. L. Kimbles (eds) *The Cultural Complex: contemporary Jungian perspectives on psyche and society.* New York, NY: Brunner-Routledge, pp. 199–211.

Kupperman, J. J. (1999) *Learning from Asian Philosophy.* New York and Oxford: Oxford University Press.

Loy, D. R. (1999) Loving the world as our own body: the non-dualist ethics of Taoism, Buddhism, and deep ecology. In C. B. Becker (ed.) *Asian and Jungian Views of Ethics.* Westport, CT: Greenwood Press, pp. 85–112.

Matthews, R. (2002) Competition archetypes and creative imagination. *Journal of Organisational Change, 15*(5): 461–76.

Miller, W. A. (1989/1991) Finding the shadow in everyday life. In J. Abrams and C. Zweig (eds) *Meeting the Shadow: the hidden power of the dark side of human nature.* New York, NY: Tarcher Penguin, pp. 38–44.

Neville, B. (2010) The polytheistic organization. *Personality Type in Depth, 1* (October).

Papadopoulos, R. K. (2006) *The Handbook of Jungian Psychology: theory, practice and applications.* London: Routledge.

Proulx, C. (1994) On Jung's theory of ethics. *Journal of Analytic Psychology, 39*(1): 101–19.

Robinson, D. W. (2005) *Conscience and Jung's Moral Vision: from Id to Thou.* New York, NY: Paulist Press.

Samuels, A. (1985) *Jung and the Post-Jungians.* London: Routledge & Kegan Paul.

Samuels, A. (1989) *The Plural Psyche: personality, morality and the father.* London: Routledge.

Samuels, A. (1993) *The Political Psyche.* London: Routledge.

Samuels, A. (1998) Will the post-Jungians survive? In A. Casement (ed.) *Post-Jungians Today: key papers in contemporary analytical psychology.* London: Routledge, pp. 15–32.

Schweiker, W. (2004) *Theological Ethics and Global Dynamics: in the time of many worlds.* Malden, MA and Oxford: Blackwell.

Singer, T. (2004) The cultural complex and archetypal defenses of the group spirit. In T. Singer and S. L. Kimbles (eds) *The Cultural Complex: contemporary Jungian perspectives on psyche and society.* New York, NY: Brunner-Routledge, pp. 13–34.

Singer, T. and Kimbles, S. L. (eds) (2004) *The Cultural Complex: contemporary Jungian perspectives on psyche and society.* New York, NY: Brunner-Routledge.

Solomon, H. M. (2000) The ethical self. In E. Christopher and H. M. Solomon (eds) *Jungian Thought in the Modern World.* London: Free Association Books, pp. 191–216.

Solomon, H. M. (2001) Origins of the ethical attitude. *Journal of Analytic Psychology, 46*(3): 443–54.

Stein, M. (1997) Individuation. In P. Young-Eisendrath and T. Dawson (eds) *Cambridge Companion to Jung.* Cambridge: Cambridge University Press, pp. 196–214.

Stein, M. (1998) *Jung's Map of the Soul: an introduction.* Chicago, IL: Open Court.

Stevens, A. (1990) *On Jung.* London: Routledge.

Stevens, A. (2001) *Jung: a very short introduction.* Oxford: Oxford University Press.

Stevens, A. (ed.) (2002) *Archetype Revisited: an updated natural history of the self* (2nd edn) London: Brunner-Routledge.

Storr, A. (1999) Foreword. In P. Bishop (ed.) *Jung in Contexts: a reader.* London: Routledge, pp. xi–xvii.

Tacey, D. (1998) Twisting and turning with James Hillman: from anima to world soul, from academia to pop. In A. Casement (ed.) *Post-Jungians Today: key papers in contemporary analytical psychology.* London: Routledge, pp. 215–34.

Whitmont, E. C. (1969/1991) The evolution of the shadow. In C. Zweig and J. Abrams (eds) *Meeting the Shadow.* New York, NY: Tarcher/Penguin, pp. 12–19.

Whitmont, E. C. (1978) *The Symbolic Quest: basic concepts of analytical psychology.* Princeton: Princeton University Press.

Wilson, E. O. (1998) *Consilience: the unity of knowledge.* New York, NY: Knopf.

Yandell, J. (1990) Foreword (E. Rolfe, trans.) In E. Neumann *Depth Psychology and a New Ethic.* Boston: Shambala, pp. 1–6.

8 Re-imagining professional ethics

Introduction

The last two chapters outlined the principles of Jungian psychology and suggested the foundation for a new approach to ethics; this chapter brings us back to the domain of professions and professional ethics. The discussion at the end of the last chapter about cultural complexes and the operation of Jungian dynamics in organizations and groups is particularly relevant here, as we transfer some of the key concepts to professions and their ethics. The aim is to address, if not resolve, some of the issues raised in earlier chapters problematizing these areas.

The first half of the chapter revisits some of the ethical approaches outlined in Chapter 4 to consider what impact a Jungian approach might have and consider anew the relevance of Jungian ethics to professions; it then re-imagines professions as entities, possessing a collective culture, established by processes reminiscent of individual human consciousness; concluding with discussion of how a profession might come to a new understanding of its own shadow material as a prerequisite for developing an ethic based on wholeness rather than goodness. This sets the scene for returning to public relations (PR) in Chapter 9, where the generalizations here will be applied to a particular professional group, generating new observations and directions for research.

Jungian concepts and the sociology of professions

There are striking similarities in world view between Jung and Durkheim (though there is little cross-referencing in sources); born in Europe in the mid-nineteenth century at a time of vast social change and increasing emphasis on absolute knowledge, both were concerned about the loss of the deeper meaning from everyday life and sought to provide moral guidance in turbulent times. But more like Freud than Jung, Durkheim emphasized the role of self-discipline as a framework for personal and social freedom, to control and mitigate the forces of egoism through moral conduct (Turner, 1992). Giddens (1978) describes Durkheim's attempt to found a 'science of morality' (1978: 63) and Turner (1992) also stresses the moral purpose of his sociology: 'Durkheim's purpose was to explore the moral problems of an advanced, differentiated, and complex society, in which the economy had become somewhat detached from other social institutions' (1992: xiii). Both

Durkheim and Jung saw this contemporary upheaval in knowledge and value as threatening to the 'sacred'; there is even a superficial similarity between Durkheim's 'collective conscience' and Jung's 'collective unconscious', although the former is seen as the aggregate of individual consciences rather than the well-spring of consciousness. Durkheim also saw society as 'organic' rather than mechanistic in its formation and development (Turner, 1992). The essential difference is that Durkheim looked out, to social institutions such as professions for moral agency, while Jung primarily looked in, to the psyche, as the route to human flourishing.

Jung and Durkheim are sometimes described as conservative, partly because of this resistance to the modernist project. They also shared an interest in the form and function of religion in society, at a time of declining church power; William James's (1905) *Varieties of Religious Experience* was profoundly influential, and European interest in Eastern faith systems was on the rise. Turner (1992) suggests that this interest in faith may be the reason Durkheim has been so misread, though Giddens (1978) does highlight his reliance on social structures to maintain rather than challenge social order. From this perspective, Durkheim notes the religious origins of many professional (formerly guild) practices and the importance of shared rituals in creating social bonds, finding moral force in that which goes beyond the individual (Turner, 1992). While Jung also engaged with religion and spirituality, his views on these matters consistently defied social convention. Indeed, Hauke (2000) argues that Jung's resistance to modernity marks him out not as a conservative but as a postmodernist, though others disagree (see below).

Max Weber also reflected on the 'disenchantment of the world' by which value was removed from objects in society and re-located to personal spheres of religion and personal relationships (Bishop, 1999: 224). Main (2007) explores the connections with Jung, emphasizing Weber's critique of the 'desacralised' modern world and its loss of collective myths. He contests that Jung's and Weber's analyses of modern capitalism and materialism are broadly similar, and wonders why Jung's work has been consistently ignored by sociologists, despite psychological approaches such as Freud's being welcomed by many. Main concludes that Jung's emphasis on religious and non-rational perspectives is incompatible with sociological approaches. This incompatibility is interesting as it seems to me that the socio-cultural approaches outlined earlier seek to deepen understanding of social change, embracing inner experience as well as the outward manifestations. Jung is not alone in wishing to move beyond the Marxist–Weberian tradition (Jarrett, 1999). An example of a new thought-partnership can be seen by highlighting the points of connection between Bourdieu's *habitus* and Jung's cultural complexes. As noted in Chapter 3, Bourdieu's thought has influenced writing on professions, in particular his concept of *habitus,* the means by which society reproduces itself, by generating in the individual and collective a set of behaviours, expectations and relations that are not absolutely fixed, or indeed conscious, but which tend to repetition unless consciously examined (Ihlen, 2007). Gray (2008) explores the Jung–Bourdieu connection, pointing out that Bourdieu's concept of *habitus* requires that its structures – such as professions – operate rather like complexes in the collective:

> What agents are actually doing exceeds their conscious intentions because they are engaged in reproducing the objective ends of habitus. They are part of a self-replicating network of relations and structures over which they have little control and the meaning of which depends on their lack of epistemic awareness. 'It is because subjects do not know, strictly speaking, what they are doing that what they do has more meaning than they know'.
>
> (Bourdieu, 1977, cited in Gray, 2008: 70)

Bourdieu shares Jung's sense that raising awareness of social conditioning to consciousness is an act of agency with the potential for transformation. Moreover, Gray suggests that this concept of unconsciousness, together with Bourdieu's idea of forgotten history, constitutes a kind of collective unconscious, not dissimilar to Jung's, though the former locates the structures of the forgotten in social history, in time, not the transcendent. Reay (2004: 438), writing about Bourdieu, not Jung, also highlights the role of the unconscious in determining *habitus*: 'Implicit in the concept is that habitus operates at an unconscious level unless individuals confront events that cause self-questioning, whereupon habitus begins to operate at the level of consciousness and the person develops new facets of the self.'

I would also argue that the circuit-of-culture approach, introduced by Curtin and Gaither (2005, 2007) to PR, is compatible with a Jungian philosophy, and this will be explored in the next chapter. Nevertheless, it is difficult to position Jung as a critical or social theorist, not least because his concept of self is so radically different. Whereas the social constructivists see self as existing primarily in the social world, co-created through relationship with and observation of others, the Jungian self, as explored in previous chapters, is seen (by some Jungian scholars) as synonymous with the transcendent. Tacey (1998: 232) illustrates this tension:

> The continuing value of Jung's Self, that 'umbrella' archetype which brings warring elements into dialogue and relationship, may not be in its bad currency in intellectual society, but in its *efficacy* in psychic and public life. The fact is that we do need very large concepts, ideals or deities to deal with the primal opposites such as inner and outer, masculine and feminine, which threaten to tear us apart if we side with one at the expense of the other. To be sure, these unities do become corrupt and have to be turned aside. But to worship plurality (the postmodern deity) as an end in itself is a perversity that the psyche will not tolerate.

One of the liveliest current debates in Jungian scholarship concerns a struggle to include or exclude his work in a postmodern paradigm: Hauke (2000) and Jones (2007) explore the relationship between Jungian and postmodern thinking, with widely varying conclusions. As suggested earlier, Hauke places Jung as a critic of modernity:

Jung's psychology challenged the splitting tendency of modernity: the splitting of the 'rational' and 'irrational', the splitting of the social, collective norm and individual, subjective experience, the splitting of the Human and the Natural, of mind and matter and, perhaps above all, the splitting of the conscious and unconscious psyche itself.

(Hauke, 2000: 2)

In his book, *Jung and the Postmodern*, (2000), Hauke argues that Jung's enthusiasm for complexity, ambiguity and symbolic meaning suggest an affinity between Jungian (or rather post-Jungian) thought and postmodernism, as does his rejection of the constraints of the collective. In the other corner, Raya Jones's (2007) book, *Jung, Psychology, Postmodernity*, notes that in postmodern discourse, the creation of a meaning-world is seen as an 'object' outside the individual, who generates but does not own the meaning: 'The idea of the self as a grammatical operator is incommensurable with Jung's view of the self as arising from the natural psyche and encompassing "both the experienceable and the inexperienceable"' (2007: 17). Jones traces shifts in psychology from its roots in natural sciences to social constructivist and other postmodern approaches, finding shared concerns from divergent perspectives. For example, she argues that 'human subjectivity is inextricably interlaced with the flow of action and its intersubjective construction' (2007: 45), but stresses the materialism underpinning most constructivist approaches.

While there is little cross-referencing between professionalism studies and Jung, the above comments suggest interesting points of convergence, as well as highlighting important differences in concept. Building on the socio-cultural approach, I am re-imagining the profession as a psychic entity, comprising the elements of the individual psyche and subject to complexes and archetypal dynamics, particularly those of persona and shadow, as will be seen later in the chapter. First, the threads between Jungian and previously explored approaches to ethics are followed.

Jungian and professional ethics

Chapter 4 set out current debates in professional ethics, suggesting that while virtue and discourse ethics had made an impact on the field, newer developments from postmodernism and feminist approaches were not yet reflected. Themes emerged from this discussion such as the overreliance of professional ethics on traditional (consequentialist and deontological) approaches; the use of virtue ethics as act-based rather than agent-based, reflecting preference for act rather than agent ethics; where agent approaches are deployed they tend to assume an internal, rational consistency not always found in human experience. It also suggested that ethics tended to be seen either as statements of ideal character or detailed situation-specific advice, with discussion of moral leadership in professions limited to descriptions of successful (or charismatic) leaders, or requiring greater reflexivity than currently exists. Professions rely on extra-strong moral standards for social status and approval, but individual members are held responsible for observance with little scrutiny of profession-wide ethical issues, increasing the gulf between professional declarations of ethical standards and the ethical complexity of practice. Questions also arose that were unresolved, such as, is there a need for separate professional ethics or will ordinary ethics 'do'; can professional bodies play a more active role in developing reflexive ethics at the professional as well as the individual level; and is there space to resolve some of the issues of internal inconsistency *and* construct a global approach to professional ethics?

I am suggesting that a Jungian approach to ethics can help with some of these issues; to quote ethicist Kwame Appiah, this 'will be an encounter, not a conquest' (2008: 73). The Jungian approach to ethics was summarized in Chapter 7 as raising and integrating aspects of the unconscious, particularly elements from the shadow, to consciousness – itself a moral challenge; recognizing projections onto other groups as aspects of the projector; and building internal relationships with previously disregarded aspects and shifting the centre of consciousness from one of gratifying (weak) ego demands to encouraging dialogue between a (strong) ego and the unconscious, within a greater, transcendent framework, which may be secular or divine. At the heart of a Jungian approach to ethics is a shift away from the dualities of right/wrong, good/bad that underpins so much Anglo-American ethics, towards a more complex ethical negotiation between multiple perspectives, within a unifying (but not homogenizing) framework. This is esoteric, inward-looking, as in Asian ethics, rather than exoteric, rules-based ethics. While Jung's definitions are not always consistent, it is clear that the ethical is linked to the integral, in that the whole person or, here, profession is less ego-driven, seeking balance between the needs of the individual and the needs of the collective, the hallmark of intrinsic ethics (CW6/356).1 Indeed, Jung contrasts the eastern philosophy of going inwards for ethical guidance with the Christian tradition of reliance on externals, such as rules, law and texts (CW10/167–70; Jones, 2007: 32), though he doubts the ability of the post-Enlightenment European ego to embrace an eastern approach and instead urges acceptance of both the order of the rational mind and the chaos of the unconscious (CW9i/489–524).

This leads into a discussion of Jungian and Asian ethics, and it is worth repeating Koehn's (2001: 170) summary of the core issues, which she applies to business ethics:

1) the multiplicity of incommensurate human goods serves as a basis for the practice of giving reasons and for virtue;
2) thoughtful human beings (note the plural) are the standard for ethically good actions, but we lack a model for the prudent man or woman; and
3) evil consists not in violating some overarching ethical rule but in pretending that only one good exists.

Koehn is building a bridge between Asian and virtue ethics, which is discussed below, but her summary also makes points of contact with Jungian ideas (not explicitly), namely the recognition of conflict as an essential human experience from which ethical struggle emerges, the emphasis on the reflective (and multiple) persons who cannot be summarized into one model of 'prudence', and the shift away from attempts to define and limit ideas of 'goodness'. This is a different emphasis than is commonly found in virtue approaches, and suggests how the latter might be expanded to take in some Asian (and Jungian) concepts, as Koehn suggests. The Jungian writer Beebe (1992) identifies integrity as the core virtue in Jungian ethics and shows how individuation offers a process by which integrity might be achieved. He also discusses the question of character from a virtue ethics perspective, as was discussed in Chapter 6, making a strong argument for an ethics based on integrity, not only as an end goal, but as the means by which an individual can continue to work on the persistent shadow material that can never be fully integrated:

> I have defined integrity as accountability emerging out of a willing sensitivity to the needs of the whole, meaning the entire matrix of self-objects in which any self is embedded. It is the self's willingness to be responsible to all its objects, and accountable for its impact upon them.
>
> (Beebe, 1998: 60–1)

This reflects one of the central arguments of this book, though I do not take the virtue approach to frame it, being reluctant to enter a competition between virtues and believing that a Jungian ethic has contributions to make beyond that paradigm. There does seem to be a correlation between Aristotle's *eudemonia*, or flourishing, and Jung's individuation in that both reside in the person not the act, though Aristotle calls this 'character', and Jung's sense of psyche is far wider and deeper than personality. Virtue ethics also recognizes the imperfection of human acts and the contradictions between desires and duties, but while Jung urges the conflicted to enter the conflict wholly because it contains the seeds of a transcendent solution (Solomon, 2001), virtue ethics refers the conflicted to the imaginary 'good man' for guidance. Appiah (2008) notes that virtue ethics has become a set of short cuts, heuristics, to guide the performance of good acts, when Aristotle actually encouraged his audience to become good people; it has morphed from agent to act, as was discussed in Chapter 4.

Revisiting discourse ethics from a Jungian perspective also reveals new insights: as outlined in Chapter 4, discourse ethics rests on the equal access of all parties to debates on issues that will affect them and is seen as Kantian in origin (Benhabib, 1992), though others see it as founded in critical theory by Jürgen Habermas, who sought to move ethics from earlier foundations in universal norms and traditions to a relational approach wherein clashes can be resolved through agreed procedures (Crawford, 1998). A Jungian approach does not focus on procedure (though this resurfaces as an issue towards the end of this chapter) but there is the sense of a dialogic 'space' within which conflict can be contained, not resolved, while deeper insights surface, allowing a new path out of the impasse, one not accessible by reasoned argument alone. Discourse ethicists may of course reject a Jungian approach because it assumes that there are 'deeper' realities beyond the socially constructed. Postmodernists (a loose term for a range of thinkers, as was made clear in earlier chapters) also argue that 'social construction ... materially reproduces the world's norms, hierarchies and values' (Crawford, 1998: 139), but as Hauke (2000) and Jones (2007) explore at book-length, there is connective tissue between these approaches and Jungian ideas. Jones contrasts the postmodernist Hermans' (1993) 'dialogic self' with Jung's dynamical psyche, pointing out that Hermans is the 'only major postmodern psychologist to make contact with the Jungian world' (2007: 85). She finds convergence in concepts of self and internal dialogue, quoting:

> The dialogic self, in contrast to the individualistic self, is based on the assumption that there are many *I* positions that can be subsumed by the same person. The *I* in one position can agree, disagree, understand, misunderstand, oppose, contradict, question and even ridicule the *I* in another position.
>
> (Hermans *et al.*, 1992, cited in Jones, 2007: 86)

This postmodern approach resonates with Jung's multiplicity of self, according to Hauke (2000), in contrast with many of the approaches to ethical decision-making outlined earlier, which presume coherent rationality as the basis for ethics. Coherent rationality might be the ideal condition for describing and codifying ethical approaches, but an ethical life is not experienced in such conditions, according to both Jungian and postmodernist thinking. Nevertheless, it is worth remembering that, for Jung, this fragmentation was illusory, caused by complexes that lose power during the process of individuation.

While neither of these writers addresses the issue of ethics (there is no index entry in either book), their explorations of the points of contact and divergence between Jungian and postmodern ideas do generate insight into ethical issues, particularly in the light of Benhabib's (1992) work on postmodernism and ethics, and Crawford (1998) on critical and postmodern ethics and international affairs (neither of which mentions Jung). Crawford rejects criticisms (see Bauman and others, below) that postmodernist ethics is nihilistic, arguing that the more recent emphasis on relation and care offers opportunities for ethical development across cultures. Benhabib argues against Habermas and others on the grounds that discourse ethics, for example, assumes universalizable and normative understanding of moral goods, an assumption that postmodernist and critical perspectives will not accept.

This raises the question: to what extent is a Jungian ethic universalizable and/or normative? In that the psychic unfolding of individuals and groups takes places within a transcendental psychic framework that includes the collective consciousness, it would seem that there is a universality to Jung's ethics, though it is also non-prescriptive about outcome, lacking the more prescriptive idea of virtue ethics' 'good man'. Indeed the *telos* of the Jungian ethical process is wholeness *not* goodness; it is not a process of identifying and shunning the 'bad' but rather of integrating and understanding it so that it loses its unconscious power. This is closer to the deep hermeneutics explored in Chapter 4; the fusion of horizons through the fluid search for shared meaning. It is also clear that each individual or group has to discover its own ethical foundation through engaging with its specific shadow, a process that cannot be ordained by edict but must be experienced. This suggests that the *process* may be universal even if the outcomes are not.

Other writers looking for this deeper connection include Bauman (1993) and Schweiker (2004, 2007), who tend to emphasize the wholeness that postmodernists reject, though neither references Jung, calling for a renewal of engagement with deeper, shared values, rather than their continued abandonment. For example, Schweiker (2007: 425) explores moral frameworks for diverse cultures and expresses concern at the instrumental use of ethics in modern business:

> Most contemporary forms of ethics have forsaken attention to the dynamics of moral consciousness and perception in order to focus on rules and principles of just social interaction or, in a related way, to explore the discourse a community uses to shape character. The turn to action and language in modern thought has virtually eclipsed the focus in ancient ethics on moral consciousness and spiritual practices.

Schweiker's exploration of the core and uniting values that might underpin twenty-first-century pluralist approaches to ethics appears to belong to the same debate that Jung was engaged with a century ago:

> For anyone concerned to develop a global ethic, the root question becomes how, if at all, global forces can be rendered accountable to norms and values aimed at respecting and enhancing the integrity of human and nonhuman life. The challenge is to live responsibly amid powers that shape the destiny of this world.
>
> (Schweiker, 2007: 425)

Having demonstrated the connections between Jungian and a range of other approaches to ethics, I want to return to the issue of professions and consider how they might benefit from these insights. In order to apply Jungian ethics to professions, I am building on the ideas of group and cultural complexes considered in the last chapter to envisage professions as 'psychic entities' containing elements analogous to persona, self, shadow and therefore capable of ethical maturity.

The profession as a psychic entity

Despite the critical deconstruction of professions offered by Weber, Freidson, Larson and other writers explored in Chapter 3 and above, Durkheim's conceptualization of professions as 'pillars of society' underpins the self-image of most professional bodies, as is evidenced by the claims they make in their codes of conduct (see Chapter 3 for details and below for discussion). This constitutes the 'ideal-typical' image outlined earlier, which Larson (1977) sees as a screen for ideological claims. It is this self-image of professions that I am suggesting acts as a persona role for the 'community of practice', presenting the field's arguments (or at least, desire) for social approval, and that this ideal-typical 'mask' reflects what Kultgen calls the '*ur-mythos* of the ... professional's service to humanity' (1988: 120). In critiquing the role of professional persona it should be remembered that this is not a moral judgement; the persona plays a crucial part in the development of the social self in the individual, the system for managing relations with others. The problem lies in over-identification with 'appearances' over reality and this is echoed in some of the pressures facing professions, as outlined in Chapter 3. For example, as suggested there, the professional is seen as an actor fulfilling their socially determined script rather than, as in traditional definitions, acquiring knowledge or expertise (Goffman, 1959; Lyotard, 1984). This can lead to an existential emptiness in which

> the 'real world' exists as a discourse within our imaginings, yet with the capacity to discipline or seduce organizational members to the rules of the larger corporate club. The first rule of membership of this club, for professional players, is that they must never speak of the emptiness, absence of foundation and paucity of purpose at its heart, for to do so puts all at risk.
>
> (Dent and Whitehead, 2002: 4)

This resonates with Jung's concept of persona, the public construction of conformity and quiescence, behind which the unlived aspects of the self lurk in the shadows. Or, to be more precise, the mask becomes oppressive when the (weak) ego identifies with persona. Where the profession constructs a version of the field on which to build its relationship to society through participation in the 'promotional ' culture (Wernick, 1991) and *believes that to be well-founded*, then Jungian psychology suggests that there will be conflict potentially leading to crisis. This also moves the discussion on from the critique of professional emptiness to entertain the possibility of healing, which Hauke (2000) stresses as Jung's core contribution.

The professional persona, as in the individual, may well be established or defended in terms of what it is not: the other. Chapter 3 briefly mentioned the issue of jurisdictional contests in defining professions, as suggested by Abbott (1988) and Freidson (1994). Pieczka (2006) describes such contests as essential for the creation of a profession and other writers have considered jurisdictional issues in particular fields (Halpern, 1992; Hutton, 2010). This can be reconceptualized as the struggle to assert the persona by rejecting the other, the not-us. Thus journalists become heated when confused with PR officers; PR workers, in turn, distance themselves from marketing and advertising personnel. It may even be that the closer the territory, the more blurred the boundaries, the more intense the rejection. Singer's (2004) description of the 'false self' and the group's inability to see itself, quoted in Chapter 5, echoes this tension, as do observations of the shadow in organizations (Feldman, 2004; Hede, 2007) discussed in the last chapter. These descriptions help illuminate the development and maintenance of group persona roles, shaped from shared experience, and reinforced by unconscious rejection of negative or unwanted aspects of the group. Cultural complexes in groups replicate the bipolarities of individual complexes, and the creation of positive and negative groups is consistent with this:

> so that when they are activated, the group ego or the individual ego of a group member becomes identified with one part of the unconscious cultural complex, while the other part is projected out onto the suitable hook of another group or one of its members. Individuals and groups in the grips of a particular cultural complex automatically take on a shared body language and postures.
> (Singer and Kimbles, 2004: 6)

The role of the professional body in enhancing or modifying such identity constructions is also worth exploring. Professional associations are charged with creating, maintaining and defending the professional identity of its members, as a collective. Of course, as Bauman and Vecchi (2004) point out, the fluidity of social forces means that identity can no longer be anchored in structures (such as professions), leading to an anxious search for groups, including virtual groups, to provide collective meaning, 'while on the move' (2004: 26). Bauman coins the term 'cloakroom communities' to describe these fleeting gatherings around issues or topics, but it is possible that professional identities are more durable, not least because they outlive particular periods of employment. And it may be the thirst for secure identity that encourages the over-identification with the persona against which Jung warns so clearly: 'Identification is an alienation of the subject from himself for the sake of the object, in which he is, so to speak, disguised' (Jung CW6/738). Yet the responsibility of the professional association is to speak up for the 'community of practice' and extol its members' virtues and contribution to society. This claim, as suggested earlier, is challenged by its economic responsibility to act primarily on behalf of members in order to maintain existing membership and attract new members. Institutes of Accounting across the world must speak up for accountants, architectural bodies for architects and so on. At the same time, as will be explored in the next section, they must also be the agents of control and accountability, both promotional and policing. As discussed in earlier chapters, over-identification with persona aspects can create a conflict when ethical demands threaten membership interests – a potential source of the friction which may lead to the crisis that fuels the desire for change. Jung saw the mid-life crisis as triggered when the emphasis on public approval becomes increasingly hollow and the need for more 'authentic' experience surfaces. In the case of professions, the performance of ethics without substance is no longer sustainable and indeed threatens the entire professional 'project'. At this point, an over-attachment to the self-congratulatory persona aspects in the face of external criticism deflects the truths that may be contained in the accusations and prevents the professional body from learning from experience or integrating its own shadow aspects. 'The difficulty in changing the persona is proportional to the stake one has in the roles one plays in family, work situation and community at large' (Mattoon, 2005: 18). Thus, the more resistant a profession is to external, or internal, criticism, the more difficulty it will have in shifting its relationship to the persona role. However, the profession has a choice of reactions: defensive and aggrandising in its threatened persona role, or reflexive and accommodating in its ego functions.

The control function of professional bodies is poorly exercised (Freidson, 1994), suggesting that the defensive reaction dominates, but it could be reconceptualized as an ego function, offering a potential way forward for enhancing the self-awareness of professions. Jung called ego the 'organising principle' (though he also uses the same term to describe the self) and if one considers the role of the professional body as an ego function, the negotiation between conflicting demands such as promotion and discipline looks suddenly familiar. A willingness to engage with difficult, challenging aspects of the field and incorporate such insights would indicate the presence of a well-functioning ego willing to engage in some degree of integration in order to establish a more mature profession. As summarized in Chapter 6, the well-functioning ego plays a crucial role in developing dialogue between the conscious and unconscious, and in facilitating the process of individuation. As suggested earlier, to effect this role the ego has to surrender its sense of being (and controlling) the whole psyche and accept its position within the transcendent whole, the moved not the mover, a challenge that is considered later in the chapter.

The developmental school of Jungian thought explores the shaping of ego functions as the fruitful struggle between the infant and their environment (Mattoon, 2005); it is worth comparing this approach with the development of professional bodies outlined in Chapter 3 (Oliver and Montgomery, 2005). The gestation in professional bodies and humans from dim awareness of the existence of shared interests to identification of component parts (members and non-members for the profession, body parts and other persons for the infant) through declarations of identity to recognition as an 'entity' are strikingly common, echoing Abbott's (1995) call for professions to be seen as social entities that are biologically driven, if only metaphorically. Abbott is clear that a profession is defined by its boundaries and by difference: different exams, different areas of expertise and bodies of knowledge. The concept of the professional body as fulfilling the ego rather than the persona function allows for a discussion about issues of control. The tension described earlier between the promotional and policing roles might be mitigated if the remit is reconceptualized as 'accountability' rather than promotion. It is worth sketching here a new role for professional bodies as incorporating ego rather than persona functions in the area of control. It could be seen from the discussion of managerialism in Chapter 3 that external bodies have sought to impose new external control mechanisms through management structures to compensate for the perceived loss of control by professional bodies (Dent and Whitehead, 2002; Freidson, 1984). Non-specialists have replaced experts, and all are expected to quantify their behaviour to satisfy a range of targets and performance indicators, areas that used to be 'left to the professional'. A profession with a well-functioning ego would be able to exercise authority with members, improve transparency internally and to external publics, and build membership through attraction rather than promotion. A start could be made, methodologically, by deploying the insights from Jung's psychological typology of inferior/superior functions (sensation, thinking, feeling and intuition) and attitudes (introvert/ extravert) which analysts use to help identify the aspects of the person that require primary attention. As suggested in the previous chapter, this schema has been applied to organizations (Corlett and Pearson, 2003; Neville, 2010), so it should be possible to develop a diagnostic tool for professions based on this typology. As the first stage of any such process involves working with the shadow, the chapter next explores how a profession might engage with its own shadow material.

Individuation as professional development

The first stage of Jungian integration and the most feasible for a profession is to become conscious of the shadow aspects of the group or field, whether that's nursing, law or politics; what's called 'doing your laundry in public'. It means accepting that as well as bad apples there may be bad barrels (Zimbardo, 2007), that the hidden abuses of power may be systemic rather than attributable to deviant individuals. This approach challenges the normative, predictive aspects of professional status management, hence the requirement for a well-founded ego. The mechanisms for generating shadow material are primarily denial and projection: disowning aspects of the profession, in this case, and projecting them onto other groups or professions. There is little literature on the shadow dynamics of professions, with the exception of Guggenbühl-Craig (1972/1991), who uses Jungian concepts to reveal the false prophet behind the preacher, the quack behind the doctor, the charlatan healer. Other writers do explore shadow aspects in workplaces and organizations though not always acknowledging Jung's contribution to this approach. For example, Egan's (1994) book *Working the Shadow Side*, a management guide to shadow aspects of organizations, groups and individual employees, does not mention Jung either in the references or index. However, Corlett and Pearson (2003) make explicit use of Jungian psychology to assess and address organizational tensions, invoking the archetype of the leader as storyteller, for example. As described in the previous chapter, Hede synthesizes Jungian literature with theories of emotional intelligence and management theory regarding workplace disputes, suggesting Jungian approaches to conceptualizing and managing shadow-based workplace conflict:

> It is proposed that projection plays a major role in emotionally-based relationship conflict that is seen as the basis of most intragroup dysfunctionality in organizational settings. By its very nature the shadow self is impossible to observe directly. Similarly, the process of projection can be only inferred rather than directly observed from behaviour.
>
> (Hede, 2007: 16)

While such an analysis of hidden emotional forces may be possible in a workgroup, asking a professional field to embrace these concepts is a tall order. The discussion on working with the shadow in the previous chapter made it clear that this a painful process, often entered into reluctantly or resisted at all costs. So why might a profession embark on such a journey? One suggestion is offered by a consortium of leading business executives (Arthur W. Page Society, 2009) as their 'project' for regaining lost public trust and re-establishing legitimacy. They see the turmoil in global capitalism as 'a unique opportunity for leaders to step forward and make business better' (2009: 3), and while I may not share their imperative, it is indicative of responses to current crises. Thus the crisis that triggers the mid-life review of persona and shadow in individuals may have its echoes in the corporate and professional culture.

So, given that many professions, from surgeons to journalists, have heroic self-images, the question is: how might one find the shadow? Drawing on theoretical insights explored in the previous chapter, it would seem that the first place to look is at the point of most irritation, a view shared by Corlett and Pearson (2003), who locate organizational problems at four different levels of consciousness, from external to the organization, to deep in the collective unconscious. One issue they identify is the 'public face seen as being same thing as organization' (2003: 39), citing a company that insisted it recruited the 'best and the brightest', despite contradictory evidence, because, they speculate, it 'confused the image it was trying to project with an inner reality about which it was oblivious, or chose to ignore' (2003: 39). Identifying the object of most revulsion/hostility may well yield insights into the shadow material that is projected outward rather than owned. Jurisdictional battles may offer some awareness, as would examination of texts, symbols and images promoted by the professional body as embodying the preferred ideal of that particular occupational group: 'Organizational individuation would then involve the integration of the other, as well as those aspects of group experience that are related to the impact of marginalization, power dynamics, and ideological differences' (Feldman, 2004: 251).

Such a shift would mean surrendering to the confusion between functions, status and roles found in many professional groups today (Watson, 2002) as they strive to adapt to changing communication and social structures. Given that much professional identity is based on jurisdictional definitions, a Jungian attempt to reconsider the other as an aspect of one's self might challenge even the notion of a profession itself. There are positive and negative reasons for suggesting individuation as a response to the current crisis in professions: the positives lie in the potential for realizing a greater vision of the field, even if the demarcation between one professional group and another becomes more blurred. However, it should also be remembered that Jung does not envisage an amorphous mass of humanity; on the contrary, he emphasizes that individuation is about allowing the 'incomparable uniqueness' to be realized. A profession prepared to re-assess its hidden qualities, construct an identity based in wholeness rather than denial, projection and jurisdictional competition might discover its incomparable uniqueness. This could even reclaim professions as the social good Durkheim envisaged, if professional ethics are truly addressed. The negative reasons are the multiple threats to the continuation of the professional project, outlined in Chapter 3 and manifest in the massive withdrawal of public trust from all professions.

The previous chapters made clear that the shift in ego from a state identified with the persona to one in relationship with the shadow and the unconscious is only possible within some concept of a transcendent function, that is, something greater than the ego's concept of itself. Jung often sees this as the god-function or god archetype but, as Chapter 6 made clear, there are disputes among Jungian scholars regarding the divine and secular interpretations of the transcendent. What was emphasized by all scholars was the importance of invoking a framework both beyond personal gratification and with real meaning (glib references to the 'greater good' will probably not suffice) to the participants. The profession itself might provide this overarching role, though there may be dangers with identification with the idealized or persona version, as suggested earlier. If one goal of the transcendent is to induce a sense of humility, I believe the role of society or polity offers a meaningful framework, as suggested by Davey (2004). This is particularly resonant with the multiple references in codes of ethics to working for 'social harmony', 'humanity' and so on (see Chapter 4). Davey's focus is not Jung but hermeneutics and in particular Gadamer's invocation of the transcendent as a framework or container for the multiplicity of interpretation. Davey argues that whereas over-deconstruction of text can lead to nihilistic fragmentation, Gadamer posits a more universal approach in which all perspectives may be included as aspects of the whole, as long as there is a binding, transcendent whole, which Davey suggests can be found in the concept of *polis*. This offers a secular alternative to a divine transcendent, though it is clearly not a question of trusting in external social structures or 'any traditional conception of a consensus formed by social contract' (2004: 217):

> Gadamer's political thinking can move away from modern subjectivism because it is transcendental in style. It pursues the question of how an individual subject is mediated by and can come to have a feeling for that which at the same time exists both within it and yet also reaches far beyond it, i.e. the polis.
>
> (Davey, 2004: 217)

This is then made meaningful for individuals, Davey suggests, 'by continuity between an individual's immediate horizon and the broader historical and linguistic horizons which sustain it' (2004: 217), which, if applied to professions, would encourage a deeper relationship between the interests of the field and those of society, as is implied in much professional rhetoric, as a 'shared community of experience'. The starting point for this argument is hermeneutic, but the sense of shared humanity, of the borderlessness between entities, feels Jungian, reinforcing earlier connections between Jung and hermeneutics. This also would provide a new foundation for trust: if professions were to operate as communities of skills, bordered by shared interests and concerns (of knowledge and practice), within a wider framework of the *polis*, to which it is accountable and transparent, trustworthiness would surely be enhanced. This sounds somewhat idealistic, given warnings (Hauke, 2000; Samuels, 1993) against Jungian theorizing with normative tendencies. Such a charge would be valid if the ideas outlined here were prescriptive, but they are presented in the spirit of Jung's commitment to healing, the contribution that Hauke (2000: 1) says distinguishes him from other cultural and social theorists. What seems to matter in Jungian psychology is not the exact nature of the transcendent, whether deity, self or society, but that the dominant ego-consciousness shifts its position from one of absolute centrality and control to a profound recognition of its own limitations. Returning to Amir's (2005) description of this individuation process, this would mean that professions would be required to:

a) recognize that its dealings with its members and the wider world are not wholly driven by rational reflection, but by forces within its collective field, mostly outside the current consciousness of members or leaders of that profession;
b) acknowledge the imperfections of the profession, its fallibilities and pretensions (without falling into despair);
c) construct a new sense of identity based on a deeper understanding of human failing and aspiration;
d) within a greater, transcendent framework, placing the needs and desires of the profession and its members in a more meaningful context.

In this sense, a profession's approach to ethics undergoes radical re-appraisal; not least because the locus of debate shifts from the individual practitioner to the collective, correcting the undue onus on individuals identified in earlier chapters, particularly the 'regressive ethics' (Abbott, 1983) whereby professional bodies avoid ethical dilemmas by devolving moral issues to the membership level, an evasion noted by others. While each individual member may or may not carry aspects of the collective ethical dynamic of persona and shadow, its primary locus is at the collective level, in the shared history, jurisdictional disputes and aspirations of the profession. It is at the professional level that a Jungian approach offers the opportunity for healing. This raises questions of ethical leadership, which are discussed below.

The second re-appraisal requires the professional body to reframe its priorities, moving from a defensive position on the profession to one more encouraging of debate and discussion. Professions have been known to do this after major crises, such as those faced by engineers experiencing conflicts of duty in the NASA Challenger case (Robinson, 2002) or general practitioners (GPs), coroners and other professional groups deceived by serial killer GP Harold Shipman over decades (Kaye, 2006). Other incentives for improving internal processes have usually been external threats, such as that of legal intervention in disciplinary and other procedures. Chapter 3 argued that the incentive in this instance is the loss of trust in professions and the imperative that, in turning to ethics to alleviate this loss, professions engage more deeply in the issues raised by the wider public and by members. Adopting a Jungian ethic requires this level of scrutiny because the aim is to raise hidden aspects of the profession, which have been operating as a brake to ethical development or even fuelling unethical behaviours. It is worth recalling the indictment that 'professional ethics instrumentalise moral concern; and in doing so, both take morality out of the picture and depoliticise the object of what might have been moral concern' (Brecher, 2010: 353).

There are two paths here (at least), both consistent with a Jungian approach: the first, outlined above, is to raise the shadow elements to consciousness, insofar as this is possible, in order to construct a new approach to ethics that recognizes the impulses, temptations and illusions particular to that profession; the second is to stop making the inflated and unsubstantiated claims to 'serve humanity' found in most codes of conduct (Kultgen, 1988). Given Brecher's (2010) suggestion that claims to ethical standards may mask indifference to ethical concerns, it would be an ethical improvement to stop generating such rhetoric and simply embrace the promotional remit of protecting members' interests. This would also be consistent with the reluctance of most professional associations to discipline their members and the view held by members that codes are for reputation rather than enforcement (Parkinson, 2001). The implications of such a stance would be the loss of the implicit benefits of the 'social contract' aspects of professionalism through which professions gain legitimacy from their declared commitment to extra-strong ethical standards (Cooper, 2004). But as the loss of public trust in professions indicates that this claim to legitimacy is not endorsed, it would seem sensible either to re-gain trust by grounding the claims in altered ethical attitudes or to accept the loss of trust in ethical claims and rebuild professional purpose along more modest lines. It might be harder to resist government regulation on this path – after all, the failure of sections of the banking industry to regulate their own ethical practices has led to greater legal controls in Anglo-American societies (Kaye, 2006). But more honest statements of responsibility – that is, members' interests take precedence over those of wider society – would at least offer the advantage of credibility. Trade unions, for example, clearly work primarily for their members, without claiming to benefit wider society, except indirectly by articulating the concerns of groups of workers. In fact, their contribution through pressure for equality, health and safety, holiday and pension rights is substantial set aside the more nebulous claims of many emerging professions. However, the literature on professions suggests that most will not wish to pursue this route, because to relinquish the claim to an ethic is to undermine the very notion of professionalism, as least as set out from the functionalist perspective. After all, the professional ethic is 'not just an ideological stalking horse ... It is also a response to a genuine social need' (Broadbent, Dietrich, and Roberts, 1997: 145). Even Kultgen (1988), who demolishes many claims to professional ethics, concludes that 'some such notion is desirable, if only in order to encourage professionals to aim higher' (1988: 259).

Which leaves the alternative course of engaging more deeply with issues of professional ethics. It is interesting to note that while major organizations have embraced the concept of Corporate Social Responsibility (CSR), there has not been a corresponding project in professional bodies, perhaps because they do not demand the same degree of public support (political and consumer) for their existence. While there has been a certain amount of scepticism about the sincerity of some CSR programmes, it is clear that there is an urgent debate in management and organizational literature and practice about the impact of their culture on ethical behaviour. For example: 'At the organisational level it is necessary to identify the norms and values that are central to the organisation and to determine whether these values are promoting or discouraging ethical behaviour' (McDonald and Nijhof, 1999: 135). There is no reason why such a debate should not take place across professions. If the concept of *polis* offers a transcendent function then professions could reposition themselves, de-centred within the overarching framework of society. This also chimes with the pledges made by most professions to serve society, but now with the purpose of deflation rather than grandiosity. Reframing professional ethics within the *polis* can offer meaning beyond the profession's group interests and releases the potential significance of the phrases routinely embedded in most professional codes concerning service to humanity or wider society. A Jungian perspective allows for the interpretation that these formulae *do* have meaning, one that has not yet been embodied in the professional discourse. However, if professions are going to bring this into consciousness, they will need to offer ethical leadership, the subject of the closing section of this chapter, which also considers how such insights might be facilitated in professional ethical discourse.

The professional body as ethical leader

There is extensive literature on ethical leadership, some of which was discussed in Chapter 4, with a tendency either to produce prescriptive guidelines for leadership or describe the characteristics of public figures who are deemed to be good, often basing the former on the actions of the latter. There is little on the group as an ethical leader and less on professions as leaders, so this section tries to bring together several threads from the leadership literature and from Jungian approaches to ethics to consider the role of the professional body as a moral (not business) leader.

First of all, the concept of leader in Jungian psychology is in itself problematic: the archetype of hero is one model for leadership, that of mother or father another; both of course contain opposing shadows. Every hero may conceal a coward or a martyr; for every supportive and encouraging parent role there is the controlling, invasive forebear. Hollis (2007) suggests that corporations suffer cultural complexes generated by the history of the organization and the 'dominant com–plexes of the leadership' (2007: 121), citing the traditional equation of the king with the state and the correlation between the monarch's health and the success or failure of crops, for example. In particular, he says, parental images attract shadow energy as 'people look to the group entity to meet their emotional needs' (2007: 121), and grow depressed or enraged if these needs are not met, reproducing the family drama in the workplace. Professional groups may attract less intense expectations as they do not engage members each day, but leading members may find similar tensions playing out in their relations with the group and its leaders. This approach also indicates that the relationship between leaders and followers is more complex than is sometimes recognized, an observation that has implications for ethical leadership. What could be more counter-productive, after all, than a parental figure lecturing members on their ethical behaviour? There may be a longing for a Plato's philosopher-King, Hollis (2007) says, who will offer wise, reflective leadership, but leaders often attain leadership precisely because they are overwhelmingly driven, often resistant to criticism or reflection. He concludes:

> the Shadow of any organisation is constituted by that which threatens the ego in charge, that which carries the unexamined, unconsciousness of leadership. Thus even the most benign group may covertly be controlled by greed, by immaturity, or by the narcissistic needs of the boss.
>
> (2007: 124)

The business ethicist Goodpaster (2007) calls this kind of drive 'teleopathy', the distorted drive for ends, and urges leaders to engage with a moral agenda because, he says, it is the leader who 'is the principal architect of corporate conscience' (2007: 3). He suggests that this engagement occurs in three phases: orienteering, steering the organization towards ethical values; institutionalizing, making sure they are structurally embedded; and sustaining, maintaining the ethical commitment over time. Goodpaster also proposes three levels of ethical education to assist this project: business schools, in-house training programmes and leadership associations. While ethics in education is outside the scope of this book, the central arguments and the suggestions for leadership networks are relevant to the discussion of professional ethics. There are also interesting overlaps with Jungian ideas; Goodpaster (2007: 19) sees organizations as 'macro-versions (projections) of ourselves as individuals'; his use of 'mindsets' is similar to Jungian complexes, including the cultural complexes occurring in groups (Singer and Kimbles, 2004); his diagnosis of teleopathy, a term he first coined in 1986, following the Ivan Boesky and Challenger scandals, is close to the condition of over-identification with the persona, in that other considerations, such as risk to self or others, take second place to achieving stated, or unconscious, goals. One difference is that Goodpaster is seeking to construct a normative prescriptive ethics for business by encouraging a 'corporate conscience' (and is aiming for a more trustworthy form of capitalism); Jung seeks to facilitate the realization of the different aspects of the self, a process in which undue emphasis on being 'good' can render true motivation invisible, and does not instrumentalize this. But both stress the centrality of consciousness to the ethical process, and the first two of Goodpaster's four attributes of ethical awareness – reflectiveness, humility, anticipation, and community involvement – are shared by the individuation process.

While the goals may be different pragmatically, professional organizations might find useful insights into how to instil ethical attitudes in their organizations. These attributes can also be compared to those offered by Ketola (2008), who has written about the role of the shadow in corporate social responsibility from a Jungian perspective. More recently (2010), he has explored concepts of responsible leadership, drawing on the work of Erikson, not Jung, and using Gandhi and Hitler as his positive and negative role models. Erikson's approach is summarized as consisting of (1) value basis, (2) self-image vs. external-image, (3) time perspective, (4) role experimentation, (5) anticipation of achievement and (6) leader–follower relations (2010: 173). The elements that are relevant here are (2) and (6), though there is scope for further work on the connections between Jung, Erikson, Ketola and Goodpaster. Ketola extrapolates the aspects of responsible leadership to produce a table showing the attributes for individuals, organizations and society (recalling the *micro, meso,* and *macro* levels of ethics considered earlier). While he deploys Erikson's approach for identifying the dimensions of responsible leadership, a Jungian approach to reconciling self-image and external image might be a valuable addition to this work. As mentioned above, Corlett and Pearson (2003) focus on the role of leader as storyteller, an approach that enriches the discursive and constructivist approaches to professions outlined in Chapter 3. To add to the elements of ethical leadership, it is also worth revisiting the ideas put forward by Rest and Narvaez (1994) and discussed in Chapter 4. They suggested that ethical leadership comprises (1) moral sensitivity – interpreting the situation, (2) moral judgement – judging which action is morally right/wrong, (3) moral motivation – prioritizing moral values relative to other values and (4) moral character – having courage, persisting, overcoming distractions, implementing skills (1994: 23). Again, it can be seen that a Jungian approach to professional ethics would embrace some of these qualities, such as sensitivity, character and motivation, though it would question what is meant by 'moral values' and ideas of 'right/wrong'. As Jung says: 'Such being the power of the unconscious, the process of coming to terms with it, in the ethical sense, acquires a special character' (1949/1990: 17–18). One exploration of Jungian archetypes in leadership (Abramson, 2007) cites literature which confirms that leaders play a crucial part in establishing the 'ethical tone' of the organization both as role models and as the arbiters of rewards and punishments for ethical/unethical behaviours, particularly in the early years of an organization and particularly when embodied in the founders. However, it is not clear how or why leaders suffering from teleopathy or over-identified with persona aspects would wish to engage with the scrutiny essential for change. Hollis (2007: 126) argues that

> managers must risk change, personal confrontation and redirection of energies ...each group, to recover its original energy and sense of purpose, must ask how the soul is enlarged or diminished by the current practices and attitudes. This takes either courage on the part of leadership, or desperation.

The Arthur W. Page Society (2009) report into trust in business referred to in Chapter 3 recognizes that there is a moral imperative in regaining public trust:

> Real change requires moral imagination, the ability to recognise problems and re-imagine our roles in ways that fill responsibility gaps. One way of understanding the crisis is to realise that people relied on the system and the market to a much greater extent than was warranted. What is required now is leadership that will foster mutuality, balance power, and develop effective trust safeguards.
>
> (2009: 8)

The loss of trust described earlier may create the imperative for change, the desperation Hollis (2007) recommends as the catalyst for change. To repeat Jung (1949/1990: 15):

> We might therefore define 'new ethic' as a development and differentiation within the old ethic, confined at present to those uncommon individuals who, driven by unavoidable conflicts of duty, endeavour to bring the conscious and the unconscious into responsible relationship.

A professional body, unlike a corporation, is run largely by its activists, usually with a small group of employees servicing the organization, and a secretariat shaping and implementing policy. Given that most members of professional bodies have their employment elsewhere, there is a greater likelihood that they will become aware of ethical shortcomings or reputational issues than might be the case among full-time employees. There is scope then for Jung's 'uncommon individuals' to come from the lay members rather than the leadership, or that leaders will stand on an 'ethics' ticket (such as Professor Anne Gregory as President of the UK Chartered Institute of Public Relations, 2004). Respected members of the profession may also take a lead in raising ethical issues, whether or not they hold an official position in the professional body. Moreover, applying a Jungian dimension to professional ethics engages the community of practice at a collective level, rather than place total responsibility for maintaining impossible demands on the shoulders of individual members of particular bodies (Abbott, 1983; Mount, 1990). As Bauman (2008: 62) says, 'morality is nothing but an innately prompted manifestation of humanity', a statement close to a Jungian perspective on ethics. The detailed collaborative and participative work in producing a new code of ethics for an emerging professional body (Messikomer and Cirka, 2010), outlined below, demonstrates that this kind of approach can be achieved if the parties are willing.

Jungian analyst Andrew Samuels (2006) has written a long and thoughtful piece about professional ethics in psychotherapy, and Barnes (2003) has a chapter on ethics in analytic relationships; while there is much literature on ethics within specific professions (especially health and law), the use of literature on this subject from Jungian writers is doubly salient and, moreover, was produced in response to moves to increase the regulatory control of psychotherapy, an issue that faces many professions. Samuels (2006: 182) argues that sociological and political considerations should also constitute the ethics of a profession, including diversity as a question of professional ethics:

> The new ethics remit I am proposing would engage directly and in a socially responsible way with questions of power in the profession, educational and otherwise. It would be essentially emancipatory in the sense of making available for challenge the underlying assumptions and purposes of psychotherapy.

Samuels also proposes an ethics committee to conduct reflexive research, which would examine the profession's economic, social and cultural structures and assumptions, and wonders if psychotherapists have modelled themselves on doctors (Barnes, 2003, suggests that the model is closer to priests in some cases). Are these reasonable or self-aggrandizing claims? How are psychotherapeutic services marketed, Samuels (2006) asks, and what do these choices say about the priorities and self-image of the profession? These are the kind of questions that all professions might ask of themselves. Samuels also addresses profession-specific questions, such as concerning the potential deterrent of a number of required therapy sessions per week for trainees without considerable economic resources; again, each grouping will have its own parallel issues. Barnes (2003) is also concerned with ethical issues at the level of the profession as well as the individual practitioner, as is this book. Her description of the ethical issues involved in the latter go deeper into clinical issues such as transference than Samuels does, highlighting the profound ethical responsibility involved in this psychic exchange, which demands high levels of consciousness from the analyst. At the professional level, Barnes (2003) notes a failure to address the philosophical underpinnings of codes of conduct in analytical and other professional organizations, echoing points made in Chapter 4 about limited, confused or conflicted theorizing in most codes of ethics. She suggests that the analytic organization's shared ethos consists of the collective ethos of the individual members, past and present, but that if this ethos is assumed to be shared but never discussed, it may in fact be illusory. In this way the pressures and uncertainties facing the individual practitioner are then reproduced at the institutional level. It is interesting to note that the organization for analysts, whose very profession involves reflection, challenge and shadow work in practice, has not brought those qualities to bear in its representative bodies. (Similarly, communication professions have had problems explaining themselves to members.) Perhaps some of the shadow material and complexes that arise in individual practice are projected onto the collective organization and 'parked' there. She also quotes Guggenbühl-Craig (1972/1991), who was cited in earlier chapters, concerning the shadow aspects of any profession and concludes: 'Ethical illusions can mask a profound uncertainty that will be reflected in our work with patients, in our analytic organisations and with one another' (Barnes, 2003: 47).

Beyond codes

The last question addressed in this chapter is whether, if professional bodies do take up the challenge of ethical leadership, codes of ethics will be of any value.

> The formulation of ethical rules is not only difficult but actually impossible because one can hardly think of a single rule that would not have to be reversed under certain conditions. Even the simple proposition 'conscious realisation is good' is only of limited validity, since we not infrequently meet with situations in which conscious realisation would have the worst possible consequences.
>
> (Jung, 1949/1990: 13)

A Jungian approach cannot yield a code of conduct, prescribing correct and incorrect actions, as the quote above illustrates. The Jungian ethical journey is inwards to realization rather than outwards for instruction. But this does not mean that nothing can be said. Rather it suggests that a Jungian ethic might be implemented through statements of principles and through guided ethical dialogue – probably based in questions rather than answers. Jung follows the quote above with a discussion of the subjectivity of ethical decision-making and the inadequacy of external 'old ethics' to resolve such dilemmas. However, he says: 'Despite their subjective nature, they cannot very well be formulated except as collective concepts … [which] will exhibit certain regular features' (Jung 1949/1990: 14). As Samuels and Barnes suggest for their field, ethics must be grounded in collective reflection and awareness. One example of how such an ethic might be generated is provided by Messikomer and Cirka (2010), who describe how an emerging professional body in the USA, the National Association of Senior Move Managers, involved with care for the ageing, built its purpose around ethics by consulting throughout the membership until there was consensus. They argue that codes can only shift from 'dead rules to living dialogue' (2010: 86) if those who must live by the rules participate in their construction. Illustrating the potential for ethical leadership in professional bodies referred to earlier, the association's leaders conducted a series of workshops involving members over a period of two years, first establishing shared values, then building a code. While the end result appears similar to Potter Box approaches for analysing the values and interests in a given ethical dilemma, Messikomer and Cirka's process is interesting and encouraging. They conclude that '[f]or a code to achieve sense validity, and realize the potential to be a living document, the code development process must be participative, the content must be values-based, and leaders must be authentic ethical managers' (2010: 59).

Translating these insights from a Jungian perspective, it seems worth summarizing the tools already identified for working with the shadow in groups and considering their implications for framing ethical approaches across professions (the particular implications for PR are considered in the next chapter and some of these issues are revisited in the final chapter):

- Analysis of corporate and promotional literature to identify tropes of language, symbolism and imagery – does the professional body present itself as part of the establishment, as an outsider, a grass-roots or an elite organization? What other institutions does it resemble?
- Identification of dominant narratives in and of the profession – are the profession's founders and leaders, past and present, seen as heroes, martyrs, healers? Even in one field, medicine, there are conflicting images, such as angelic nurses and heroic sword-wielding surgeons. Journalism has its 'sword of truth' – last waved by soon-to-be convicted perjurer, Jonathan Aitken; law has the goddess of blind justice.
- Demographic analysis – what are the gender balances, are ethnic minorities subtly dissuaded at early stages of career planning, is diversity given lip service

but resisted in practice? Is there a 'common sense' view that say, architects are male, childcare workers female?

- De-construction of notable, especially repeated, crises – what was seen, what was not? Were the crises concerned with failure to penetrate the dominant 'mindset' such as the NASA disasters or Enron? Was their misplaced complacency about the trustworthiness of fellow professionals, like the failure to challenge the death rate of Harold Shipman's patients? How do Members of Parliament, journalists, priests, accountants all fail to interrogate their own behaviour for so long? Importantly, what happens to whistleblowers?

- Examination of external evaluation of profession, by survey, poll or media (including social media) coverage – how does the profession rate in annual trust surveys, is it the regular butt of cartoons, jokes or online forums?

- Analysis of core texts used in teaching the profession, scrutiny of critical responses – what is the central 'story' being told about the profession – what is the story that is not being told? Is someone else, such as a critic, telling the untold story?

- Assessment of core curriculum and means of control of teaching – which stories are being taught and discussed in the classroom, in faculty and conference meetings? Are these different perspectives reflected in syllabi? Is there over-control of the curriculum or a general lack of interest? How does the profession engage with its educators? What are its attitudes to theory?

- Identification of the main out-groups, external, adjacent and internal to the profession – which groups attract the most intense reactions, jealousies and resentments? Where are they located in proximity to the profession? Is there are shared history, a split in perspectives? Have they gained more status in the struggle for jurisdictional control? Or is the group emerging within the profession, like an upsurge in women in science? What is under threat?

- Observation of the normal workings of the professional body, its structure and hierarchy, decision-making procedures, culture, physical surroundings, use of symbols – what kind of offices, how are they run and staffed, how accessible are they to members, what sub-groups operate in the office and elected positions? How is the communication organized, what is the attitude to ordinary members?

- Interviews with members of the profession and/or professional body can yield insights into which topics are off-limits, which groups or organizations attract common hostility, which complaints occur regularly from members and/or staff, and what happens to such comments?

The section on reflection suggested some routes for inventory-taking and it seems inappropriate to prejudge the outcome of such investigation, particularly as a central precept of the Jungian approach is the willingness to let the 'patient' evolve their own solutions. However, it is not unreasonable to suppose that such enquiry could lead to the production of a set of ethical statements, perhaps less defined than principles, constructed along Jungian lines, broadly similar to the following:

- Wherever there is a claim of goodness, excellence, service or other virtue, there will be a corresponding hidden aspect, including greed, selfishness, manipulation and deception. These are human qualities. This profession attempts to be aware of its shortcomings so that the public/society/clients are not damaged by thoughtless or routinized abuse of responsibility.
- In particular, reflection has led this profession to believe that it is at particular risk of a), b) c) and therefore strives to avoid these temptations by undertaking x), y) and z).
- Although this profession possesses and practices a body of knowledge, acquired through special training and/or education, it actively monitors how members use this knowledge, to ensure, so far as is possible, that those it serves are well-served.
- To this end, an ethical committee regularly reviews the profession's performance across a range of indicators and places its reports in the public domain. This review applies to the profession as a whole as well as to individual members, recognizing that not all professionals in this field belong to this professional body.
- The ethical committee is also closely involved in the design of the curriculum, which is (or may be) required for entry to the profession.
- The professional body has a range of responsibilities: to its members, to its clients/other fee payers, and to society generally. These responsibilities are sometimes in conflict. This profession aims to honour its commitment to society, through dialogue, reflection and accountability, but recognizes that it discharges its widest duty best when encouraging ethical debate – including disagreement – within its ranks.

The question raised in Chapter 4, as to whether special ethics are required by professionals, is best answered by proposing that a professional's ethical conduct is determined by his or her ethics as a person among persons, a member of society, with moral agency and responsibility, but that the particular responsibilities of a profession – to issues of health, law, education, accounting, engineering and so on – should be stated, together with awareness of the shadow aspects of that profession, the particular archetypes and complexes that have evolved in that field. It is worth remembering that Confucian and Buddhist ethics do not distinguish between the public and private sphere. Being a member of a profession may indicate special responsibilities but it does not morally separate, let alone elevate, the practitioner from the rest of humanity.

The next chapter returns, for the last time, to the profession of PR to consider the impact of the last three chapters on the issues raised earlier in this book.

Conclusions

This chapter set out to generate insights into how a Jungian ethic might be adopted by those professions seeking to practice ethical leadership. It considered points of contact and divergence with existing approaches in professional ethics and the wider field of global and postmodernist ethics, highlighting the common ground between, for example, virtue and Jungian ethics or with postmodernism, but also identifying the fundamental grounds of disagreement. The role of the professional body in a new kind of ethical leadership was then explored, in which ethical responsibility was shared at the collective level, not merely devolved down to members, picking up a point made clearly in Chapter 4. The challenges facing ethical leaders were stressed, together with the difficulty of raising the shadow material and cultural complexes of the profession to consciousness. Suggestions were made, following discussion in earlier chapters, for conducting a reflective inventory and for the kinds of statements that might result from such enquiry.

It was clear that recurring themes and questions from a variety of ethical perspectives are addressed, if not resolved, by a Jungian approach, suggesting scope for further research and investigation, as will be further considered in the concluding chapter.

Note

1   All references to Jung cite the *Collected Works* and the relevant paragraph, not page.

References

Abbott, A. (1983) Professional ethics. *The American Journal of Sociology, 88*(5): 855–85.
Abbott, A. (1988) *The System of Professions: an essay on the division of expert labor.* Chicago, IL: University of Chicago Press.
Abbott, A. (1995) Things of boundaries. *Social Research, 62*(4): 857–82.
Abramson, N. R. (2007) The leadership archetype: a Jungian analysis of similarities between modern leadership theory and the Abraham myth in the Judaic-Christian tradition. *Journal of Business Ethics, 72*(2): 115–29.
Amir, L. B. (2005) Morality, psychology, philosophy. *Philosophical Practice, 1*(1): 43–57.
Appiah, K. (2008) *Experiments in Ethics.* Cambridge, MA and London: Harvard University Press.
Arthur W. Page Society (2009) *The dynamics of public trust in business – emerging opportunities for leaders.* Arthur W. Page Society.
Barnes, F. P. (2003) Ethics in practice. In H. M. Solomon and M. Twyman (eds) *The Ethical Attitude in Analytic Practice.* London and New York, NY: Free Association Books, pp. 38–47.
Bauman, Z. (1993) *Postmodern Ethics.* Oxford: Blackwell.
Bauman, Z. (2008) *Does Ethics have a Chance in a World of Consumers?* Cambridge, MA: Harvard University Press.
Bauman, Z. and Vecchi, B. (2004) *Identity: conversations with Benedetto Vecchi.* Cambridge: Polity.
Beebe, J. (1992) *Integrity in Depth.* College Station, TX: Texas A&M University.
Beebe, J. (1998) Towards a Jungian analysis of character. In A. Casement (ed.) *Post-Jungians Today: key papers in analytical psychology.* London: Routledge, pp. 53–66.
Benhabib, S. (1992) *Situating the Self: gender, community, and postmodernism in contemporary ethics.* New York, NY: Routledge.
Bishop, P. (1999) C. G. Jung and Nietzsche – Dionysos and analytical psychology. In P.

Bishop (ed.) *Jung in Contexts: a reader*. London and New York, NY: Routledge, pp. 205–41.

Brecher, B. (2010) The politics of professional ethics. *The Journal of Clinical Evaluation in Practice, 16:* 351–5.

Broadbent, J., Dietrich, M. and Roberts, J. (1997) *The End of the Professions?: the restructuring of professional work*. London: Routledge.

Cooper, D. E. (2004) *Ethics for Professionals in a Multicultural World*. Upper Saddle River, NJ: Prentice Hall.

Corlett, J. G. and Pearson, C. (2003) *Mapping the Organizational Psyche: a Jungian theory of organizational dynamics and change*. Gainesville, FL: Center for Applications of Psychological Type.

Crawford, N. C. (1998) Postmodern ethical conditions and a critical response. *Ethics and International Affairs, 12*(1): 121–40.

Curtin, P. A. and Gaither, T. K. (2005) Privileging identity, difference and power: the circuit of culture as a basis for public relations theory. *Journal of Public Relations Research, 17*(2): 91–115.

Curtin, P. A. and Gaither, T. K. (2007) *International Public Relations: negotiating culture, identity and power*. Thousand Oaks, CA: Sage.

Davey, N. (2004) Towards a hermeneutics of attentiveness. *Renascence: Essays on Values in Literature, 56*(4): 217–34.

Dent, M. and Whitehead, S. (2002) *Managing Professional Identities: knowledge, performativity and the "new" professional*. London: Routledge.

Egan, G. (1994) *Working the Shadow Side: a guide to positive behind-the-scenes management*. San Francisco, CA: Jossey-Bass.

Feldman, B. (2004) Towards a theory of organizational culture: integrating the 'other' from a post-Jungian perspective. In T. Singer and S. L. Kimbles (eds) *The Cultural Complex: contemporary Jungian perspectives on psyche and society*. New York, NY: Brunner-Routledge, pp. 251–61.

Freidson, E. (1994) *Professionalism Reborn: theory, prophecy, and policy*. Cambridge: Polity.

Giddens, A. (1978) *Durkheim*. Hassocks: Harvester Press.

Goffman, E. (1959) *The Presentation of Self in Everyday Life*. New York, NY: Doubleday Anchor.

Goodpaster, K. E. (2007) *Conscience and Corporate Culture*. Malden, MA and Oxford: Blackwell.

Gray, F. (2008) *Jung, Irigaray, Individuation: philosophy, analytical psychology, and the question of the feminine*. London: Routledge.

Guggenbühl-Craig, A. (1972/1991) Quacks, charlatans and false prophets. In C. Zweig and J. Abrams (eds) *Meeting the Shadow: the hidden power of the dark side of human nature*. New York, NY: Tarcher/Penguin, pp. 110–16.

Halpern, S. A. (1992) Dynamics of professional control: internal coalitions and cross-professional boundaries. *American Journal of Sociology, 97*(4): 994–1021.

Hauke, C. (2000) *Jung and the Postmodern: the interpretation of realities*. London: Routledge.

Hede, A. (2007) The shadow group: towards an explanation of interpersonal conflict in work groups. *Journal of Managerial Psychology, 22*(1): 25–39.

Hermans, H. J. M. and Kempen, H. J. G. (1993) *The Dialogical Self: meaning as movement*. San Diego, CA and London: Academic Press.

Hollis, J. (2007) *Why Good People do Bad Things*. New York, NY: Gotham Books.

Hutton, J. G. (2010) Defining the relationship between public relations and marketing: public relations' most important challenge. In R. L. Heath (ed.) *The SAGE Handbook of Public Relations*. Thousand Oaks, CA: Sage, pp. 509–22.

Ihlen, Ø. (2007) Building on Bourdieu: a sociological grasp of public relations. *Public Relations Review, 33*(3): 269–74.

James, W. (1905) *Varieties of Religious Experience: a study in human nature*. London: Longmans.

Jarrett, J. (1999) Schopenhauer and Jung. In P. Bishop (ed.) *Jung in Contexts: a reader*. London: Routledge, pp. 193–204.

Jones, R. A. (2007) *Jung, Psychology, Postmodernity*. Hove, East Sussex: Routledge.

Jung, C. G. (1949/1990) Foreword, in Neumann, E., *Depth Psychology and a New Ethic*. Boston, MA: Shambala Press. pp 11–18.

Jung, C. G. *Civilisation in Transition*, Vol. 10, *Collected Works* (eds Read, H., Adler, G. A., Fordham, and M.; trans. R. F. C. Hull). London: Routledge & Kegan Paul.

Jung, C. G. *Aion*, Vol. 9ii, *Collected Works* (eds Read, H., Adler, G. A. and Fordham, M.; trans. R. F. C. Hull). London: Routledge & Kegan Paul.

Jung, C. G. *Psychological Types*, Vol. 6, *Collected Works* (eds Read, H., Adler, G. A. and Fordham, M.; trans. R. F. C. Hull). London: Routledge & Kegan Paul.

Kaye, R. P. (2006) Regulated (self-)regulation: a new paradigm for controlling the professions. *Public Policy and Administration, 21*(3): 105–19.

Ketola, T. (2008) Taming the shadow: corporate responsibility in a Jungian context. *Corporate Social Responsibility and Environmental Management, 15*(4): 199–209.

Ketola, T. (2010) Responsible leadership: building blocks of individual, organisational and societal behaviour. *Corporate Social Responsibility and Environmental Management, 17*(3): 173–84.

Koehn, D. (2001) *Local Insights, Global Ethics for Business*. Amsterdam: Rodopi.

Kultgen, J. (1988) *Ethics and Professionalism*. Philadeplhia: University of Philadelphia Press.

Larson, M. S. (1977) *The Rise of Professionalism: a sociological analysis*. Berkeley, CA and London: University of California Press.

Lyotard, J.-F. (1984) *The Postmodern Condition: a report on knowledge*. Manchester: Manchester University Press.

McDonald, G. and Nijhof, A. (1999) Beyond codes of ethics: an integrated framework for stimulating morally responsible behaviour in organisations. *Leadership & Organization Development Journal, 20*(3): 133–47.

Main, R. (2007) Ruptured time and the re-enchantment of modernity. In A. Casement (ed.) *Who owns Jung?* London: Karnac, pp. 19–38.

Mattoon, M. A. (2005) *Jung and the Human Psyche: an understandable introduction*. London: Routledge.

Messikomer, C. M. and Cirka, C. C. (2010) Constructing a code of ethics: an experiential case of a national professional organization. *Journal of Business Ethics, 95:* 55–71.

Mount, E. (1990) *Professional Ethics in Context: institutions, images, and empathy*. Louisville, KY: Westminster/John Knox Press.

Neville, B. (2010) The polytheistic organization. *Personality Type in Depth, 1* (October).

Oliver, A. L. and Montgomery, K. (2005) Toward the construction of a profession's boundaries: creating a networking agenda. *Human Relations, 58*(9): 1167–84.

Parkinson, M. (2001) The PRSA Code of Professional Standards and Member Code of Ethics: why they are neither professional nor ethical. *Public Relations Quarterly, 46*(3): 27–31.

Pieczka, M. (2006) Chemistry and the public relations industry: an exploration of the concept of jurisdiction and issues arising. In J. L'Etang and M. Pieczka (eds) *Public Relations, Critical Debates and Contemporary Practice*. Mahwah, NJ: Lawrence Erlbaum Associates, pp. 303–27.

Reay, D. (2004) *Special Issue: Pierre Bourdieu's sociology of education: the theory of practice and the practice of theory*. Abingdon: Carfax.

Rest, J. R. and Narvaez, D. (1994) *Moral Development in the Professions: psychology and applied ethics*. Hillsdale, NJ and Hove, East Sussex: Lawrence Erlbaum Associates.

Robinson, S. (2002) Challenger Flight 51-L. In C. Megone and S. Robinson (eds) *Case Studies in Business Ethics*. London: Routledge, pp. 108–22.

Samuels, A. (1993) *The Political Psyche*. London: Routledge.

Samuels, A. (2006) Socially responsible roles of professional ethics: inclusivity, psychotherapy and 'the protection of the public'. *International Review of Sociology, 16*(2): 175–89.

Schweiker, W. (2004) *Theological Ethics and Global Dynamics: in the time of many worlds*. Malden, MA and Oxford: Blackwell.

Schweiker, W. (2007) Whither global ethics? Moral consciousness and global cultural flows. *Journal of Ecumenical Studies, 42*(3): 425–39.

Singer, T. (2004) The cultural complex and archetypal defenses of the group spirit. In T. Singer and S. L. Kimbles (eds) *The Cultural Complex: contemporary Jungian perspectives on psyche and society*. New York, NY: Brunner-Routledge, pp. 13–34.

Singer, T. and Kimbles, S. L. (eds) (2004) *The Cultural Complex: contemporary Jungian perspectives on psyche and society*. New York, NY: Brunner-Routledge.

Solomon, H. M. (2001) Origins of the ethical attitude. *Journal of Analytic Psychology, 46*(3): 443–54.

Tacey, D. (1998) Twisting and turning with James Hillman: from anima to world soul, from academia to pop. In A. Casement (ed.) *Post-Jungians Today: key papers in contemporary analytical psychology*. London: Routledge, pp. 215–34.

Turner, B. S. (1992) Preface to the second edition. In B. S. Turner and C. Brookfield (eds) *Professional Ethics and Civic Morals*. London: Routledge, pp. xiii–xlii.

Watson, T. (2002) Speaking professionally: occupational anxiety and discursive ingenuity in human resourcing specialists. In M. Dent and S. Whitehead (eds) *Managing Professional Identities: knowledge, performativity and the 'new' professional*. London: Routledge, pp. 99–115.

Wernick, A. (1991) *Promotional Culture: advertising, ideology and symbolic expression*. London: Sage.

Zimbardo, P. G. (2007) *The Lucifer Effect: how good people turn evil*. London: Rider.

9   The shadow of excellence

Introduction

This is the third visit to the domain of public relations (PR): the first sketched an overview of the field, suggested a typology of approaches, identified some recurring issues with its approach to ethics and indicated divisions between the theoretical ethical perspectives promoted by texts and professional associations and those often expressed by practitioners. The second excursion added depth by taking on board a range of sociological literature on professions and philosophical literature on ethics. Now, the final adventure (in this book, anyway) reframes PR ethics in the light of the Jungian concepts explored in previous chapters.

I suspect I am raising more hares than I can chase, or burrowing down more tunnels than necessary (to mix metaphors), but I am trying to demonstrate the richness of these ideas and their potential for transforming our understanding of PR as a profession and its conflicted attitudes towards ethics. As the final chapter illustrates, these indicate areas for future research and cannot come to conclusions here, or even perhaps anywhere, given the fluidity of both subject and approach. One of the challenges in a Jungian approach is to resist the urge to fix things – so there will be no new codes, no models, no '10 ways' of doing anything. As I said at the beginning of the book – it's time to get messy.

Public relations – a Jungian approach

Chapter 8 suggested that professions could be viewed as psychic entities, containing the same components Jung ascribed to the individual psyche, namely ego, persona, shadow, and other archetypes that have the potential to be brought into conscious relationship with each other during the process of individuation. As with individuals, the first stage of group individuation is recognizing the shadow elements that were previously attributed to others, followed by engagements with this shadow material and finally the reconceptualizing of the whole as the sum of many, often contradictory, parts contained in a greater entity or field, often called the transcendent, which may or may not be secular. In this schema, it would appear that PR, like many other relatively new professional groups, has invested heavily in its persona aspects, while shadow material has accumulated outside its acknowledged range of vision. It would also appear, from the confusion about identity and lack of coherent central narrative (Hutton, 2010), that it may have an underdeveloped ego function, causing it to become unduly defensive (Stein, 1998). The indicators of persona function can be found in the many claims, particularly from those supporting the excellence approach, to enhance democracy, serve society and so on. Sample quotes include: 'Public relations has a moral purpose, which is social harmony' (Seib and Fitzpatrick, 1995: 1); or more recently, 'Public Relations is the champion of democracy and the guardian of common sense' (Vercic, 2005: n.p.). Bowen's statement, cited earlier, reinforces this: 'public relations is serving a larger and more ethically responsible role by communicating for the good of society, both for the benefit of specific groups and for the maintenance of society itself' (Bowen, 2007: 279). As suggested in earlier chapters, core textbooks, the professional organizations and trade magazines are notably lacking in self-criticism (Holtzhausen, 2000; McKie, 2001; Moloney, 2006). I'm suggesting – and it was one of the insights that fuelled my thesis and this book – that the core shadow material in PR concerns propaganda and persuasion. Just look at the absence of propaganda from core texts: Wilcox *et al.* (2003) devote two pages out of over 650 to the subject of propaganda and Cutlip avoids what he calls 'that dirty word' by describing US war efforts as 'organised promotion to kindle fervent patriotism' (1985: 31). Moloney notes that 'favourable literature (by academics and authors who have worked in PR) adopts various approaches to the propaganda link: ignore it and/or define PR in a way which dissolves or reduces the linkage' (2000: 85). These issues were raised in Chapter 5, and are reframed in terms of persona and shadow below. PR codes of ethics, also explored in Chapter 5, embody this persona role, in their promotional role for establishing the reputation and goals of the profession, rather than as instruments for controlling ethical behaviour of members. In many ways, professional PR bodies are so aligned with the excellence approach that they are almost synonymous and both can be said to perform the persona function. To repeat, Jung is clear that a persona is necessary to conduct business in the world, to behave in ways acceptable to society and that elements of the individual (or group) are properly selected for presentation and others kept back as private. The danger is in over-identifying with this public face, and forgetting it is not the whole story. So, the elements of the psyche corresponding to persona and shadow can be seen in the dualistic dynamics between PR's self-aggrandisement and the unacknowledged voices both of critics and many practitioners who feel that persuasion lies at the heart of the field.

The applicability of Jung's approach is further evidenced by the intensity with which the critics pick up the rejected, shadow material and fling it back at PR. 'Today's PR industry is related to democracy in the same way prostitution is related to sex', according to Miller and Dinan (2008: 14). Their book *A Century of Spin* provides copious illustrations of PR deployment of deception and misrepresentation in government and corporate communications, examples that are updated on www.spinwatch.org. It is worth noting that Miller and Dinan are unable to come up with any defence of PR – there is no discussion of the communication tactics used by voluntary organizations, trade unions or environmental campaigners, for example, nor any discussion of how a corporation might legitimately defend its own interests. This is also characteristic of shadow dynamics – the emphasis on the otherness of the other precludes connection, shared ownership or recognition of the self in the other:

> Intense collective emotion is the hallmark of an activated cultural complex at the core of which is an archetypal pattern ... Like individual complexes, cultural complexes tend to be repetitive, autonomous, resist consciousness, and collect experience that confirms their historical point of view.
>
> (Singer and Kimbles, 2004: 6)

I am therefore suggesting that a Jungian approach allows us to reconceptualize PR as follows: a) like other kinds of groups, PR can be considered as a psychic entity consisting of contradictory elements that will undermine the whole until brought into conscious – but not fixed – relationship with each other; b) that the cultural complex operating in PR as a community of practice embracing practitioners, academics and students may be centred on the 'problem' of persuasion; c) that engaging with this complex may reveal the seeds of its own healing; and d) that PR cannot claim meaningful ethics without examining its own shadow, an observation that applies at both individual and collective levels. The next section goes deeper into the shadow aspects of the field, in particular issues of the other, jurisdiction and persuasion as a central practice.

The other, in a Jungian conceptualization of PR, may be external or internal. To take the internal schisms first: the past half-century has seen a sustained effort to emphasize strategic communication and boardroom counsel over the older versions of promotion and publicity commonly associated with the field. As a consequence those practising PR in the areas of sports, celebrity and music, for example, are not welcome in the club. The tone of comments from the Chartered Institute of Public Relations, indicated in Chapter 2, in response to practitioners espousing advocacy ethics (or the 'cab for hire' version thereof) also indicates internal disputes. Bowen's (2008) grouping of practitioners into ethical and anti-ethical splits the field into right and wrong in ways that are rejected by Jungians. Amongst scholars, the tensions between Grunigians and critical scholars are palpable, and these and other schools of thought have been explored throughout this book. The point here is not to argue for peace and reconciliation but to embrace recent writing such as Edwards' (2012: 20) argument for PR's positions or schools to be seen as continua rather than divisions: 'The notion of continua rather than categories makes space for the "grey" area between the extremes of each scholarly group'. This is also echoed in recent discussion of communication ethics (Arnett, 2011), which starts from the premise that ethics are multiple. I am suggesting that a Jungian framework encourages acceptance of such grey areas, recognizing that conflict sometimes has to be 'held' rather than resolved. However, in order to bring hidden aspects to light, some digging into the shadow of the field is required.

The role of the other within the profession is explored by Edwards (2011), who demonstrates how diversity is 'ironed' out of core images, causing black and minority ethnic entrants to minimize their racial and/or cultural differences to fit in; the role of the professional body in generating such norms was discussed earlier in the book. In Jungian ethics, as well as other ethical approaches, the other is always an aspect of oneself. Individuation requires the subject to recognize that the aspects of other people that he or she finds most difficult are actually shadow projections, disowned elements of the self which are forcibly attached to groups or individuals so that the subject need not confront their hidden desires. The erotic ambiguity of the homophobe is one example in individuals; the casting of race, gender, sexuality, disability or other group identity as 'other' illustrates how this works on a larger scale. A Jungian approach is genuinely founded in diversity, requiring willingness to engage with rather than reject the other in the self, both individually and collectively.

However, instead of recognition and negotiation, the other, in current professional ethics, is usually designated scapegoat. The penalties meted out to whistleblowers illustrate this, no matter that they are enacting the service to society that so many professional bodies claim then ignore. Thus problems of fabrication and distortion, as reported in the Westminster debate (see Chapter 2) and on critical websites, are loaded onto individual 'deviants' in order to maintain the purity of the primary vision. That this is not unique to PR can be demonstrated by the extraordinary reluctance to admit that illegal phone tapping at the late UK newspaper, the *News of the World,* was not merely conducted by a few isolated individuals who have been, or will be, punished, but was endemic in normal practice. The 2012 Leveson Inquiry blew the lid off that collective fantasy, just as the 1999 McPherson report into racism in the Metropolitan Police following the murder of Stephen Lawrence revealed institutional rather than individual culpability. In the past year in the UK, an investigation into Mid Staffordshire NHS Foundation Trust has found several hundreds of unnecessary deaths, the result of cultural norms and institutional neglect and at the time of writing; and a Royal Commission in Australia is investigating abuse, particularly of children, in a variety of institutions entrusted with care of the vulnerable. Such examples involve professional groups, checking systems and regulations (light in journalism, heavy in health); all proved inadequate. Closer to home, in 2011, it was revealed that Facebook had hired the public relations agency Burson-Marsteller to 'bad mouth' Google; Burson-Marsteller then pressured journalists to write negative copy, until the transactions were revealed by internal emails. Responses in various blogs included: 'called a spade a spade', 'smearing is an integral part of PR' and, more thoughtfully from a senior member of the Public Relations Society of America (PRSA):

> Will our profession use this as a teachable moment—an opportunity to reassess our commitment to serving the public interest and being ethical counselors to our clients? Or will we just brush it aside as yet another instance of an ethical lapse taking center stage for a couple of news cycles?
>
> (Treviit, 2011)

In these examples, the tension between developing an ethical approach and protecting the group's reputation are palpable, and recall earlier reflections on

Jungian cultural complexes (Feldman, 2004), particularly the defensive strategies taken by groups that perceive themselves to be under attack, and then shut down alternative perspectives. Feldman (2004) concludes that tension is necessary for development and should be welcomed; insights from infant development can be applied to groups, so that 'organizational culture can grow, develop and mature, as dialogue is facilitated between opposing opinions and viewpoints' (2004: 254). It is also worth repeating here Ketola's (2008) use of Jungian theory to illuminate shadow dynamics in corporate social responsibility (CSR), also known as corporate responsibility (CR), a field closely aligned with and often under the remit of PR. Like this book, Ketola's paper, one of a series, relates Jungian concepts of ego, persona, shadow and self to the corporate world, arguing that CR issues often trigger denial and/or projection of the problem onto others:

> This is the shadow working … It is almost impossible for any individual to resist the luring shadow's aggressive and defensive behaviour patterns … and try to respond in the ego's rational way to CR challenges because the feelings of guilt and shame overwhelm us. This is why company representatives go blind to the facts and to their own behaviour. It may take months for them to accept the truth and sublimate by admitting liability … Yet concession is the only way forward.
>
> (2008: 201)

Ketola suggests that successful chief executive officers (CEOs) respond to a CR issue by making concessions, because 'the ego of mentally developed individuals has accepted its shadow' (2008: 201) and is therefore able to make more mature and responsible decisions. Ketola's summary of individuation and characterization of some aspects of Jungian psychology appear somewhat simplistic (for example, he sees archetypes as originating in the self, which in turn is presented as synonymous with personal character), but the application of Jungian thought to corporate situations, particularly those involving responsibility, helps illustrate the applicability of my arguments, and takes them into the world of ethics and responsible decision-making. Ketola also raises the question of personal and collective responsibility in corporate decisions when company actions conflict with personal values, as do Corlett and Pearson (2003). They also suggest a range of rituals for organizations experiencing change, with an emphasis on storytelling to help understand and adjust to such transitions – including the interesting recommendation to reflect a crisis as a series of stories in order to raise awareness of the multiple interpretations available to every situation.

Having looked at internal 'others', it is worth examining the issues of jurisdiction in PR from this Jungian perspective. Earlier chapters have set out the main principles of this analysis, as evolved in professions (Abbott, 1988, 1995) and applied to PR (Pieczka and L'Etang, 2001). The tensions with marketing and journalism are the most marked as they compete directly for organizational resources, respect and seats on the board. Each sees the other as a subset of itself, a kind of sibling 'King of the Castle' rivalry. One can observe attempts to borrow each other's clothes as PR emulates marketing's superior quantitative attributes by seeking to introduce Return on Investment, for example, while marketing moves into the field of relationships, hitherto secured by PR, by promoting social marketing and relationship marketing as the next innovation in management theory and practice. Work on CSR was developed as an aspect of PR theory but has not been located in PR departments (Bowen *et al.*, 2006). The relationship with journalism is also a struggle for resources but these are not concerned with the internal organizational goods but with access to the public sphere. Traditionally, PR sought to control information reaching media audiences while journalists resisted such attempts; this is a history of mutual dependency conducted in terms of abuse. PR people and operations are seen by journalists as barriers to 'truth'; the media is blamed by PR for distorting all communication efforts (indeed this distortion was used to justify lying in the 2007 Westminster debate). The advent of new media and the marginalization of the 'gatekeeper' role do not seem to have diminished these antagonisms.

There is also the other in PR identities – not a struggle for work but for definition. As suggested earlier, PR identities have polarized into moral guardians vs. amoral advocates (Fawkes, 2012); calling one group ethical and the other anti-ethical (Bowen, 2008) creates an 'other' out of many practitioners. Baker's (2008) opposing archetypes of advocate and partisan are presented as a continuum, rather that binary opposites, and her work helps delineate the characteristics of these positions. What a Jungian perspective offers is something more welcoming than the rejection practitioners sometimes experience, as expressed by one Canadian practitioner:

> the Code of Professional Conduct of the Canadian Public Relations Society …
> preaches that ethical professional conduct for public relations practitioners
> has something to do with promoting 'honesty, accuracy, integrity and truth' in
> public communications. While this notion might be truly inspiring, it none-
> theless ignores what public relations actually is all about – namely, the
> advocacy and dissemination of the partisan viewpoints of those who engage
> our services, for the benefit of those who engage our services.
>
> (O'Malley, n.d.)

L'Etang (2011) also notes the contradiction between codes that exalt both transparency and confidentiality without acknowledging that the latter is usually secured at the expense of the former.

Reclaiming persuasion

I have long believed that the central shadow issue to PR is persuasion, and its murky relationship to propaganda. I have written on this elsewhere (Fawkes, 2006, 2007, 2009), as have others (L'Etang, 2006; Moloney, 2006; Pfau and Wan, 2006; Porter, 2010; Weaver *et al.*, 2006). As Chapters 2 and 5 made clear, the excellence approach bases its ethics in the structure of symmetrical communication and condemns persuasion as unethical. And while persuasive ethics is considered in (primarily US) schools of rhetoric, core PR texts rarely examine persuasion in any depth. I suggest that the idea of persuasion is threatening to the self-image or persona of excellence and that collective energy is expended, ensuring that PR keeps its distance from this contagious concept; after all, if we let persuasion in, propaganda can't be far behind. Indeed, the boundaries between definitions of PR, propaganda and persuasion, as offered by historians and social psychologists, are blurred to the point of interchangeability (Fawkes, 2006). PR pioneers saw no problem with trying to 'organize' the responses of mass audiences; indeed, they saw it as democratic leadership, in Lippman's (1995/1925) phrase. Bernays opens *Propaganda* (Bernays and Miller, 2005: 38) with the sentence: 'The conscious and intelligent manipulation of the organised habits and opinions of the masses is an important element in democratic society'. There is a linkage between this statement and the claims that PR contributes to democratic process examined throughout this book; the organization-centred view of the field does call for 'intelligent manipulation' of the masses, even if such terminology is now seen as toxic. After all, 'the real value of propaganda lies *not* in its dissemination and promotion of *ideas* but in its ability to orchestrate public opinion and social action that supported the ruling elite' (Weaver *et al.*, 2006: 9 emphasis in original). Isn't what Moloney (2000: 84) calls, 'weak propaganda' a central aspect of everyday PR? The denial of PR's roots in propaganda leads to the denial of persuasion, even though 'it cannot be seriously maintained that all persuasion is bad or undesirable' (Jaksa and Pritchard, 1994: 128). If this is brought more fully into the light, the suspicion grows that the real darkness lies not in persuasion but power. If communication, including persuasion, is viewed as neutral in itself, then the ideological deployment of these tools comes into focus. It is not the persuasive nature of communication that causes imbalance but the inequalities of resources and access to media, where constraints on transparency and disclosure act to the advantage of one party that is unavailable to the other. The question is not only 'what are PR people doing?' but 'to what ends?', as Porter (2010) points out. Blaming persuasion for what is wrong with PR is missing the point.

In practice it seems to me that the unwillingness to engage with this aspect of the field has exacerbated the abuse; failure to acknowledge the widespread, contemporary use of propaganda techniques, including front organizations, deceptive use of PR people as journalists, withholding of significant information from affected publics, corruption of democratic processes, and so on, compounds the problem. Moloney (2006) provides a measured insight into these issues and is a better guide than the shriller Stauber and Rampton (2004) or Miller and Dinan (2008). These are the aspects of PR that are familiar to the general public and no amount of statistics regarding excellent practice can really make a difference until some kind of ownership takes place. Moreover, this is the heart of the field as recognized by practitioners, who consistently place promotion of client interests as their key concern, as was explored in Chapters 2 and 5. As suggested there, the chasm between the concept of ethical guardian and advocate undermines the field's attempts to evolve a meaningful approach to ethics.

And to refer to my own experience, professional and personal: when I look back 30 years at my role as a campaigner on trade union issues, civil rights and local government, I see someone so committed to the cause that I unconsciously selected those messages that would advance it, and rejected those that wouldn't. It was adversarial and fairly brutal at times, but we were fighting for collective rights (we lost). Persuasion is an essential tool when trying to redress imbalances of power – it may be all you have. I put my heart and soul into persuading others – union members, councillors and ratepayers – to resist cuts. This was not a cool presentation of options to the executive. I made no claims to objectivity and embraced partisan positions. However, what strikes me now is the degree of self-persuasion that fuelled my non-stop activity; opposition was simply intolerable. I lived in a very black and white world. Not long before, I had confronted my own addiction and understood the extraordinary ability to delude oneself in the face of overwhelming evidence. I'm fine, I insisted, as everything fell apart. I use this experience to explore how people at Enron, the *News of the World* or the Catholic hierarchy might convince themselves that they are the victims, despite the evidence of abuse. I know that it is possible to construct a view of oneself and resist counter-positions until the situation becomes critical. I also know that it is not possible to recover, in my experience anyway, without reconceptualizing past behaviour, acknowledging the damage done to others, as well as oneself, in these years and recognizing that some kind of vigilance (benevolent, not punitive) will be necessary to prevent repetition of such patterns. This involves what Jung calls individuation.

So the danger in persuasion it seems to me is not in persuading others but in persuading oneself to the point where other perspectives are marginalized, creating a sense of self that is predicated on the rightness of a particular position. To reconsider that position is extremely difficult once the ego is involved; people go to great lengths to avoid such adjustments (Festinger, 1962; Fishbein, 1975). One disillusioned environmentalist wrote of his pain at discovering the truth behind his employer's claims to go 'Beyond Petroleum' during the Gulf of Mexico oil spill:

> I couldn't get the images of the brown pelicans out of my head – every inch of their bodies covered in oil, with only their eyes peering out from the thick, brown goo. Like everyone else, I felt outrage that BP could let this happen. But unlike everyone else, I also felt personally betrayed by BP. Like many of us who spend eight to 12 hours a day building brands, I believed in the story I was helping to craft, no matter how small my contribution was … The idea is to ask how to deal with situations where the brands we work on not only disappoint us, but lead us astray.
>
> (Torres, 2010)

This is both personal and professional; you can feel the pain of confronting this shadow. I felt the same way when the Council I had campaigned for started implementing the cuts they had been opposing. I had to learn that I could not place my personal identity in the hands of politicians; that people mean what they say when they promise one thing and also mean it when they do the opposite; it was my naïvety not human nature that was misplaced. I now see how, in Jungian terms, these stances lead to extreme antagonism, where opposing views are characterized as idiotic or malign (the 2013 Australian election provides plenty of illustration, but this discourse is even more polarized in the USA).

Given that rejected material often contains the seeds of what is missing from the whole person, what they need to grow up, it may be that failure to acknowledge the persuasion at the heart of most PR has infantilized our ethical approaches. What if persuasion is an asset rather than a liability? Practitioners see it as their main offering; perhaps a wider discussion could re-envision the persuader in the old rhetorical approach, a skilled deployer of text and symbol to serve a particular end. After all, a Jungian approach encourages engagement with, rather than rejection of, these elements of the whole: what do they have to tell PR about itself? How can one have a professional internal dialogue if there is no capacity to listen (Pieczka, 2011)? And how can one have professional ethics if they are based on the denial of large swathes of practice? Perhaps we will be better able to examine power imbalances in communication if we accept the reality of persuasion than if we insist on an illusory ideal of equality (Moloney, 2006). The collective self-examination recommended in a Jungian approach would surely involve painful but honest appraisals of PR's involvement with propaganda, past *and* present. As Jung (CW14/706)[1] points out, shadow material contains what we need to be whole, if only we can claim it:

> This process of coming to terms with the Other in us is well worthwhile, because in this way we get to know aspects of our nature which we would not allow anybody else to show us and which we would never have admitted.

This also illustrates how such complexes work at both the personal and collective level; the practitioner is engaging with ethical conflicts in their personal domain that reflect absolutely those taking place at the collective level. Unfortunately the quality of debate often serves to prevent rather than encourage wider discussion of these conflicts, despite the evidence that silence causes stress in individuals (Kang, 2010), and, I argue, professions. The next section revisits the dominant approaches to PR, set out in Chapter 2, in the light of the above discussion and earlier reflections on Jungian approaches to professions and professional ethics. Finally the chapter ends with discussion on the role of professional bodies in taking up these issues.

Revisiting approaches to public relations

Looking at excellence through a Jungian lens reveals an over-insistent emphasis on professional probity and a reluctance to admit to the seamier side of PR that resembles the reactions of the persona to shadow material. As stated several times, this is only bad news if the idealized version is seen as the totality of the entity, all that can be said about a person or group. The evidence lies in the manner, detailed above and in earlier chapters, that excellence constructs itself not as one story in many about PR but as a benchmark against which behaviours can be categorized as Good or Bad PR. This is the 'optimal approach [that] has stunted public relations scholarship' (Pfau and Wan, 2006: 102). Not only that, but in exporting these benchmarks globally, excellence has become universally accepted by professional bodies and a proliferation of educational institutes as the foundation of PR practice and education (Moloney, 2000; Parkinson, 2001). It is a remarkable achievement, but not necessarily an *entirely* healthy one.

The dis-ease, it seems to me – hence the subtitle of this book – is in its difficulty in engaging with the shadow side of PR and the consequential superficial engagement with ethics. As mentioned earlier, most PR core texts may include a page or two on ethics at most, but provide nothing of real help to the novice practitioner, preferring to rely on codes for guidance, although, as earlier discussion of codes suggested, these are rhetorical statements designed more for external consumption than internal monitoring or support of ethical behaviour. The philosophical underpinning is Kantian, according to Bowen (2007), though that is disputed by L'Etang (2003), with a central claim that communication constitutes a social good (Bowen, 2010). Thus ethics emerges from 'collaborative decision making, listening and appreciating, social value and meaning' (Bowen, 2010: 571) among other positive aspects of communication. This returns the discussion to Baker's (2008) good and bad practitioners, with positive characteristics celebrated and negative traits ignored.

There is little discussion of power, feminist, post-colonial or postmodern ethics, because they raise awkward questions that challenge the worldview of excellence – a worldview predicated on professional progress, self-improvement and ultimately social harmony. This looks like a Newtonian, Enlightenment vision increasingly at odds with our complex, quantum century. And as outlined above, the resistance to persuasion leads to an emphasis on the idealized aspects of the field, rather than the messier realities, despite modification of the original model (Grunig, 2001). But as Jung suggests, conflict is an essential trigger to moral examination, forcing dialogue with the unconscious. Moreover, according to Jung's ideas of compensation, the more a group insists on its idealized self-image (and blames others for misrepresentation or, if pushed, 'bad apples' in its own ranks), the more obscure – and potent – its own shadow becomes.

While I have avoided viewing Jungian ideas from a therapeutic perspective, it is worth imagining PR as a client. The difficulty therapists have with people who have become over attached to their persona aspects is in convincing them (or rather encouraging them to discover) that there are other perspectives, and, moreover, that these may not be as threatening as first appears. It means shifting from a singular to a multiple understanding of self and other, and if PR were a client (remember, I have *no* qualifications as a therapist) I would be concerned at its resistance to this possibility. Instead, all new ideas are vacuumed into the excellence ideal, to bolster its primary premises. Indeed, I remember being at a conference when members of the excellence team reported on how well the rest of the world was doing, and their disappointment that so many still didn't see PR their way. Oh *dear*, I thought, we've failed! Perhaps too it reminds me of the years I spent lying on a couch wondering why my therapist couldn't understand that I was a Very Nice Person and she should just *stop* asking me if control was an issue. I guess it takes one to know one. The common thread is the lack of reflexivity, the inability to enter into a dialogue with aspects of the field as aspects of the whole.

Of course the aim of a Jungian approach is one of healing, should the parties wish it, and there are interesting threads that connect the story of excellence with a deeper archetypal approach. For example, the definition of the practitioner as a 'boundary spanner', negotiating communication between the organization and its internal and external publics, generates a resonance with the figure of Hermes, who gives his name to hermeneutics, the messenger between the gods and man (one suspects many PR practitioners treat the boardroom like Olympus):

> Hermes is a god: Guide of souls to the underworld, the divinity of olive cultivation, athletics, boundaries, commerce, and messenger of the gods. Hermes stands as a liminal presence, on the threshold or boundary of depth psychology and politics, of psychic reality and social reality, of the personal and the political.
>
> (Samuels, 1993: 89)

I have mentioned hermeneutic ethics in Chapter 4 and from the beginning stressed my own role as interpretive; hermeneutic philosophy and methodology also seems, as I suggested in Chapter 5, appropriate to reimagining PR. In the proper Jungian tradition of exploring the meaning of Greek gods in western culture, PR could embrace the meanings associated with Hermes, the messenger-god,

> associated with the function of transmuting what is beyond human understanding into a form that human intelligence can grasp. The whole idea suggests a process of bringing a thing or situation from unintelligibility to understanding. Hermes was not a simple deliverer of messages, but was an interpreter of the messages he delivered. His character interacted with the literal aspects of the message to create meaning. He was the original Hermeneutic catalyst, bringing about a meaningful connection between the what, the how and the why.
>
> (Berci and Griffith, 2006)

Interestingly, Greek mythology is more sanguine about the consequences of mediating between gods and men, as Hermes resorts to extended trickery to protect mankind from vengeful immortals. A boundary spanner who favours those weaker than his masters! Interestingly, he is also the figure who accompanies souls to the underworld, making him an ideal archetype to invoke in seeking to understand the shadow side of PR. Of course, Hermes is also the arch-Trickster in Greek mythology, the deceiver, double-sayer, unreliable guide; every archetype contains its own shadow. The film *The Yes Men* (Smith and Ollman, 2005) illustrates how effective such deception can be: the protagonists borrow the clothes, language and logos from corporate PR to destabilize norms, a very Trickster activity indeed, with PR at its chill heart. The metaphorical richness of Hermes points to the ability of classical figures to contain the contradictions we seem so keen to categorize out of existence today. It means restoring *ambiguity* to the position of PR. Freed from the management straitjacket of excellence, a real boundary spanner can switch roles, swap sides, confront and confound earlier statements, echoing the calls for an activist perspective and engagement with complexity (Coombs and Holladay, 2010; Holtzhausen, 2012; McKie and Willis, 2012).

The boundary spanner is also a metaphor for relationship, although Relationship Management (RM) has in some ways become an extension of the excellence approach, with many shared publications (including the key text by Hon and Grunig, 1999). In the process it has become aligned with a kind of liberal management theory, where concern for publics is designed to facilitate alignment with management goals. It has also become another tool for quantitative analysis: by offering dimensions of relationship that allows those who must measure everything to measure that elusive concept, human relationship. From a Jungian perspective it is at risk of reducing the complexity of human interactions and contradictions into spreadsheets. In this way it resembles the transformation of Jung's compass of personality types into the Myers-Brigg Type Indicator matrix, despite the idea of superior/inferior aspects of feeling, thinking, sensing and cognition being to aid diagnosis not fix labels on people. Similarly the application of RM assumes that parties can both identify the key aspects of a relationship and, importantly, quantify those aspects. It does not allow for multiple, contradictory experience and so limits its usefulness. Pieczka's (2010) exploration of the deeper foundations and implications of dialogue theory demonstrates how superficially it has been deployed in PR. Those who genuinely practised listening and exchanging shifted their position to incorporate aspects of the other rather than 'manage' them. Moreover, like the excellence approach, RM theory marginalizes the obstacles created by power imbalances, despite the fact that many of the most important communication issues facing this century, from climate change to religious fundamentalism, raise questions concerning the relative power of the parties seeking relationship.

In earlier consideration of RM, I placed dialogic theory, discourse ethics and hermeneutics (see Smith, 1997 for an exploration of the relationship between these bodies of thought) in the RM 'tent', though others may find another home for this approach. In any event, from either a hermeneutic or Jungian perspective, RM will need to consider internal relationships – of self with self, as well as self with other. Habermas is often cited in discussions about discourse ethics, but his early (1972) call for critical self-understanding in order to minimize barriers to communication is disregarded. The opportunity, to my mind, is that the uptake of RM in PR theory strikes a chord because it is in relationships that so many communicators excel; it offers something of a way forward, or could, if stripped of its positivist elements. It creates a space where real discussion could take place about how we as PR practitioners, educators and commentators engage with those who use our services.

Instead of emphasizing the management aspect, getting publics to line up behind organizational goals, a Jungian approach could foster a shift in the balance of power.

The First Amendment version of the advocacy model (Fitzpatrick and Bronstein, 2006), which emphasizes the speaker's right to state a case in the court of public opinion, rather than the ability to learn from the perspectives or experiences of others, assumes the existence of an objective truth that can be ascertained through this process, and is therefore unlikely to be harmonious with a Jungian view. Nothing is more indicative of the duality that saturates western culture than the binary settings of courts, to say nothing of the cultural bias inherent in basing an approach to PR on one country's constitution. In court one is guilty or innocent, right or wrong. Models of reconciliation rather than confrontation might be more useful for advocates, and would also encourage reflection on the difference between courtroom debate and communicative dialogue and the ethical implications of these stances. The warnings about the need for transparency in advocates has an air of exhortation rather than engagement. Of course, advocates should be transparent about their clients, their income, the brief, but in practice they are often not. The material that fuels sites such as Spin-watch.com illustrates *a* (not necessarily *the*) truth about PR. So how might a Jungian approach help here? Many of the quotes from practitioners cited in Chapter 2 illustrate the allure of the legal model; just as excellence attracts academics, advocacy resonates with practitioners. What we need is a concept of the field that acknowledges *both* these types (not clustered into ethical and anti-ethical, such as Bowen, 2008) as legitimate aspects of PR, each of which call for nuanced ethical responses. Useful insights for such a project can be gleaned by the less materialistic, more philosophical ethics taught in schools of rhetoric (to repeat, this is a mainly a US phenomenon). As mentioned before, it is important because it recognizes the centrality of persuasion to practice and seeks to evolve an ethical approach to this reality. It also concentrates on the communication itself – whether the message is for health or arms promotion, the act of persuasion is seen as having at least the *potential* to be ethical – a refreshing change from some of the earlier approaches outlined above. However, de-contextualizing communication can lead to a focus on speech acts rather than power relationships, for example. The relationship between virtue ethics, the main ethical philosophy of this approach, and Jungian ideas is explored in Beebe (1992) and described above. The elevation of integrity as the core virtue above justice or care has the effect of shining the spotlight on the person doing the communication rather than their acts or intentions and deepens the discussion of PR from a virtue ethics perspective. Introducing Beebe's (1992) text, with its emphasis on self-awareness and self-scrutiny, to PR scholarship would be a considerable contribution, I believe. The other tension between Jungian and virtue ethics is the polarizing interpretation of virtues and vices, as seen in the contrast between the archetypes of principled advocates and pathological partisans in PR and advertising (Baker, 2008). Explorations of the sliding scale between loyalty and uncritical adherence help advance understanding of these issues and indicate how practitioners might monitor their own position on such a scale, though there is still a danger of polarization here. The effect of persuasion on the persuader as well as persuadee is a key question, but a Jungian approach would cast them as persona and shadow, opposing aspects of the same entity, thus moving beyond duality. I have described the field as comprising saints *and* sinners (Fawkes, 2012), and my argument is that both are aspects of the whole and cannot be divided one from another. Nevertheless, bringing a Jungian dimension to virtue ethics provides a framework for deeper analysis of the nature of virtue and indeed self, and could help shift the focus back from act to agent, as intended. There are still problems, and it may be hard to reinstate this depth, but the gap between virtue ethics and a Jungian approach is probably the narrowest of all those canvassed.

As suggested earlier, critical theory approaches take a variety of attitudes towards PR, from the Chomskian perspective that the concept is an oxymoron to Moloney's (2006) call for funding for minority groups to enable them to participate more equally in public communication and thus revive the democratic discourse. Much critical writing is more concerned with materialism, from a post-Marxist, Weberian perspective, than the experiential, even spiritual values embodied in Jungian writing. As power is so often the unacknowledged aspect of PR theory, critical approaches, which bring it into the centre of discussion, offer a healthy counter-balance to the promotional and non-reflexive discourses outlined earlier and play a role more akin to the mature ego of Jungian theory than others. However, the stance is by definition oppositional – more the hermeneutics of suspicion than conversation. Indeed, some critics of PR (Miller and Dinan, 2008; Stauber and Rampton, 2004) act as mirror images to the upbeat messages of excellence. Like the research underpinning excellence, the examples provided by these authors and similar websites are based on real events, recorded in the public domain. But both only tell partial stories about the field: just as PR cannot be described by its ideals, it cannot either be comprehended merely as relentless propaganda.

The introduction of social theory approaches to PR (Ihlen *et al.*, 2009) makes such arguments easier to place in a wider context. The last chapter explored resonances between Jung, Durkheim and Weber and their convergent concerns about society, concerns that were well founded at the start of the twentieth century and seem even more apposite a century later. In particular the Jungian concept of cultural complexes seems a useful analytic tool for understanding some of the deeper issues in social change today. It offers insights that move away from the blame and confrontation that characterize most political discourse, and allows us to witness the turmoil as a manifestation of the collective unconscious of the individual, group or profession. The addition of cultural approaches to the critical discourse reflects this search for inner as well as outer meaning, for the inclusion of the experiential as well as the observable. So work on PR and the circuit of culture (Curtin and Gaither, 2007) would undoubtedly be considered as part of the hermeneutics of conversation, offering points of contact with Jungian concepts of self, identity and representation. Given the resemblance, noted earlier, between the circuit of culture and the hermeneutic circle of understanding, it is not surprising that both offer world views of fluidity, complexity and interrelatedness. Edwards' (2012) observations on the need for PR fields of research to be seen as continua rather than fixed, opposed positions, is a move towards a holistic approach to the field. Adding the Jungian perspective provides a set of well-used tools for investigation and engagement, which deepens the value of this approach. The dynamic elements of the psyche spelled out in Chapter 7 can be brought to the circuit of culture to help us see more clearly how the process of generating identity, meaning and culture operates, bringing these elements together as 'a synergistic whole in constant flux' (Curtin and Gaither, 2005: 98).

A Jungian approach to PR ethics shares with critical theorists the need to deconstruct the current claims found in many codes and in much writing from the excellence perspective that PR serves society. It looks beyond the insistence that ethics resides in symmetry, recognizing the essentially asymmetric, fluid and contradictory nature of most human relationships. But it also moves past the critical to consider how to engage with, rather than simply reject, those holding other views. The concept of a synergistic whole in constant flux could also be applied to the field of PR (and other professional disciplines); the theoretical positions taken by most scholars are seen as antagonistic of each other, and certainly excellence claims (or at least is given by many followers) a kind of absolute authority that creates an exclusivity of thought. Jungian, like hermeneutic analysis, offers a metatheoretical view, suggesting that these are complementary aspects of the whole, rather than competing views.

The next question concerns the potential for the professional body in encouraging a renewed engagement with ethics, and the consequences for PR codes of a Jungian approach.

Professional codes and leadership

The last chapter suggested the possibility of asking professions to live up to their own ideals in re-working their relationship and responsibility in society. Instead of insisting on Excellence as a descriptor rather than an ideal, professional bodies, could, for example, follow Goodpaster's (2007) elements of ethical leadership: orienteering, steering the organization towards ethical values; institutionalizing, making sure they are structurally embedded; and sustaining, maintaining the ethical commitment over time. They could also explore dimensions of ethical leadership (Rest and Narvaez, 1994), or consider the role of individuated CEOs in managing collective shadow material in organizations (Ketola, 2010), enacting the mature ego function. But in order to establish its own ethical values, PR's professional organizations would need, as this book has argued throughout, to engage with its own shadow in order to reach a collective psychological maturity. That this can be achieved is clear from the literature (see Corlett and Pearson, 2003). As laid out in Chapter 8, the professional body can choose the path of ethical transformation if it chooses, not least by creating space for reflexivity rather than triumphalism concerning the tensions and directions for the field. The loss of public trust in professions may offer a real motivation and create an opportunity for change.

As earlier chapters made clear, the professional body has a key role in managing cultural complexes, the specific dynamics of the group, as the public representation of the profession in society as well as the designer and promoter of its ethical standards. In the case of PR, the professional bodies in the Anglo-American sphere have been largely promotional, speaking up for the 'community of practice' and extolling members' virtues and contribution to society. Economically, they must be seen to be acting in the interests of members in order to maintain existing membership and attract new members. The assertion that the excellence project has shaped PRSA and, by extension, international codes of conduct, means that this approach is now institutionalized in many countries (Parkinson, 2001). The professional bodies have thus taken on or formalized the persona functions embedded in the excellence ideals, the '*ur-mythos* of the ... professional's service to humanity' (Kultgen, 1988: 120). The persona role, with its concerns for social acceptance, can also be illustrated by the accessories of professions, such as Coats of Arms, Royal Patrons, splendid headquarters, as well as the acquisition of institutional recognition such as Charter status (in the UK). But rather than dismiss these show-pieces as irrelevant to the development of a deeper ethical approach in PR, I am suggesting that a Jungian approach encourages professional associations to play a more mature ego role. This function is analogous to the developed ego role outlined in earlier chapters, which can only operate if it has become relativized by awareness of a greater body to which it has accountability. In the previous chapter, it was suggested that this might be conceived as the *polis*, a claim that would resonate with PR's many claims to serve society (Heath, 2006; Taylor, 2010; Valentini *et al.*, 2012). Building a new relationship with the wider community, based on acknowledgement of what was previously denied (but often suspected by others, in the way of shadow material) would create a new foundation for PR ethics. Such reflection involves the acceptance that on the one hand excellence is a laudable goal and genuinely reflects the experience and aspirations of many practitioners throughout the field; and on the other that their colleagues (or themselves in different circumstances) are often actively involved in using decidedly non-excellent methods to promote their employer's views.

So what would a professional body have to change to encourage collective ethical decision-making? Abbott's (1983) suggestion that attention needs to be given to questions of 'mediocre practice' across a whole profession provides a starting point perhaps. Just as organizations conduct ethical audits, why shouldn't professional bodies do the same? I sense a growing urgency to such debates, as shifts in the collective culture and economy undermine the last vestiges of professional responsibility. There is a need for ethics that reaches beyond profession or firm, beyond corporate or even global culture to take up 'planetary responsibility' (Bauman, 2008: 227). I hope that a Jungian approach to professional ethics might contribute to such a new approach.

One of the first steps must be to get rid of Codes. Chapter 5 showed that leading PR codes use excellence as their guide, emphasizing ideal generalities with pitifully little guidance as to how to manage the contradictions they contain. Only the International Association of Business Communicators research (Bowen *et al.*, 2006) raised the issue of being honest with oneself as a precondition for honesty with others. All these codes and principles share a reliance on external guidance for ethical decision-making. The inner dynamics of ethics have been relegated to religion or mysticism and appear to me to be wholly absent from debate. Yet, surely, it is the physical, social even spiritual experience of discomfort that prompts many of us to consider the ethical nature of our acts. PR practitioners who experience ethical conflict manifest a series of physical and emotional symptoms, and often change employers to resolve their inner discomfort, one of the prime exacerbating factors being the inability to discuss ethical issues openly with management (Kang, 2010). Earlier discussion illuminated the emptiness of codes, and worse, their capacity to minimize the messiness of actual ethical dilemmas by placing professional reputation above professional guidance.

Jungian individuation requires the development of a mature approach, in which the individual or group owns dissociated elements and starts asking questions such as: what actions in the individual/organization/profession have created a culture where such behaviour is seen as acceptable? Are we susceptible to particular temptations that have been denied rather than engaged with critically? So, groups dealing with financial transactions might heighten their awareness of fiscal irresponsibility and the desire to transgress; groups dealing with the vulnerable might reflect on the danger of abusing their powers and so on. In the PR field, my sense is that we want things to be better, to emphasize the positive, to stress the ideal over the real. We also, clearly, want to be seen to be doing the right thing, to be working for a better society. The temptation is to believe our own propaganda and blame those who don't for their 'cynicism'. Like all such denials, it becomes a block to dialogue. Codes thus embody that denial and act as obstacles to ethical dialogue. Reframing Baker's model of PR's virtues and vices (2008: 241) in a Jungian context allows us to look at what might be attractive in the vices, unattractive in the virtues. Are we (sometimes) drawn to situations that seem to sanction manipulation, deceit or secrecy? Are transparency, humility and respect too *difficult* to bring to everyday work, where cultures and organizations ask for the opposite?

The key argument presented here for embarking on such a dialogue is the concept that through this process a new professional ethic can emerge. A Jungian ethic would not lead to a new code of conduct, nor even a decision-making model, though there might be some similarities. I think of it more as a moral inventory and return to the checklist based on the stages of individuation outlined in the previous chapter (Amir, 2005). Here I amend that generic approach to be more specific to PR. So, a Jungian approach to PR as a profession would:

a) recognize that its dealings with its members and the wider world are not wholly driven by rational reflection, but by forces within its collective field, mostly outside the current consciousness of members or leaders of that profession; thus, despite claims to serve society and enhance democracy, it must be acknowledged that not all PR activity lives up to that ideal;

b) acknowledge the imperfections of the profession, its fallibilities and pretensions (without falling into despair); in particular, the PR practitioner is often closer to the organization that employs or contracts him or her and may consciously or unconsciously privilege that interest over the wider demands of society;

c) construct a new sense of identity based on a deeper understanding of human failing and aspiration, moving away from the idealized symmetrical communicator based in excellence, or the principled advocate from virtue approaches and recognize that both are contained within the field, often within individuals;

d) recognize the centrality of persuasion to PR practice and start a profession-wide discussion of what this means for individual practitioners, the organizations that employ them and society; and

e) locate the profession within a greater, transcendent framework, such as the interests of society, placing the needs and desires of its members in a more meaningful context, by encouraging them to remember that while serving organizations above society offers short-term benefits, in times of continuing global crisis, such as the present, the costs are long-term and high.

Individual and collective ethical dialogue would offer a release of the tension between the idealized self-image underpinning the promotional aspects of the professional body and its codes of conduct and the actual experience of ethics in the workplace. Instead of the contempt for those trumpeting impossible ideals, on the one hand, and the 'disappointment' of those upholding such ideas, on the other, as evidenced in the Westminster debate, a new ethic would recognize the reality of both as aspects of the whole.

The final chapter looks at how such ideas might be put into operation and where further research is required to develop this approach.

Conclusions

This chapter has sought to integrate observations from the literature of professional ethics and Jungian psychology into the field of PR in order to make some key points that offer a new direction for PR ethics:

a) Critics reflect back unpalatable truths about the field of PR: they do not tell the whole truth; but they do tell *a* truth that some PR activity is devoted to the corruption of the democratic process and/or uses deceptive and manipulative methods to promote goods, services and organizations. This material needs to be brought into the debate about the field by the professional body, not excluded or denied.

b) The dominance of idealized images in the texts, speeches, positions and websites of the professional body forms a barrier to discussion about the sub-ideal actualities, which lie between the ethical image promoted and the abuses exposed by critics. Given that rejected material often contains the seeds of what is missing from the whole person (i.e. what they need to grow up), it may be that failure to acknowledge the persuasion at the heart of most PR has infantilized ethical approaches and rendered persuasion a liability rather than, as many practitioners see it, our central asset.

c)   Professional bodies have the opportunity to change the ethical culture of PR, by shifting responsibility from individual practitioners to the collective in order to conduct a real audit of practice – and not merely technical acts of communication, but of our role in society.

A Jungian approach means shifting away from rationality and certainty and becoming prepared to live with internal conflict for a period, both in the group and the member. Thus, an ethical approach starts with the recognition of conflict as an essential human experience, rather than looking to codes of ethics as means of avoiding conflict. To repeat one of Jung's (Jung 1949/1990: 17) comments on individuation as an ethical process:

> If a man is endowed with an ethical sense and is convinced of the sanctity of ethical values, he is on the surest road to a conflict of duty. And although this looks desperately like a moral catastrophe, it alone makes possible a higher differentiation of ethics and a broadening of consciousness. A conflict of duty forces us to examine our conscience and thereby to discover the shadow. This then forces us to come to terms with the unconscious.

Note

1   All references to Jung cite the *Collected Works* and the relevant paragraph, not page.

References

Abbott, A. (1983) Professional ethics. *The American Journal of Sociology, 88*(5): 855–85.
Abbott, A. (1988) *The System of Professions: an essay on the division of expert labor.* Chicago, IL: University of Chicago Press.
Abbott, A. (1995) Things of boundaries. *Social Research, 62*(4): 857–82.
Amir, L. B. (2005) Morality, psychology, philosophy. *Philosophical Practice, 1*(1): 43–57.
Arnett, R. C. (2011) Situating a dialogic ethics – a dialogic confession. In G. Cheney, S. May and D. Munshi (eds) *The Handbook of Communication Ethics.* New York, NY: Routledge, pp. 45–63.
Baker, S. (2008) The model of the principled advocate and the pathological partisan: a virtue ethics construct of opposing archetypes of public relations and advertising practitioners. *Journal of Mass Media Ethics, 23*(3): 235–53.
Bauman, Z. (2008) *Does Ethics have a Chance in a World of Consumers?* Cambridge, MA: Harvard University Press.
Beebe, J. (1992) *Integrity in Depth.* College Station, TX: Texas A&M University.
Berci, M. E. and Griffith, B. (2006) Social studies methodology viewed as in a hermeneutic perspective. *Journal of Thought, 41*(4): 45–64.
Bernays, E. L. and Miller, M. C. (2005) *Propaganda.* Brooklyn, NY: Ig Publishing.

Bowen, S. A. (2010) The nature of good in public relations. In R. L. Heath (ed.) *The SAGE Handbook of Public Relations*. Thousand Oaks, CA: Sage, pp. 569–83.

Bowen, S. A. (2007) The extent of ethics. In E. L. Toth (ed.) *The Future of Excellence in Public Relations and Communication Management*. Mahweh, NJ: Lawrence Erlbaum Associates, pp. 275–97.

Bowen, S. A. (2008) A state of neglect: public relations as 'corporate conscience' or ethics counsel. *Journal of Public Relations Research, 20*(3): 271–96. doi: 10.1080/10627260801962749

Bowen, S. A., Heath, R. L., Lee, J., Painter, G., Agraz, F. J., McKie, D. and Toledano, M. (2006) *The Business of Truth: a guide to ethical communication*. San Francisco: International Association of Business Communicators.

Coombs, W. T. and Holladay, S. J. (2010) *PR Strategy and Application: managing influence*. Chichester, West Sussex: John Wiley & Sons.

Corlett, J. G. and Pearson, C. (2003) *Mapping the Organizational Psyche: a Jungian theory of organizational dynamics and change*. Gainesville, FL: Center for Applications of Psychological Type.

Curtin, P. A. and Gaither, T. K. (2005) Privileging identity, difference and power: the circuit of culture as a basis for public relations theory. *Journal of Public Relations Research, 17*(2): 91–115.

Curtin, P. A. and Gaither, T. K. (2007) *International Public Relations: negotiating culture, identity and power*. Thousand Oaks, CA: Sage.

Cutlip, S. M., Center, A. H. and Broom, G. M. (eds) (1985) *Effective Public Relations* (6th edn) London: Prentice-Hall International.

Edwards, L. (2011) Critical perspectives in global public relations: theorizing power. In N. Bardhan and C. K. Weaver (eds) *Public Relations in Global Cultural Contexts*. New York, NY: Routledge, pp. 29–49.

Edwards, L. (2012) Defining the 'object' of public relations research: a new starting point. *Public Relations Inquiry, 1*(1): 7–30.

Fawkes, J. (2006) Can ethics save public relations from the charge of propaganda? *Ethical Space, 3*(1): 38–42.

Fawkes, J. (2007) Public relations models and persuasion ethics: a new approach. *Journal of Communication Management, 11*(4): 313–31.

Fawkes, J. (2009) Public relations, propaganda and the psychology of persuasion. In R. Tench and L. Yeomans (eds) *Exploring Public Relations*. Harlow, Essex: Pearson, pp. 252–72.

Fawkes, J. (2012) Saints and sinners: competing identities in public relations ethics. *Public Relations Review, 38*(5): 865–72. doi: 10.1016/j.pubrev.2012.07.004

Feldman, B. (2004) Towards a theory of organizational culture: integrating the 'other' from a post-Jungian perspective. In T. Singer and S. L. Kimbles (eds) *The Cultural Complex: contemporary Jungian perspectives on psyche and society*. New York, NY: Brunner-Routledge, pp. 251–61.

Festinger, L. (1962) *A Theory of Cognitive Dissonance*. Stanford, CA: Stanford University Press.

Fishbein, M. A. I. (1975) *Belief, Attitude, Intention, and Behavior: an introduction to theory and research*. Reading, MA: Addison-Wesley.

Fitzpatrick, K. and Bronstein, C. (2006) *Ethics in Public Relations: responsible advocacy*. Thousand Oaks, CA and London: Sage.

Goodpaster, K. E. (2007) *Conscience and Corporate Culture*. Malden, MA and Oxford: Blackwell.

Grunig, J. E. (2001) Two-way symmetrical public relations: past, present and future. In R. L. Heath (ed.) *Handbook of Public Relations*. Thousands Oaks, CA: Sage, pp. 11–30.

Habermas, J. (1972) *Knowledge and Human Interests*. Boston: Beacon Press.

Heath, R. L. (2006) Onward into more fog: thoughts on public relations' research directions. *Journal of Public Relations Research, 18*(2): 93–114.

Holtzhausen, D. (2000) Postmodern values in public relations. *Journal of Public Relations Research, 12*(1): 251–64.

Holtzhausen, D. (2012) *Public Relations as Activisim: postmodern approaches to theory and practice*. New York, NY: Routledge.

Hon, L. C. and Grunig, J. E. (1999) Guidelines for measuring relationships in public relations. *The Institute for PR*. Online. Available at www.instituteforpr.org/ research_single/guidelines_measuring_relationships

Hutton, J. G. (2010) Defining the relationship between public relations and marketing: public relations' most important challenge. In R. L. Heath (ed.) *The SAGE Handbook of Public Relations*. Thousand Oaks, CA: Sage, pp. 509–22.

Ihlen, Ø., Fredriksson, M. and Ruler, B. v. (2009) *Public Relations and Social Theory: key figures and concepts*. New York and London: Routledge.

Jaksa, J. A. and Pritchard, M. S. (1994) *Communication Ethics: methods of analysis*. Belmont, CA: Wadsworth.

Jung, C. G. *Mysterium Coniunctionis*, Vol. 14, *Collected Works* (eds Read, H., Adler, G. A. and Fordham, M.; trans. R. F. C. Hull). London: Routledge & Kegan Paul.

Jung, C. G. (1949/1990) Foreword, Neumann, E. *Depth Psychology and a New Ethic*. Boston: Shambala Press. pp. 11–18.

Kang, J. -A. (2010) Ethical conflict and job satisfaction of public relations practitioners. *Public Relations Review, 36*(2): 152–6.

Ketola, T. (2008) Taming the shadow: corporate responsiblity in a Jungian context. *Corporate Social Responsibility and Environmental Management, 15*(4): 199–209.

Ketola, T. (2010) Responsible leadership: building blocks of individual, organisational and societal behaviour. *Corporate Social Responsibility and Environmental Management, 17*(3): 173–84.

Kultgen, J. (1988) *Ethics and Professionalism*. Philadelphia: University of Philadelphia Press.

L'Etang, J. (2003) The myth of the 'ethical guardian': an examination of its origins, potency and illusions. *Journal of Communication Management, 8*(1): 53–67.

L'Etang, J. (2006) Public relations and propaganda: conceptual issues, methodological problems and public relations discourse. In J. L'Etang and M. Pieczka (eds) *Public Relations, Critical Debates and Contemporary Practice*. Mahweh, NJ: Lawrence Erlbaum Associates, pp. 23–40.

L'Etang, J. (2011) Public relations and marketing: ethical isues and professional practice in society. In G. Cheney, S. May and D. Munshi (eds) *The Handbook of Communication Ethics*. New York, NY: Routledge, pp. 221–40.

Lippman, W. (1995[1925]) The phantom public. In Jackall, R. (ed.) *Propaganda*. New York, NY: New York University Press, pp. 351–99.

McKie, D. (2001) Updating public relations: 'new science' research paradigms and uneven developments. In R. L. Heath (ed.) *Handbook of Public Relations*. Thousand Oaks, CA: Sage, pp. 75–91.

McKie, D. and Willis, P. (2012) Renegotiating the terms of engagement: public relations, marketing, and contemporary challenges. *Public Relations Review, 38*(5): 846–52. doi: http://dx.doi.org/10.1016/j.pubrev.2012.03.008

Miller, D. and Dinan, W. (2008) *A Century of Spin: how public relations became the cutting edge of corporate power*. London: Pluto.

Moloney, K. (2000) *Rethinking Public Relations: the spin and the substance*. London: Routledge.

Moloney, K. (2006) *Rethinking Public Relations: PR propaganda and democracy* (2nd edn) London: Routledge.

Neumann, E. (1949/1990) *Depth Psychology and a New Ethic*. C. G. Jung (Foreword) Boston, MA: Shambala Press.

O'Malley, P. (n.d.) In praise of secrecy. Online. Available at www.aboutpublicrelations. net/ucomalleyb.htm, retrieved 8 October, 2012.

Parkinson, M. (2001) The PRSA Code of Professional Standards and Member Code of Ethics: why they are neither professional nor ethical. *Public Relations Quarterly, 46*(3): 27–31.

Pfau, M. and Wan, H. (2006) Persuasion: an intrinsic function in public relations. In C. H. Botan and V. Hazleton (eds) *Public Relations Theory II*. Mahweh, NJ: Lawrence Erlbaum Associates, pp. 101–36.

Pieczka, M. (2011) Public relations as dialogic expertise? *Journal of Communication Management, 15*(2): 108–24.

Pieczka, M. and L'Etang, J. (2001) Public relations and the question of professionalism. In R. L. Heath (ed.) *Handbook of Public Relations*. Thousand Oaks, CA: Sage, pp. 223–35.

Porter, L. (2010) Communicating for the good of the state: a post-symmetrical polemic on persuasion in ethical public relations. *Public Relations Review, 36*(2): 127–33.

Rest, J. R. and Narvaez, D. (1994) *Moral Development in the Professions: psychology and applied ethics*. Hillsdale, NJ and Hove, East Sussex: Lawrence Erlbaum Associates.

Samuels, A. (1993) *The Political Psyche*. London: Routledge.

Seib, P. M. and Fitzpatrick, K. (1995) *Public Relations Ethics*. Fort Worth, TX and London: Harcourt Brace College Publishers.

Singer, T. and Kimbles, S. L. (eds) (2004) *The Cultural Complex: contemporary Jungian perspectives on psyche and society*. New York, NY: Brunner-Routledge.

Smith, N. H. (1997) *Strong Hermeneutics: contingency and moral identity*. London: Routledge.

Smith, C. and Ollman, D. (2005) *The Yes Men*. Los Angeles, CA: MGM Home Entertainment.

Stauber, J. C. and Rampton, S. (2004) *Toxic Sludge is Good For You: lies, damn lies and the public relations industry*. London: Robinson.

Stein, M. (1998) *Jung's Map of the Soul: an introduction*. Chicago, IL: Open Court.

Taylor, M. (2010) Public relations in the enactment of civil society. In R. L. Heath (ed.) *The SAGE Handbook of Public Relations*. Thousand Oaks, CA: Sage, pp. 5–15.

Torres, M. (2010) What happens when the brands we work for disappoint us? *Ad Age*. Online. Available at http://adage.com/article/guest-columnists/brands-work-disappoint/ 144750/, retrieved 8 August, 2011.

Treviit, K. (2011) Smear campaigns have no place in PR. Online. Available at www.prdaily.com/Main/Articles/8288.aspx, retrieved 13 November, 2011.

Valentini, C., Kruckeberg, D. and Starck, K. (2012) Public relations and community: a persistent covenant. *Public Relations Review, 38*(5): 873–9.

Vercic, D. (2005) Public relations is the champion of democracy and guardian of common sense. *Behind the Spin*. Online. Available at http://publicsphere.typepad.com/behind thespin/current_affairs/index.html, retrieved 23 June, 2006.

Weaver, C. K., Motion, J. and Reaper, J. (2006) From propaganda to discourse (and back again): truth, power, the public interrest and public relations. In J. L'Etang and M. Pieczka (eds) *Public Relations, Critical Debates and Contemporary Practice*. Mahwah, NJ: Lawrence Erlbaum Associates, pp. 7–21.

Wilcox, D. L., Cameron, G. T., Ault, P. H. and Agee, W. K. (2003) *Public Relations, Strategies and Tactics* (7th edn) Boston, MA: Allyn and Bacon.

10 What next?

Reflections and directions

This final chapter brings together the threads woven throughout this book, summarizing the key arguments, suggesting avenues for operationalizing some of the insights generated and indicating areas for further research.

The introduction set out a list of questions that were presented as subsets of the main research question: can a Jungian approach to ethics make a contribution to the field of professional ethics in general and public relations (PR) ethics in particular? This chapter returns to those questions and considers the degree to which they have been answered.

- Can ethics be purely rational, and if not, how can we know our own motives in seeking to act ethically when self-delusion is endemic?
- Can Jung's welcoming of psychological complexity and contradiction help in this dilemma; does the move away from good/bad ease or complicate ethical understanding? Is a non-normative ethics possible?
- How does hermeneutic philosophy enrich or challenge our understanding of ethics and ourselves?
- To what degree do approaches to PR ethics confine themselves to 'rational' choice-making, avoiding philosophical engagement?
- Is this true of other professions? What are professions, is PR one, how do they fit into society? What are their claims to ethical standards based on? What makes them tick?
- What would professional ethics in general and PR ethics in particular look like if a non-rational approach were taken? What next?

Throughout the book I have argued that a Jungian approach to ethics has a real contribution to make to current debates, in particular that working with the shadow aspects of professions would provide a more robust foundation for ethics than the idealized codes of conduct currently offered. Mapping concepts of professions, highlighting debates in early sociology regarding the role of the professions in society, showed how tenuous the claim to be professional really is, particularly in emerging professions. This also showed how the claim to serve society, by upholding a set of ethical standards, is central to the Anglo-American idea of professions. This relationship was examined throughout as an explicitly ethical one, the claim to ethics being central to the professional 'project', whereby certain occupational groups are granted status and the autonomy to manage their own affairs with minimal state interference. The concerns of early sociologists that core values or shared moral meanings were becoming lost in the reliance on reason and procedure was also explored – a set of concerns shared by Jung and revived in recent years by others in a range of different contexts. In other words, the discussion on ethics moved beyond attention to codes before returning to the mechanisms by which professions enact and police (or fail to) their ethical values. The ethical relationship between professions and wider society can be dismissed as self-serving, or, I argue, reinvigorated as a real ground for ethics. The chapter on professional ethics explored a variety of ethical approaches, finding a continued preference for traditional, rational-based decision-making, despite postmodern and other developments in the field. While ethicists raise age-old problems of how to live, how to relate to others and what it means to live well, professions tend to reduce such debates to instrumental lists based on idealized versions of the group, which in turn are largely ignored by those they are explicitly designed to regulate.

Problems with PR and its various approaches to ethics were set out at the beginning, and then re-examined in the light of the literature on professions and ethics. Like other emerging occupations, PR has constructed a dominant image of its practice based on an ideal, in our case the acknowledged ideal of symmetrical communication, in which ethics is structurally guaranteed by equality of access to communication and decision-making. This model of excellence depends on the marginalization of persuasion, which is then relegated to the 'vice' category, despite being the avowed purpose of many practitioners. I suggested in Chapter 5 that this partial, idealized set of ethics exacerbates a gap in understanding between academics and practitioners, and leads to a disregard for the principles the former seek to impose on the latter, through their influence in professional associations worldwide. I identified a particular polarity between what I call 'saints and sinners' (Fawkes, 2012b) and what Baker (2008) calls 'principled advocates and pathological partisans', which affects concepts of ethics and which is based in a binary good/bad division that shuts down the very conversations that need opening up.

The central chapters of this book then set out Jung's view of the psyche, emphasizing throughout that no single view can be called definitive, and highlighting the intra-disciplinary disputes concerning aspects such as the relationship between the ego and the self. As with establishing professional ethics in its wider professional context, sketching the Jungian landscape was important both to raise and question the unfamiliar concepts of psyche and also to introduce the central idea of individuation as the teleology of the human soul. This was described as involving the integration of shadow material, and coming into a relationship with the unconscious, within a greater, transcendent framework. This chapter on the Jungian psyche also established the validity of extrapolating from the individual to the collective psyche, with particular interest in the 'cultural complex' that occupies a middle ground and is applicable to groups (Singer and Kimbles, 2004).

The Jungian psyche forms the foundation for a new approach to professional ethics, constructed from a range of sources but rooted in Jung's sense that wholeness, not goodness, is the wellspring of moral maturity. Jung emphasized the capacity to see the other in oneself as the prerequisite for ethical human relations, available through the journey of individuation. In particular, he emphasized the centrality of working with the shadow as the first stage in individuation, and that has been echoed here. Only through willingness to engage with aspects of the individual or group that were previously rejected as unacceptable and/or projected onto reviled others is the delusion-prone ego able to develop a mature role. The challenge of working with the shadow in groups was considered, prior to the application of these ideas to professions and their ethics.

Interpreting discussion of professions through a Jungian lens led to reconceptualizing them as psychic entities based in the collective of each group, comprising functions such as ego, persona and shadow, each of which will be differently configured, according to cultural, historical and other factors. This built on earlier writing about applying Jungian concepts to groups and organizations as well as individuals. The integration of a profession's disparate elements was then posited, through recognition of shadow aspects, as a new foundation for a professional ethic. New insights from a Jungian perspective were brought to professional ethics, demonstrating the congruence, and dissonance, between the dominant approaches already established and the newly introduced concepts of Jungian ethics. This discussion raised issues outlined in earlier chapters, such as trust and moral leadership, suggesting that regaining lost trust offers an incentive for undertaking the rigours of Jungian scrutiny. Of course, such an undertaking requires ethical leadership if professions are to rebuild their relationship with society, which, in its highest conceptualization, as *polis*, might offer a transcendent framework for collective individuation.

Returning to the field of PR offered in-depth illumination of what a Jungian perspective can bring to a specific field, particularly by seeing the good/bad divisions outlined earlier as aspects of the whole. This examination led to suggestions that the excellence project plays a persona role, with persuasion as the rejected shadow material, identifiable by others outside and some within the field, but denied by those with a strong, uncritical, attachment to an idealized version of the profession and its contribution to society. Looking at the field through a Jungian lens reveals advocates and advisers as elements of the whole, suggesting that engagement with persuasion is a prerequisite for developing a depth approach to ethics. Work already undertaken from the schools of rhetoric, largely based in virtue ethics approaches, offers some grounding, but there is still a tendency to idealization or polarizing practice into vice and virtue categories, when a mature overview requires initial acceptance of all aspects before any developmental activity can begin. Again, it is important to stress that the goal is not compliance, a shrugging 'what do you expect' attitude, but that, in seeing more clearly what actually constitutes this body, there will be acknowledgement that not all persuasion is evil and that most practitioners spend a great deal of time, as do most humans perhaps, putting the best case forward, for themselves and their clients. It is by raising fears and temptations to consciousness that individual practitioners and the profession as a whole can best make thoughtful choices.

Each profession will have to confront its own rejected material, but it is not too great a jump to speculate that journalists' insistence on an idealized service to 'truth' has been used to disguise, even justify, unethical and even criminal information-gathering practices. The charlatan, quack and false prophets identified in Jungian thinking can be found behind many shiny professional fronts. Reflecting on the literature examined in this book, it seems that the more a group insists on a particular virtue, whether that's care or justice, the more likely it is to indicate where the shadow aspects lie. In the last two chapters I raised some general ideas about how a professional body might examine these aspects; here, I offer a little more detail, and indicate potential directions for future research.

Implications for practice

In previous chapters, several suggestions were made for working with the shadow aspects of professions, drawing on ideas from Jungian therapy with individuals and the application of Jungian ideas in organizations and workgroups. This section revisits these possibilities and applies them to the field of PR, indicating areas for future investigation.

In order to clarify the persona of PR, particularly if investigating socio-cultural differences between PR in various nations, one place to start is by analysing corporate and promotional literature produced by the professional body, in order to identify tropes of language, symbolism and imagery – does the professional body present itself as part of the establishment, as an outsider, a grass-roots or an elite organization? What other institutions does it resemble? The contrast between the HQ of the Chartered Institute of Public Relations (CIPR) (UK) and the Public Relations Institute of Australia, for example, is striking, with the former located in the heart of London's establishment, particularly when it was in St. James's Square, the home of the gentlemen's club. The latter was in a somewhat run-down part of Sydney, opposite a couple of sex shops, but in an interesting 1930s block of shops and apartments. A discourse analysis of professional body websites would be worth investigating. In addition to critical analysis of literature, websites and so on, it would be worth studying the normal workings of the professional body, its structure and hierarchy, decision-making procedures, culture, physical surroundings, use of symbols. What kind of offices, how are they run and staffed, how accessible are they to members, what sub-groups operate in the office and elected positions? How is the communication organized, what is the attitude to ordinary members? Again, my own experience is largely UK based and in my extensive dealings with the CIPR I found people to be civil and pleasant, in a relaxed but slightly formal setting. However, as was discussed in earlier chapters, professional bodies are largely run by self-selected elites and, compared to the transparency with which trade unions are obliged to operate, such bodies have enormous scope for self-determination and self-serving, with familiar names occupying top positions over decades.

There are other means for identifying dominant narratives in and of the profession, through examining key texts or conducting interviews with leading practitioners (L'Etang, 2004). How do we see the profession's founders and leaders, past and present; as heroes, martyrs or healers (Corlett and Pearson, 2003)? Even in one field, medicine, there are conflicting images, such as angelic nurses and 'heroic' scalpel-wielding surgeons. Journalism has its 'sword of truth'; law has the goddess of blind justice. So many of the stories about PR's leaders emerge from US histories and are highly sanitized (Ewen, 1996), though new writing (L'Etang, 2004; Sriramesh and Vercic, 2009) is redressing that imbalance. So even our stories about ourselves are 'spun'. This echoes the tension, described throughout this book, between the idealized founders and the scoundrel 'bad apples'. Allegations that Joseph Goebbels had a copy of founding father Edward Bernays' *Propaganda* tend not to appear in PR-driven histories (Curtis, 2002; Ewen, 1996). Equally, critical scholars may disregard narratives that describe the contribution that PR has made to reducing conflict between warring parties (Rice and Somerville, 2013).

Another approach at understanding the realities of a profession is through demographic analysis – what are the gender balances, are ethnic minorities subtly dissuaded at early stages of career planning, is diversity given lip service but resisted in practice? Corlett and Pearson (2003: 108) stress the damage that patriarchal organizations have done in repressing the feminine, both to their female employees and their overall psychic health, 'relegating otherness in general to the shadow of organizations'. The CIPR has taken a lead on diversity issues, recognizing that a profession which excludes potential practitioners is moribund. This built on research (Edwards, 2010) which found that the accepted notion of a PR worker is young, white and female, and that black and minority ethnic practitioners go to great lengths to minimize their differences from this 'norm'. Again the point of such data is to identify not only who is currently practising, but which groups are not.

De-construction of notable, especially repeated, crises – what was seen, what was not – can also help expose the 'underbelly' of any organization, as demonstrated in previous chapters. Again, I would highlight the abuses reported in websites such as Spinwatch.org and contrast their detailed accounts of PR manipulation of the media and democratic processes with the very low number of disciplinary procedures, suggesting that such instances are either ignored or accepted. Given that PR has striven to place itself in the boardroom, what responsibility does the profession have for the current state of the world?

It would also be worth looking at the field from others' eyes, using data from surveys, polls or media (including social media) coverage – how does the profession rate in annual trust surveys, is it the regular butt of cartoons, jokes or online forums? In the UK, for example, the rise of the term 'spin doctor' extended beyond political communication into the general field of PR, leading to much resistance from some practitioners. How many PR people say they work in advertising (Thurlow, 2009)? Do they protest too much?

In this book, I have scrutinized some of the leading literature to understand the central 'story' being told about PR – and to expose the story that is not being told.

Is someone else, such as a critic, telling the untold story? And is it really the job of academics to work for 'the practice to be more rigorous and respected' (Gregory, 2012)? Or is this co-opting scholars into the profession's promotional campaign (Moloney, 2006)?

Another site of lost stories will be curricula; which versions of PR are being taught and discussed in the classroom, in faculty and conference meetings? Research (unpublished) I undertook for the CIPR in 2005 identified the institutional location of PR degrees as a significant factor in determining content, so that those courses run in business schools looked at organizational issues and contexts, while those located in media schools tended more towards production and publicity models. Both were called BA (Hons) Public Relations. I haven't looked at education in this book but its role in professionalization is significant and therefore deserves closer scrutiny. Are different perspectives, including national and cultural variations, reflected in syllabi? Is there over-control of the curriculum or a general lack of interest? How does the profession engage with its educators? What are its attitudes to theory?

As suggested in earlier chapters, issues of jurisdiction can be reframed from a Jungian perspective on the 'other' as containing the unlived or rejected aspects of a field. So which groups attract the most intense reactions, jealousies and resentments? Where are they located in proximity to the profession? Is there are shared history, a split in perspectives? Have they gained more status in the struggle for jurisdictional control? Or is a new group emerging within the profession, such as lobbyists or social media specialists? What is under threat? I've suggested earlier that tension with marketing within organizations and with journalism in access to various publics is of particular interest. There are also attempts at regular intervals to rename the field, to divorce itself from lobbying organizations, or campaigners or other voices that compromise the ideal. A Jungian approach embodies that hermeneutic principle of seeking a 'fusion of horizons', increasing the capacity to learn from the other.

This analysis mirrors the archaeological approach Jung brought to treating his patients, the careful excavation of meaningful images, dreams and stories that both reveal and conceal deeper complexities. And the purpose or *telos* is the theme of this book, to generate an ethics based on depth understanding and recognition of the concealed or shadow elements of a profession. While I have no direct experience of applying Jungian thinking to group dynamics, and have constructed the arguments largely from literature, I do have over 30 years of watching individuals, including myself, use versions of these principles to reconstruct their own lives, through therapy, meditation and/or 12-step programmes (the origin of which were strongly influenced by Jung, as suggested earlier). It is a slow process, the first stage of which is simply becoming conscious of all the competing impulses that arise in any number of situations and noticing which ones are acted on, which inhibited. This is not pretty, observing the extent of self-centred, narcissistic, thoughtless interactions with others, but the point is that removing whatever substance fuelled the illusions requires living in a flawed present. Eventually, most learn to step back from the hardwired reactions, consider alternative responses (often long afterwards) and acquire the capacity for choosing how to live with others, and importantly, oneself. Kindness is necessary to survive this, and one of the attractive aspects of a Jungian approach is that it counters the tendency for punishment and blame found in so many ethical frameworks, by recognizing that everything is human and that learning to listen to what others might call 'bad' may yield important insights. One of mine was the decades-long struggle to stop being so 'good', that ghastly, dutiful martyr role that traps so many hard-working women in social compliance when what we really need is to learn to accept, without courting, disapproval. (Writing this book has tested my nerve, it must be said. The armour of traditional, impersonal academic discourse has never looked so appealing.) Jung recognizes that it is necessary to withdraw from social projections in order to become whole, but that this means abandoning a range of empty claims.

Returning to the application of these ideas to professions generally and PR in particular, it can be seen that for a profession to change, it has to want to. It has to participate fully in the process of identifying and engaging with its shadow aspects because such insights cannot be imposed; this is esoteric not exoteric ethics, as was made clear from the beginning. Moreover, an external consultant who tried to force a profession to recognize its hidden aspects might find themself the object of shadow-based hostility, preventing further insight or growth. There is, nevertheless, scope for external facilitators to help construct and organize the dominant narratives of the profession, as suggested in more detail earlier, through in-depth interviews, discourse analysis of professional texts and other co-creational approaches for enabling shadow aspects to surface.

If professions are to engage with such deep reflexivity, ethical leadership will be required. This may come from leading members of the professional organization, the profession itself or from others willing to discuss such issues, whatever their status. As suggested earlier, the resulting insights are more likely to lead to statements of principle rather than codes of practice, in which the shadow aspects of the profession are brought to collective consciousness as particular temptations for that group. This may irritate those who want fixed solutions. And of course, such statements of principle will need monitoring and amending at regular intervals because a Jungian approach to ethics can only be a work in process: the goal cannot be fixed solutions as the shadow is ultimately unknowable, likely to shift and manifest itself in different ways when some part is brought to the collective consciousness. An ethical committee or adequate space in annual conferences for reflection and debate will be necessary to monitor these commitments (Samuels, 2006).

This process reflects a shift in professional ethics back from the individual to the collective, in which debate and reflection allow for a re-conceptualization of the profession and its ethical aspects, as a field, not just as an aggregate of its members. It addresses the privatisation of ethics (Bauman, 2008), whereby members carry the burden of ethical dilemmas, with only exhortations to best behaviour as guides. As Messikomer and Cirka (2010) found, such an approach can only be achieved where professions wish to engage with the rigour of developing ethical process for generating ethical principles. One recent example was the consultation with those present at the World Public Relations Forum in Melbourne, 2012, about values and ethics for the Global Alliance of Public Relations and Communications Managers. I observed the session, which was really too brief and poorly located, in the main conference venue, to allow for deeper reflection, but which nevertheless reflects a willingness to open the doors for member participation. This suggests the possibility of creating a space in the worldwide PR community for talking not about best practice but, for a change, about those decisions that members regret or wish they had handled differently. There is important research to be done into the ethical considerations involved in everyday practice, particularly those that cause discomfort (Kang, 2010). This evidence of distress indicates that practitioners need greater support in facing the ethical decisions involved in professional practice than they currently receive. A Jungian approach enables the individual practitioner to understand that professional ethics concerns being rather than doing, providing an opportunity, should they so wish, to reconfigure personal as well as professional ethical relationships with themselves as well as others.

I have suggested that the *polis*, society in its most exalted form, might form a transcendental framework in which to evaluate the relative interests of members, clients and the wider world. This seems more urgent now, as we face a range of global crises, economic, climatic and social. Any group claiming to benefit the wider community must be reflecting on its capacity to make a difference in coming times.

Most practitioners lack ethical training (Bowen, 2008), and the suggestions above indicate that wider and deeper debate across professional groups would be essential in creating the kind of reflexivity central to ethical practice. Just as I had to learn as an individual to keep asking a set of questions about my motives and desires when confronted by choices so that they were conscious and therefore disempowered, so I imagine a set of questions for individual practitioners, such as: am I comfortable with this decision? If not, why not? Is it because my pride/self-image/security is threatened or do I fear harm will come from it? Am I prepared to raise this discomfort? If not, why not? Am I in a position of power or powerlessness? Am I abusing that position/abdicating responsibility? Who do I blame for ethical failures? What does this say about me? Is there a 'safe' forum for expressing doubts? If not, why not? For PR as a whole, the issues might be: Does the professional body provide a safe forum for airing ethical dilemmas? How invested is it in protecting the image rather than changing the reality? What do the 'bad apples' tell us about the profession as a whole? How can we raise issues of wider ethical concern?

The locus for ethical decision-making has thus shifted from external rules or even comparative analysis of competing values and stakeholders, to something deeper in the individual and the collective, the old, big question: how are we to live?

Implications for theory

Various research directions are suggested in the discussion above, including interviewing individual practitioners to understand more precisely the degree to which they see their practice as ethical, possibly using critical incident methods to elicit reflections; there is a long tradition of using scenarios to engage respondents in the complexities of ethics (see Sandel, 2011 for brilliant examples). The degree to which national or global professional bodies are responsive to these suggestions will determine the extent of relevant research at this level; however, as suggested earlier, professions are well aware of the fragility of their claims to self-management and may welcome new approaches. The point is not to turn professions into Jungians, but to bring Jung's knowledge of human motivation into the wider world. Given that some writers are already using Jungian concepts to understand workplace dynamics, competitiveness in capitalism, and shadow dynamics in corporate social responsibility, there is scope for extending this work to professional associations and their members.

One possibility for further research is suggested by a co-narrative approach, in which the key stories held by leading members of a profession are gathered and shared in the hope of encouraging recognition of the main descriptors, including shadow materials. This is operationalized by Corlett and Pearson (2003) in a series of checks and tests for organizations, but has not, I believe, been applied to professions. They also provide helpful inventory-tools for consultants, as a facilitator would be needed to conduct workshops, focus groups and story-telling sessions. These could be supplemented with analyses of websites, promotional material and speeches, for example, as suggested in earlier chapters. Using Jungian analytic tools to identify the main narratives, archetypes and myths would yield insights unavailable in standard audits, raising issues that tend to be ignored in ethical scrutiny. Even stimulating such a discussion would be a contribution. Jung was clear that he learned from his patients and that healing was a co-operative project in which both parties were changed by the process. Such an ethic should inform any practical follow-up work.

There is also related scope for research into the impact of different kinds of ethical codes – professional, organizational, trade union, cultural, religious and personal – on professional practice. While this book has explored tensions between professional and practitioner approaches to ethics, there may be other, parallel tensions regarding competing codes. What happens when the corporate and professional or trade union guidance clashes? The relationship between these is well worth exploration.

In particular, it seems to me that further work is needed in PR scholarship, to elucidate the divided identities of advocate and excellent boundary spanner, and I hope to explore the role of Hermes in PR in the near future. The hermeneutic approach to ethics is underexplored in PR literature and there is scope for widening discussion of PR as interpretation, which I have attempted to do recently (Fawkes, 2012a). This is a rich vein for investigation and deserves further attention.

During the writing of this book, and the thesis that preceded it, I have become conscious of a thread of enquiry that is still evolving but which builds on socio-cultural approaches to PR and asks how Jungian engagement with the psyche contributes to understanding of society. Early writing on sociology engaged with psychology, before the split in the mid-twentieth century; perhaps it is time to re-consider the linkages rather than separation. Linkages have been found but not explored in depth between Jung and Durkheim, Bourdieu and Goffman. I have begun writing about Jung and Goffman (see below) but suspect that much more needs to be said about Jung, sociology and culture in building PR theory.

It is clear that framing PR as a social force, as a producer of culture, creates new spaces for reflection. One question I intend to research in the coming years is the part that PR has played in generating a culture which emphasizes the outer world of appearance, reputation and image over inner, experiential ways of being human. Our role in the development of free-market capitalism has served the profession well, leading to massive expansion in practitioners over the past half-century, so it seems reasonable to ask what responsibility we bear, collectively, for the current state of escalating global inequality and the despoliation of the planet's resources. This goes beyond the issue of working for oil companies, but asks for 'planetary ethics' (Bauman, 2008) to counter the impact of consumerism on culture, as was discussed in Chapter 4.

From this, another strand emerges, focusing on the ideas of performance, performativity and communication; has PR's major contribution been promotional after all, not as a management function? Or, rather, have the key organizational tasks involved a kind of theatrical presentation. In the age of 'selfies', has all communication become a performance? Is it possible to reclaim the sense of performance as creative and expressive of deeper meaning, rather than that pejorative phrase 'a PR event'?

Returning to Jung, there is more work to be done on applying the theory of cultural complexes to professions, too, and perhaps others will pick up this and other ideas introduced across this text and apply them to their own field. In presentations, conversations and conferences, examples have been offered from varying professional groups, such as the shadow dynamics of *eros* in the classroom, and the shadow of hostility in the allegedly 'caring' therapeutic relationship. Journalists also experience unexplored tensions between those who see themselves as 'seekers after truth', serving society, and those who consider themselves as 'hacks' with no moral responsibility for the content of their publications. A UK specialist currently re-envisaging the accounting profession found fruitful material in the ideas presented here and I suspect that every profession will have similar dilemmas; indeed I suggest that the failure to address the hidden aspect of professions has significantly contributed to the general loss of trust in professions.

Throughout this book, I have also stressed the consequences of the failure of professional ethics to engage with collective issues, its preference for bad apples over bad barrels. This revisioning of professional ethics moves away from blame towards responsibility. This is not about wallowing in guilt or shame but being willing to change. The Jungian approach outlined here amounts to a new theory of professional ethics, in which all the disparate elements of the field participate in a process of integration, a process of growing up.

Conclusions

In conclusion, this book has constructed a new theoretical framework for reviewing the role of professions in society and encouraging the collective reappraisal of its ethics. Drawing on a wide range of literature from the sociology of the professions, old and new approaches to ethics, philosophical debates and PR texts, I suggested that professions generally, and PR in particular, face profound ethical problems in their relationship with society. Into this situation I introduced Jungian concepts to demonstrate how a new approach to professional ethics might be constructed by identifying the hidden aspects of a profession. These were then applied to PR, revealing how tensions between academics, between academics and practitioners, and between practitioners might be reconsidered as aspects of the whole rather than mutually exclusive fragments. I suggest that persuasion is the site of most conflict and therefore a pathway to recovery; recognizing the reality of the shadow material offers the possibility of a deeper, richer relationship with society for individual practitioners and the profession as a whole, grounded in shared humanity.

References

Baker, S. (2008) The model of the principled advocate and the pathological partisan: a virtue ethics construct of opposing archetypes of public relations and advertising practitioners. *Journal of Mass Media Ethics, 23*(3): 235–53.

Bauman, Z. (2008) *Does Ethics have a Chance in a World of Consumers?* Cambridge, MA: Harvard University Press.

Bowen, S. A. (2008) A state of neglect: public relations as 'corporate conscience' or ethics counsel. *Journal of Public Relations Research, 20*(3): 271–96. doi: 10.1080/106272 60801962749

Corlett, J. G. and Pearson, C. (2003) *Mapping the Organizational Psyche: a Jungian theory of organizational dynamics and change.* Gainesville, FL: Center for Applications of Psychological Type.

Curtis, A. (2002) *The Century of the Self.* UK: BBC.

Edwards, L. (2010) 'Race' in public relations. In R. L. Heath (ed.) *The SAGE Handbook of Public Relations.* Thousand Oaks, CA: Sage, pp. 205–22.

Ewen, S. (1996) *PR!: a social history of spin.* New York, NY: BasicBooks.

Fawkes, J. (2012a) Interpreting ethics: public relations and strong hermeneutics. *Public Relations Inquiry, 1*(2): 1–24.

Fawkes, J. (2012b) Saints and sinners: competing identities in public relations ethics. *Public Relations Review, 38*(5): 865–72. doi: DOI 10.1016/j.pubrev.2012.07.004

Gregory, A. (2012) Reviewing public relations research and scholarship in the 21st century. *Public Relations Review, 38*(1): 1–4. doi: http://dx.doi.org/10.1016/j.pubrev.2011.10.003

Kang, J.-A. (2010) Ethical conflict and job satisfaction of public relations practitioners. *Public Relations Review, 36:* 152–6.

L'Etang, J. (2004) *Public Relations in Britain: a history of professional practice in the twentieth century.* Mahwah, NJ and London: Lawrence Erlbaum Associates.

Messikomer, C. M. and Cirka, C. C. (2010) Constructing a code of ethics: an experiential case of a national professional organization. *Journal of Business Ethics, 95:* 55–71.

Moloney, K. (2006) *Rethinking Public Relations: PR propaganda and democracy* (2nd edn) London: Routledge.

Rice, C. and Somerville, I. (2013) Power-sharing and political public relations: government–press relationships in Northern Ireland's developing democratic institutions. *Public Relations Review, 39*(4): 293–302.

Samuels, A. (2006) Socially responsible roles of professional ethics: inclusivity, psycho-therapy and 'the protection of the public'. *International Review of Sociology, 16*(2): 175–89.

Sandel, M. J. (2011) *Justice: what's the right thing to do?* Sydney, NSW: ABC Commercial.

Singer, T. and Kimbles, S. L. (eds) (2004) *The Cultural Complex: contemporary Jungian perspectives on psyche and society*. New York, NY: Brunner-Routledge.

Sriramesh, K. and Vercic, D. (eds) (2009) *The Global Public Relations Handbook: theory, research, and practice* (expanded and rev. edn) London: Routledge.

Thurlow, A. B. (2009) 'I just say I'm in advertising': a public relations identity crisis? *Canadian Journal of Communication, 34*(2): 245–64.

Index